The PUB

A Cultural Institution – from Country Inns to Craft Beer Bars and Corner Locals

jacqui small

PETE BROWN

To Liz, my favourite drinking buddy.

First published in 2016 by
Jacqui Small LLP
An Imprint of Aurum Press
74–77 White Lion Street
London N1 9PF

Publisher: Jacqui Small
Senior Commissioning Editor: Fritha Saunders
Commissioning Editor/Project Editor: Joanna Copestick
Managing Editor: Emma Heyworth-Dunn
Designer: Paul Palmer-Edwards, Gradedesign.com
Picture Research: Grace Morris
Illustrations: Jeremy Sancha
Production: Maeve Healy

ISBN: 978 1 910 25452 3

A catalogue record for this book is available from
the British Library.

2018 2017 2016
10 9 8 7 6 5 4 3 2 1

Printed in China

CONTENTS

INTRODUCTION

How do you sum up something as beautifully anarchic as the British pub?

PUBS HAVE BEEN the cornerstone of British social life for at least a thousand years. History books may be full of kings, queens, politics and wars, but the real history of Britain – the history of the vast majority of the population – happened in and around the pub.

There's a pub at the heart of every successful soap opera on TV. The idea of the pub as represented by the scriptwriters – common, neutral ground where all members of society mingle – is eternal. Chaucer used it in *The Canterbury Tales* in exactly the same way as it's been used by the writers of *Coronation Street* for the last 60 years. Its unique brand of humour defines and encapsulates British life.

For much of our history, the pub was the single focal point of our social lives. Anything we wanted to do, from playing games to meeting future spouses, we did there.

That's no longer the case. We now have more and varied choices for what we want to do with our leisure time – and more pressure on that leisure time – than we've ever had before. But the simple mention of the word 'pub' still makes us smile affectionately in a way that 'squash court', 'coffee shop' or 'shopping mall' never could.

There are still around 50,000 pubs in the UK, and this book contains fewer than 350. It's not an attempt to list every good pub in the UK. It doesn't even claim that the 350-ish pubs here are the 350-ish best pubs in Britain. Without visiting all 50,000, that would be an impossible claim for me to make.

So if you have a favourite pub that you're fiercely proud of, and you genuinely think it's the best pub in the world, there's a good chance it's not here. Sorry.

This book is a personal journey through the world of pubs. And it's also a slice through pubs, a representation of their diversity and character. I could easily have filled a book this size with the pubs of London, or the pubs of Yorkshire. Where I know loads of great pubs, I've had to be brutal in deciding which to leave out. In areas where I haven't really drunk before, I've had the best time following the recommendations of people I trust, discovering places unfamiliar to me and that make me see my home country in a whole new, wonderful light.

I hope you enjoy drinking in these pubs as much as I did.
Cheers.
Pete Brown

OPPOSITE: The stunning, beautifully preserved main bar at the Garden Gate in Hunslet, Leeds.

1

PUB

History

WHAT'S IN A NAME?

To write the history of the pub, you first have to define what it actually is – and that's not as easy as it might sound.

IF YOU WERE TO START compiling a list of the names of every pub you saw, you would quickly begin to see some common names and themes: The Red Lion, The White Hart, The King's Head, The Rose and Crown.

These names bear witness to the continuity of the pub over the last thousand years. If your local, say The King's Head, is old enough, it was probably once called The Pope's Head before a tactical name change following Henry VIII's Reformation. The Rose and Crown, meanwhile, dates back to the war that ended with Henry's father claiming the English throne. The Red Lion and White Hart were heraldic signifiers belonging to knights and date from even further back in time.

Originally these were not written names at all, but easily recognizable symbols to serve a population that was mostly illiterate. The symbols were painted onto signs hanging over the street, or directly onto walls, and were used to differentiate one establishment from another.

So just how old is the pub? Well, that depends on your point of view. I usually say about a thousand years. But I could also argue for an age of two thousand, or two hundred.

DRINKING PLACES

When individual old pubs stake their rival claims to be the oldest in Britain, they choose their parameters carefully. A building may be only 300 years old ('only!') but the pub may have been mentioned by name centuries before that. It probably burnt down and was rebuilt in the same spot. So is it the same pub or a different one? Another pub might be built on foundations that are 800 years old, even if most of the structure is Georgian. So is it 800 years old, or 200?

You can get into similar debates with the whole notion of the pub. Some pubs with certain characteristics are called inns. And the most famous inn of all time is the one in Judaea where there was no room on Christmas Eve 2000 years ago. Does this mean inns are at least 2000 years old? Or are we using a slightly incorrect word in our translation from ancient Hebrew?

These are the kind of questions that could keep a conversation going down the pub for an entire evening, but let's cut to the chase: if you define a pub as a place where people gather to consume alcohol and drink, laugh, chat, confide, bond and flirt, then the first pub was probably a pleasant woodland clearing or desert oasis some 50,000 years ago. If you define it as a building specifically designed for this practice, pubs of some description are as old as the earliest cities – around 10,000 years old. But if you want to know about the British pub – the institution that ostensibly serves the same function as bars and cafes, but has a quite different character – that's a story that begins in the Middle Ages and carries on evolving today.

Anyway, back to those pub names you were collecting. As you gather a few more, you might notice some subtle distinctions. You might find a King's Head Tavern and a King's Head Inn, for example. Does it make any difference? Probably not. We might refer to a pub as a hostelry, watering hole or boozer. Some pubs are developing a tedious habit of referring to themselves as a 'Bar and Kitchen' or 'Craft

OPPOSITE: Pub signs like these are the descendants of large visual icons that identified pubs when most people couldn't read.

Beer House', as if this somehow makes them more special than mere pubs. Inns, taverns and alehouses are just different words for the pub, and we frequently use them interchangeably.

But that wasn't always the case. Historically, the inn, the tavern and the alehouse were different establishments with different functions, and even had different licensing conditions. Each establishment contributed something to the DNA of the modern pub – and that at least starts to explain why the pub is so singular in its character.

THE ALEHOUSE

In medieval England most households baked their own bread and brewed their own beer.

But people are better at some things than others, and as communities grew in size, most citizens discovered a neighbour whose beer was superior to their own. Beer was a necessity at the time, as it was clean and sterile, unlike water, and it was also a vital source of nutrients. So we began buying beer from our neighbours instead of brewing our own. When we did so, we lingered for a while, and the place where we bought beer turned into a place where we drank it too.

The earliest alehouses would have been little more than people's homes, with no bar, and beer being brought up from the cellar in jugs or tankards. Gradually, the alehouse grew larger and more accommodating.

The earliest forerunner of the modern pub, the alehouse, contributed the sense of homeliness and community that's at the heart of any great local. And beer. It also gives us beer. That's very important.

THE INN

Medieval society was structured around religion, with monasteries supplying spiritual and practical guidance in many areas. Pilgrimages to the shrines of saints were the weekend breaks of the time, and monasteries were obliged to offer shelter to pilgrims. As travel around the country increased, monasteries began building inns outside the walls, and the concept spread to towns,

cities and major roads between them, becoming a commercial rather than a religious enterprise.

As roads improved, the stagecoach arrived, and it was the coaching inn that gave the modern pub much of its romantic imagery: the horse brasses and beams, and the impressive old buildings around courtyards. The inn was a multi-faceted business that provided bedrooms and dormitories, food, stabling for horses, meeting rooms, function rooms and storage for valuables. And beer, of course.

THE TAVERN

The tavern was somewhat more upmarket than the alehouse. With its roots in the Roman occupation of Britain, it began making a

comeback in wealthy cities where people wanted a broader choice of drinks, offering wine and spirits such as brandy and rum. The tavern gave these broader choices to the modern pub, and the word is still used by pubs that want to look a little classier. They also sold beer.

PUBLIC HOUSES

Towards the end of the 17th century, the distinctions between the three types of establishment began to blur, and the term 'Publick House' – probably a contraction of 'Publick Alehouse' – was applied more generally across different establishments.

In 1830, for the price of two guineas, the Beer Act allowed any householder to open their home to sell beer. The number of pubs in Britain soared, and the idea of 'the pub' – as it was increasingly known toward the end of the 19th century – as a place that in many ways resembled a private house, was reinforced.

But there was a glut of pubs. Beer drinking peaked in the 1870s, and as it began a steady decline, pubs had to fight harder to stay in business. Many took loans from the breweries that supplied them and became 'tied' to the brewery – if they weren't owned by brewers outright, they were at least committed to selling only that brewer's beers.

GIN PALACES

Pubs used the money to become more ornate, peaking with the gaudy, glamorous 'gin palaces' of the late 19th century. Their owners brought in architects from countries like Italy, who were more accustomed to designing palaces or churches, and filled pubs with bright lights, intricate tiles and carvings, marble columns and cut-glass screens. The gin palace offered people an elegance they could never have previously imagined – so long as they kept paying for drinks. Private booths with table

ABOVE: Traditional Harveys delivery dray outside The Royal Oak, South London.

OPPOSITE TOP LEFT: Branded merchandise from a time when it was classy.

OPPOSITE TOP RIGHT: The Eagle in Cambridge, ready for some gastro action.

OPPOSITE BOTTOM: The Salisbury in St Martin's Lane is one of the best-preserved gin palaces in London.

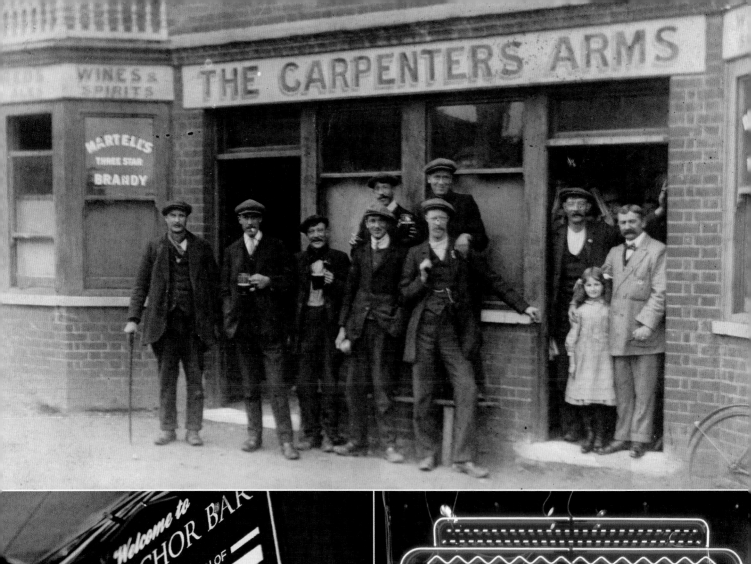

OPPOSITE TOP: Then it was the Carpenters Arms. It may or may not be called the same thing today. Pub names often reveal fascinating snippets of local history.

OPPOSITE BOTTOM LEFT: Drink craft beer and cider at the Anchor in Newcastle, Northern Ireland. But whatever you do, don't ask them to define 'craft' as an ale concept.

OPPOSITE BOTTOM RIGHT: The Draft House chain plays with retro and modern design cues but always manages to feel pubby.

service were installed for those who could afford it. For the rest, a large standing-only area replaced communal table, and the practice of 'vertical drinking' – standing with your drink in hand, which makes you drink quicker – foreshadowed modern city-centre 'circuit' pubs. There was an outcry that the poor wouldn't appreciate such luxury and so should be denied it, but surviving gin palaces are some of today's most beloved pubs.

FALL AND RISE

World War One saw tight restrictions placed on pub opening hours, so the strength of beer and pubs never really recovered their former dominance in our lives. During the 1920s our homes became pleasanter places to live in, with the general spread of heat and light, and newly acquired distractions such as the wireless and, later, the TV. The 'improved public house' movement saw pubs rebuilt as roadhouses or grander buildings with theatres and function rooms seeking to attract the whole family, challenging the idea, dominant since the Industrial Revolution, that pubs were just haunts for working class men.

World War Two, with its Home Front, strengthened the idea of the pub as a focus for the whole community, dismantling some of the class barriers that had cut it off from more affluent (or snobbish) society. In the final quarter of the 20th century, even the stigmatization of women by pubs finally began to disappear.

THE LOCAL

The vast majority of Britain's pubs evolved gently with the communities of which they were part. In the 1970s and 1980s 'theme pubs' emerged, as well as sports bars, gastropubs and branded chains, some of which became destinations you would travel to. But the majority remained somebody's 'local'. Your local is not necessarily the pub closest to your house, but it's probably within walking distance and it's the pub with which you have a relationship. It's your home from home, where you may even have friends you don't see in any

other context. You're not just a customer there, you're a 'regular'. Research shows that people who have a local pub in which they are a regular are happier, have wider social networks, and even drink more responsibly than those who only visit big town-centre pubs where nobody knows your name.

NEW TYPES OF PUB

Pubs reflect who we are and change to meet our needs. But they also anchor us in history and tradition. Gin palaces, coaching inns and roadhouses, Georgian taverns and simple alehouses, all still remain. Any of them could be an average pub going through the motions, or a treasure-trove of carefully curated drinks looked after by a publican who weaves a magical atmosphere. New types of pub – the craft beer house and the gastropub – continue to emerge. Just like gin palaces or roadhouses in their day, they're attacked by traditionalists when they first appear, but go on to join the pub's rich tapestry.

And so the pub remains different from any other commercial institution. On a typical high street, it's the only establishment that changes as you go around the country. Our shops, cafes and restaurants may be uniformly branded, but with the exception of a few town-centre chains, you never know quite what you're going to get in a high-street pub. It's a source of constant delight that there are over 4,000 pubs in the UK called The Red Lion – the most popular pub name in the UK – yet no two Red Lions are quite alike.

In terms of how we spend our leisure time, the pub will never be as important as it used to be. We have many more choices now. As a nation, we're looking to get fitter and drink less, and whatever other attractions the pub has – and a good one has many – it will always be thought of primarily as a place to get a drink. We go to the pub now when we want to *go to the pub*, rather than going because there's nothing else to do. But as an idea and an ideal, as a symbol of who we are and what we want, its power is undimmed.

DEFINING THE SPECIAL ATMOSPHERE OF THE BRITISH PUB

HOW A LITERARY GREAT (ALMOST) GAVE US THE DEFINITION OF THE PERFECT PUB

ON A GLOOMY DAY in February 1946, the *London Evening Standard* published a column from one of its regular contributors that would capture the mercurial essence of the British pub and pin it, like a butterfly, for eternity.

It's hard to imagine George Orwell – one of the greatest-ever writers in the English language – as a jobbing journalist, but that's exactly what he was at the time. He'd written often in his essays about the cultural importance of the pub, but in *The Moon Under Water* he went further and described his favourite London pub (country pubs being slightly different).

In The Moon Under Water, the members of staff know your name. There's a bit of food, but it's reassuringly basic. The beer is good and is served in the correct drinking vessels.

Orwell goes on to mention the beer garden, the Victorian architecture, the games in the public bar, and the low hubbub that enlivens the place, while leaving it quiet enough to talk.

The Moon Under Water sounds perfect, even now. But then Orwell pulls the rug from under us, admitting that, rather than describing a *real* pub, he has in fact been listing the attributes he feels make up the *ideal* pub. As far as he knows, this pub doesn't exist. The clue is in the name, a mirage that disappears when you reach out to touch it.

Orwell's perfect pub was an amalgam of several pubs in which he regularly drank. The best of them only scored eight on his list of ten attributes.

This remains a common frustration for anyone lucky enough to be surrounded by a choice of pubs. If I were to draw up my own criteria, living just a few miles up the road from where Orwell drank in Islington, every pub, even those I love dearly, would fall short.

The one with the best beer has aloof, trendier-than-thou, staff, which is offputting. The one that has the best food won't let us take our dog in. The one with the nice beer garden that is happy to accommodate four-legged Mildred has poorly kept beer. And so on. And yet I happily drink in them all, because each has something special.

The Moon Under Water still sounds idyllic today. While some of the details have changed (pink pewter tankards?) the principles still hold.

So what exactly is the magic that defines the perfect pub?

'If you are asked why you favour a particular public-house, it would seem natural to put the beer first, but the thing that most appeals to me about the Moon Under Water is what people call its "atmosphere".' replies Orwell.

Seventy years later, when market research surveys ask people why they choose a particular pub, 'atmosphere' (or words that mean the same thing) regularly comes out as the main reason why we'll walk past three pubs to get to our preferred 'local'.

Atmosphere is difficult to pin down. It's a function of the environment, the people, the time of day, and most of all, the person who orchestrates all these elements into a seamless, pubby whole. It can't be bottled and it can't be replicated.

Most people who create a perfect pub atmosphere probably couldn't tell you exactly how they do it. But most of the pubs in this book have been chosen because they excel in this simple but incredibly difficult aspect. There are many here that Orwell would recognize and acknowledge from his search. And I think there are at least two to which he would have given a full ten out of ten. The Moon Under Water still lives.

OPPOSITE TOP: 'Yeah, I don't think they should allow dogs in here. We humans have to stick together. Right, mate?'

OPPOSITE BOTTOM: Time only manages to ooze forward slowly like treacle, in London's 'Ye Olde' Cheshire Cheese, which in ye olde days, was simply called the Cheshire Cheese.

THE ANATOMY OF THE PUB

A bunch of rooms with a counter serving alcohol, the pub also offers intricate codes that reveal how the British relate to one other.

According to archaeologists and historians, our houses were once big halls where all the occupants ate and slept together. Anything else you wanted to do together, you probably tried to find somewhere nicer to do it, as our homes were utilitarian and basic at best.

For most of our history, the pub has been a nicer place to spend time in than our homes. It wasn't just the heat and light, which many people struggled to afford; pubs were better decorated, had more comfortable furniture, and, of course, a nicer atmosphere. The middle of the 20th century was the first time that most of us had homes that we actively chose to spend time in rather than go elsewhere, and the trend in home comforts continues to accelerate. Less than 20 years ago, our homes lacked plasma TVs, high-speed wireless internet, smartphones, social media, or home delivery shopping and online takeaway food ordering.

When we lived in communal rooms, pubs would give us privacy, with different rooms subdivided further inside. In Chaucer's time, pubs had screens and compartments, and this is an idea that persisted well into the 20th century. Snugs, separated from the main room by so called 'snob screens', created areas no one could see into, save the barman.

Even pubs that didn't have snugs would have separate spaces that demonstrated the British class system in physical form. A typical pub would have at least two rooms: a saloon or lounge bar, and a public bar. The public bar would be more basic than the saloon, often with bare floors and simple furniture in contrast to the carpets and upholstery of the saloon.

ABOVE: Cockney rhyming slang in Liverpool's Philharmonic Dining Rooms. See what they did there?

ABOVE LEFT: Ornamental glass was used widely in Victorian and Edwardian pub windows.

TOP RIGHT: Traditional stained-glass door panelling brought up to date in a restored pub interior.

BOTTOM RIGHT: A stained-glass panel signals the entrance to a saloon bar.

The bar would, of course, be in the middle. It served the same range of drinks to people on either side, but would charge more for those served in the saloon.

In the first half of the 20th century, the divisions between the two were fixed: it was expected that you knew your place. When the armed forces descended on the pub, it was understood that enlisted men went into one bar and officers into the other. Then, the Home Front in World War Two began to make such distinctions feel outdated.

Many pubs are still structured like this. Visiting a pub for the first time, you might enter the front door and find a door to your left and one to your right. If they're not labelled – and often they aren't – which do you choose? It's a sign of the way things have changed in Britain that many of us would be slightly disappointed if we discovered we'd opted for the saloon bar. It's likely to be quieter, more staid and a little formal. The public bar feels like the real pub, where the life is. It's certainly where the pool table, the dartboard and the TV screens are likely to be.

Over the last 30 years or so, the public bar and the saloon have begun to disappear altogether from pubs, especially urban pubs. Maybe now we have enough privacy at home that we feel an urge to be closer to other people when we visit the pub. Walls have been knocked down and the public and the saloon have become one big room.

But there's still a demarcation of space between the public, interactive area of the bar and the little nooks and corners we claim for our groups. In pubs, we want to be separate from other customers, but we still want to be closer to them, feeling a buzz at being together in the same space with people doing similar

OPPOSITE TOP: Settling in for the afternoon at the historic Lamb & Flag in London's Covent Garden.

OPPOSITE BOTTOM: The Fat Pig in Exeter is only a few years' old but you'd never guess it from this highly skilful and sympathetic pub restoration.

ABOVE LEFT: You take your thanks where you can get them at Edinburgh's Canny Man's pub.

ABOVE RIGHT: No, he doesn't want to talk to you. But that's OK, someone at the bar will do.

things, even if we don't directly interact. The regulars may stand at the bar, holding court, joking with the long-suffering staff. If you're an interloper at the bar, you may be regarded coolly, left alone or encouraged to join in the banter. If that seems intimidating, don't worry – the watchful bar staff in a decent pub will indulge regulars but stop them from making anyone else uncomfortable. A great bar person performs many roles as well as serving the drinks, from being a settler of disputes or a fount of knowledge, to a school teacher in disguise. The pub is a funny old place. Because we're a funny old bunch of people.

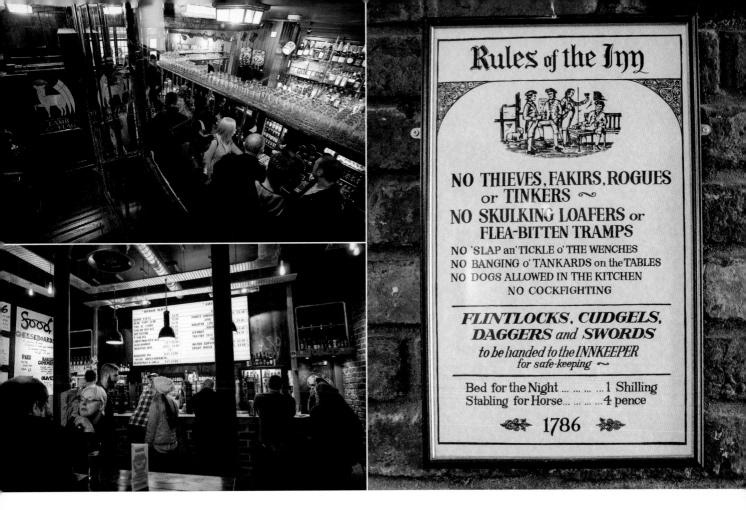

WHAT ARE YOU HAVING?

If you've grown up with pubs, you probably don't realize how strange they are until you try to explain them to a foreign tourist.

A little while ago I met an American journalist who wanted to interview me in a pub, about pubs. I was a few minutes late, and I found her at the bar, hunched over her smartphone, looking a little traumatized. Once we'd introduced ourselves, she gestured at the bar and said, 'How do you... how do you do... *this*?'

It's simple, I explained. You go up to the bar – there's no table service, except there is sometimes, but if you just sit at a table, you can wait for hours without being asked what you want. At the bar there's no queue – well, there is, but it's an invisible queue, and the bar staff and all the waiting customers are expected to know whose turn it is. You don't jump your turn, because that would be very rude. But if someone else gets served before you when it's your turn, it's also a bit rude to point this out. But don't worry, because if a member of the bar staff tries to serve you before the person who was already waiting when you arrived, and you say, 'Actually, I think this person was waiting before me,' that makes you a complete hero, and everyone loves you.

When you do get served, you just ask for what you want to drink. It's as simple as that! Although, obviously, you need to decide what you want before it's your turn, so you're not holding anyone up when you finally do get served; you order any pints of Guinness at the beginning of the round, never the end, followed by pints of cask ale and then any other drinks, giving your full order all at once rather than ordering one drink at a time, unless you're ordering a huge round and then you break it

TOP LEFT: A fly jealously watches the punters getting them in at the Lamb & Flag, Covent Garden.

BOTTOM LEFT: A BrewDog bar, redefining the visual aesthetic while retaining the core principles of the pub model.

ABOVE RIGHT: OK, so you can buy this poster on Amazon, but at The Barrels in Hereford they really do still insist you hand over your cudgels and flintlocks for safekeeping.

down a little, and never, ever order cocktails if there are more than four other people waiting at the bar.

Simple.

While it's easy to joke, pub etiquette has been studied with some seriousness by social anthropologists such as Kate Fox, bestselling author of *Watching the English*.

The pub is a place that sells alcohol, and alcohol lowers inhibitions. The pub appeals because it's an informal space, but there still has to be some kind of code that governs behaviour. Almost every aspect of pub etiquette is designed to enhance the social aspects of drinking alcohol, the unwritten rules bringing out the very best of how booze makes people feel.

Buying rounds encourages group rather than solo drinking. It also creates mutual obligation, an important foundation for social relationships. If you never buy your round, you can expect to become a social pariah. But at the same time, if you're a stickler for whose round it is and who has bought what when, you can be seen as tight, missing the point of what the round is all about.

Ordering at the bar allows bar staff to assess if someone is too drunk to be served, but also changes things around, forcing you to mingle in neutral territory rather than sticking to occupied tables that have invisible signs above them reading 'private space'.

Pub etiquette does more than allow pubgoers to police themselves, to keep the pub relatively free of regulatory meddling. The pub's unwritten code of laws enforces and perpetuates a very British idea of decency: politeness, reserve, consideration for others, quiet assertiveness, being friendly but not too showy, and, of course, always buying your round.

THE PUB AS PLAYGROUND

If you need proof of how central the pub is to British society, its intimate relationship with just about all the sports we care for – and many we don't – brings its importance vividly to life.

What's the trophy for most sports? A cup, of course. This is no coincidence: the British are far better at creating new sports than competing in them. Cricket, football, tennis and rugby were all invented in Britain. And all had the pub as their main venue until purpose-built grounds emerged.

The pub has also, in its time, been the key venue for wrestling, boxing, foot racing, bowls, and the meeting point for hunts. Popular pub names such as the Talbot, the Horse and Jockey, the Cricketers, and the Bat and Ball all have their roots in links to sport.

Pub names also remind us of 'sports' we may be less proud of in modern times. Pubs were the venue for activities such as cock fighting, bear baiting, dog fighting and duck hunting – yes, duck hunting – where a duck in the pond by the pub would have its wings tied and have a pack of dogs set upon it. It's a grisly story, and one that might make you look at the good old Dog and Duck in a different light. But it's no worse than the Fighting Cocks, the Bear, the Dog and Partridge or the Fox and Hounds.

Pubs still keep this link alive in many ways. Before football players became multi-millionaires, working in a pub after retiring from the game was a common career choice, helping drive custom from adoring fans. Pubs have their own Sunday League teams, and, of course, important games on the big screen have become a central draw to the pub more recently.

If you're not a talented athlete, the pub still provides plenty of opportunities for competitive games. For centuries, pubs have persuaded

ABOVE: It remains a source of hilarious astonishment at The Rose & Crown in Huish Episcopi, Somerset, that, in other pubs, people have abandoned the awesome game of skittles for cheap, inferior pinball and trivia machines.

people to stay longer by providing the facilities for games such as skittles (some old pubs, especially around Wiltshire, still have skittle alleys in use), dominoes, darts, bar billiards and, in the last 30 years or so, pool.

In more recent years, having a stack of battered board games that you fondly remember from your youth has become an easy shorthand for pubs to suggest they have character. For a small deposit at the bar, you can pass a couple of pleasant hours arguing over the rules for Monopoly, Scrabble, Mousetrap or Risk.

But quietly, with minimal fanfare, the most popular competitive pub pastime has undoubtedly become the pub quiz.

The early part of the week is a quiet time for pubs. A quiz ensures at least one night that can be as busy as a Friday. People might not drink as quickly, but a clever quizmaster keeps them in the pub from around 8pm – 'Get there early

to be sure of a seat!' – until closing time. A recent report from market researchers Mintel showed that one in five UK adults takes part in a pub quiz at least once a year, making it the country's second most popular form of what they call 'participative entertainment' behind that other pub staple, karaoke.

Despite its popularity, the quiz has resisted all attempts – and there have been many – to render it formalized and streamlined, sponsored and homogenized into a national event. Companies have tried to create national championships using pub TVs or even bespoke electronic equipment. They always fail.

The pub quiz is informal. Just like every other aspect of the pub, it changes to suit the pubs that host it, and the regulars who play. The pub is where we go to relax and bond. But in an instant, it can become the arena in which we compete for supremacy in any way we can.

THE MODERN PUB

Imagine a mental image of the typical English pub. What do you see?

For many of us, it's a picture informed by popular culture – a soap-opera pub where an entire community drinks together and everyone knows your name, unchanged in appearance since the shows they belong to were first aired. Then there's the country pub, with its thatched roof, babbling brook and hanging baskets.

These pubs still exist, but they're becoming less common. The traditional community boozer (a synonym for the word 'pub' that is only really appropriate for this traditional type of establishment) is being attacked from all sides. The smoking ban, the growth of different alternatives for how we spend our leisure time, the restrictive practices of the pub companies that own thousands of British pubs and the greed of property landlords have all contributed to a steep decline in the number of British pubs.

But the pub adapts. It always has done. If a pub doesn't reflect the aspirations of the drinking public, they'll drink somewhere else instead. British society is more fragmented, less homogenous than it has ever been before. And, therefore, so is the pub.

First came the much-maligned theme pubs of the 1980s. Particularly for town-centre pubs, it became the norm to refurbish as, say, a Club Tropicana-style cocktail bar. When the appeal of that faded, it might have regenerated as a fairly unconvincing Irish pub, a medieval banqueting hall or a Mexican cantina.

The problem with theme pubs was never the themes themselves, but the way they were executed. (You might disagree, but if you say you'd rather drink in a perfectly preserved coaching inn today, that's still a theme pub –

ABOVE: Birmingham's Purecraft Bar combines a fashionable industrial chic interior with the personal, attentive service expected in a decent pub.

just one that's been done very well.) As a society, we love exploration and novelty, but we need to feel the pubs are authentic to some degree.

Today's fragmented pub universe may be full of concepts that don't appeal to you personally, but they're generally done better than they used to be. A self-proclaimed sports bar will probably show everything from Champions League football to American baseball to motor sport, probably simultaneously on different screens, with signed shirts from local teams framed on the wall. It's not my idea of a great pub, but if sport is your thing, it's paradise. A high-street barn that wants to blur the line that separates pub and nightclub is no good at all to anyone looking to nurse a quiet pint, but it will no doubt have invested in talented DJs and a decent lighting system to provide a venue far superior to the pub disco of 20 or 30 years ago. The Farrow & Ball-painted gastropub will have proper restaurant-standard meals at restaurant prices or, if you're lucky, slightly cheaper fare that still retains a little of the pub's unpretentious informality. And the newly emergent craft beer bar, with its singular, faux industrial design aesthetic and complete rejection of the creative comforts that characterize traditional pubs, is nevertheless a reinvention of the original concept of the alehouse. It will, however, serve a wide range of beers you won't see in the traditional boozer across the street.

And then there's the astonishing rise of the JD Wetherspoon chain. Dismissed by many as not being 'proper pubs', thanks to their mass-market standardization, Wetherspoon's outlets serve a great range of beers, impeccably kept, at very keen prices. They also preserve local buildings from demolition and keep local history alive. You might not want to spend an

OPPOSITE TOP: If you know a heating vent, plain white tile or railway sleeper that needs a home, direct it to your nearest craft beer bar, where friends are waiting.

OPPOSITE BOTTOM: Shiny brewing vessels nestled in the background send freshly brewed beer direct to the bar of The Bridge Tavern in Newcastle.

TOP LEFT: The craft beer bar that started it all? North Bar in Leeds looks as contemporary now as when it opened twenty years ago.

ABOVE LEFT: Cambridge's Pint Shop is a modern take on the 19th-century alehouse.

ABOVE RIGHT: The Southampton Arms in North London was rocking the white-tiled wall look long before you even knew it was hip.

entire evening in one, and I was, sadly, unable to find a particular one I felt had a special enough atmosphere to feature in this book, but Wetherspoon's, while far from perfect in the eyes of many pubgoers, are an important aspect of the modern pub.

The pubs listed here are perhaps more traditional as a collection of pubs than you'd find in a British town more generally. These are pubs with character, and it means most of them tend to have changed little over the last few decades. They don't need to. But these are exceptional pubs. They prove that while the pub evolves to suit our broader world view and more corporate reality, the traditional British pub still retains a sense of magic for many of us.

THE FUTURE OF THE PUB

The pub has been around for a thousand years. So why do people worry that it's about to disappear in the next couple of decades?

Every six months, the British media runs a glut of stories about the death of the pub. This is when the figures for the net number of permanent pub closures are announced by CAMRA (the Campaign for Real Ale). In 2010, Britain was losing 50 pubs a week. The situation has since improved, but the number is unlikely to move into surplus any time soon.

Running a pub is hard work. Faced with increasing obstacles, many publicans are ground down. Often, they feel crushed by the terms of the agreements they have with big pub companies, unable to make a profit no matter how hard they work. Stumped for ideas, it's easy to head for the lowest common denominator in an attempt to rustle up

custom. It becomes a vicious cycle of cut costs and cut corners, with no money available for serious improvements, until it grinds to a halt. The pub company often then deems the pub unviable, and sells it for development.

So pubs are closing. But they're also (re-) opening, albeit at a slower rate.

Everards Brewery in the Midlands has spent the last decade rescuing 'unviable' pubs under its Project William scheme. It works with local microbrewers looking to open their first pub, refurbishing and refreshing faded community locals. The results are often staggering. People who can't remember when they last visited the pub come back. They meet friends they haven't seen since their last visit, and thank the new owners for giving them back their pub and their community.

Everards is not the only brewery taking over defunct pubs. Invariably, a model based

TOP AND BOTTOM LEFT:
The Brown Cow in Mansfield, Nottinghamshire (inside and out) – does this look like an 'unviable' pub to you?

TOP AND BOTTOM RIGHT:
The Seven Stars (inside and out) – like the Brown Cow, a pub saved by Everards' brilliant 'Project Willliam' pub regeneration scheme.

ABOVE: The guys who own The Rake in London's Borough Market are too cheap to splash out on proper decoration, so instead they came up with the brilliant idea of getting any visiting brewer to sign the wall. It's become a hall of fame to the global craft beer revolution.

on good beer and good conversation proves successful where louder music, cheaper drink, more TV screens and brighter lights have failed. The original idea of the pub still appeals. It's incredible that this is still a surprise to some.

The recent growth of craft beer bars is another example of the phenomenon. The beers and decor may be different, but many successful craft operators open in pubs that had failed as typical boozers, where the love and atmosphere had died. Their solution is different from the reinvention of the traditional local, but it's still based on the centuries-old template of good beer and good conversation.

Parallel to the rise of the craft beer bar is the arrival of the micropub. These tend to open in empty shops, in towns where local commerce has lost out to big chain brands in retail parks. The Micropub Association defines a micropub as 'a small freehouse which listens to its

customers, mainly serves cask ales, promotes conversation, shuns all forms of electronic entertainment and dabbles in traditional pub snacks'. The same idea, yet again.

So the pub of the future looks a great deal like the pub of the past – with one important caveat.

The job of running a great pub is getting harder. It's no longer enough to simply tick off the basics in a competent fashion, open the doors and polish glasses while waiting for the punters to flow in. The pubs featured in this book are all run by people who regard their pubs as a passion and a vocation, rather than just a mere job. They put in more effort than anyone could reasonably ask of them, because they want to.

It's perhaps a little worrying that running a great pub demands so much. But for as long as there are people prepared to give their all in this way, the pub will continue to thrive.

3

PUB
Types

TYPES OF PUBS

*What makes a great pub? Everyone has their own idea,
but the best pubs are a mixture of location, longevity,
love – and utter randomness.*

SINCE SOCIAL MEDIA HAPPENED, printed guidebooks are of little use unless you're going to constantly update them. That's why this book is not a guidebook. If you want to know whether a pub allows dogs inside, whether it offers Bed & Breakfast or what time it serves meals, we've provided the URL or Facebook page address where possible.

This book is about the essence and personality of a pub. It celebrates the breadth and diversity of the British pub's character. It doesn't tell you the things you need to know before deciding whether to hire a babysitter or take public transport rather than the car. Instead, it hopefully gives you the reasons that make you want to visit the pub in the first place.

Our original idea was to divide this book into sections defined by type of pub, but as soon as we started trying to do that, we realized that nearly every great pub would appear in at least two different sections. Many community pubs also serve great beer. Many country pubs are also of historical interest. And so on. Great pubs are great because they offer more than one thing. They embody a combination of factors that frustrates our natural desire to catalogue everything neatly.

So instead we've created a list of symbols that denote the aspects we most enjoy about the British pub. Every pub listed in this book has one or more symbols by its name. It would be easy to generate more, but we got to 12 pretty quickly and decided to stop there

risked pub reviews starting to look like they've been written in emoji.

Opposite is a brief description of what each symbol means. In the following section, we explore each one of these aspects of the pub in more detail, and offer a profile of one pub that we feel is a great example of each trait.

We're not necessarily saying that The Talbot in the former pit village where I grew up is the best community pub in the UK, but we are saying it's a perfect example of what makes community pubs so special. This one was chosen because I was once part of the community that still uses it, which means I'm better placed to talk about it than I am about the community pub you love just as much.

I'm not going to argue that The Gurnard's Head in Cornwall serves better food than any other pub in the country, or that The Bridge Beer Huis in Burnley serves the best beer anywhere – there are other organizations and publications that run competitions to decide these things, and even they don't make everyone happy with their choices. What we are saying is that these pubs are perfect examples of pubs that have built themselves around great food or drink respectively, and that they are great all-round pubs where food or beer happens to be the highlight.

So here are the traits we've looked for in our pub selection. It would be impossible for any one pub to exhibit them all, but you need at least one to get in this book, and it's surprising just how many symbols a few rare, special

GUIDE TO PUB SYMBOLS

HISTORIC PUBS
It's probably very old, and it may also have had some very famous visitors or even historic events that have happened on the premises. The pubs listed here are those that haven't let it go to their head.

ARCHITECTURALLY INTERESTING PUBS
Often historic, but not necessarily so. Pubs have always reflected our hopes and aspirations, and in any age, their architecture reflects that.

HUB OF THE COMMUNITY PUBS
The traditional backstreet boozer and the hub of the country village have always brought people together and nurtured the bonds between them, and they always will.

PUBS WITH LIVE ENTERTAINMENT
Most of Britain's popular entertainment can trace its roots back to the pub. These pubs are those that still nurture the talents of those who hope to be the stars of tomorrow, and sometimes allow the rest of us to get up and have a go for ourselves.

COUNTRY PUBS
There are thousands of pubs on rural roadsides, up in the hills and nestling in country villages. Those listed here do much more than simply admire the view.

COASTAL PUBS
It's not just the location, you know – there are plenty of awful pubs in seaside towns. Our selection of coastal pubs responds to their environment to create something truly special for which it's worth taking a detour.

RAILWAY PUBS
Every town with a train station has a pub either in it or nearby. The few railway pubs in this book use this particular location as inspiration for greatness.

ECCENTRIC PUBS AND PUBS IN UNUSUAL LOCATIONS
You might not 'get', or even like, all of the pubs that qualify for this listing. But this is an area where pubs form our last line of defence against the rampant, branded homogenization of our communities.

GREAT BEER PUBS
All pubs stock beer. Our great beer pubs do more than that, nurturing a range that discerning drinkers will pass many other pubs to get to.

GREAT FOOD PUBS
Not only do they not necessarily provide usual pub food offerings, but neither are they restaurants masquerading as pubs. This is about trustworthy food done brilliantly well.

Also...

GREAT CIDER PUBS
The revival in cider production and consumption means that there are now numerous pubs that offer a great cider or two among the handpumps. In some pubs you'll find a range of ciders that surpasses the beer offering.

GREAT WHISKY COLLECTION PUBS
Sometimes pubs are known as much for their range of superb artisan spirits as a great range of beer. These pubs all have an extensive and daring collection of single malt .

♜ HISTORIC PUBS

WHEN ANY ESTABLISHMENT has been in business for centuries, you know it must be doing something right.

Among Britain's 50,000 pubs, there aren't too many that are newly built. We take Victorian era or 1930s pubs almost for granted. If they go as far back as the 18th century, we start to appreciate their antiquity. But hundreds of pubs are even older than that.

A dozen or so pubs each claim to be the oldest in Britain. This is a tricky thing to prove, which is why the claim is disputed, and it ultimately comes down to a matter of interpretation. Ye Olde Trip to Jerusalem in Nottingham (pages 47, 181) is usually cited as Britain's oldest pub in most pub guides. Claiming to date back to 1189, the parts that are dug into the rocks under Nottingham Castle were probably selling beer back then, but the main building is far newer, and the name of the first pub on this site was almost certainly different. So is Ye Olde Trip the same pub, or merely a different pub on the same site?

Other historic pubs are a mishmash of patchwork construction. Not a single one of these ancient places was built with the intention that it should stand for centuries. For most of their history, these pubs were lit by naked flame, largely built from wood and full of people who had been drinking heavily. Inevitably then, fires have destroyed at least parts and, in many cases, entire buildings have had to be rebuilt. Wood also rots eventually and has to be replaced. Look closely, and even if some parts of a building feel original, there is a distinct possibility that those blackened oak beams may well have been cut by modern machinery.

But for most pubgoers, such an analytical approach misses the point. Pubs can be portals to a previous age. And unlike the castles or palaces that we can now look around, back then they were likely to have been full of ordinary people just like us. If you were to stand at the bar in a pub like Preston's Black Horse (page 190), you can almost feel an Edwardian merchant standing next to you. Gaze out of the window of The Strines Inn (page 212) and you can almost hear the clop of horses and the jingle of harness, and imagine the whiff of manure and sweat.

Pubs have always been places where life happened. Until the last few decades, the pub was a place you went to for most of your social and many of your business needs. Apart from the church, pubs were the biggest places in many communities, often the warmest and brightest, perhaps even the safest. Pubs like The Briton's Protection in Manchester (page 192) found themselves at the centre of historic events, while the rollcall of characters who drank in London's George Inn (page 138) is a history book in itself.

These two pubs are particular exceptions to the general rule that historic pubs survive better in the countryside than towns or cities. Cities are constantly being redeveloped and rebuilt, or burned or bombed. Get out onto ancient roads between them, and old pubs will invariably be dotted along the way, still welcoming tired travellers.

Old pubs age in different ways, and if you want to explore history via the pub, it's worth finding the right type. Some are preserved almost as museums: to walk into The Bridge Inn in Topsham, Devon (page 100) really does feel like stepping back in time – it's hard to spot anything that's changed.

Others (none included in this book) have been turned into tourist traps, tacky theme pubs that offer a cartoonish (and invariably poorly researched) version of the pub's history and what it means.

OPPOSITE TOP: The George at Norton St Philip (invisible ghost not pictured).

OPPOSITE BOTTOM LEFT: Edinburgh's Oxford Bar (fictitious Inspector Rebus not pictured).

OPPOSITE BOTTOM RIGHT: A pub lamp (defiinitely pictured).

My favourite historic pubs are those that are simply timeless. They haven't been self-consciously preserved; they just haven't changed. That's an important difference and an impressive feat. It means there's simply been no need to reinvent or evolve, because what worked a century ago continues to work just as well now. The pub goes on quietly doing the same thing – in the same manner that it always has.

The beer fonts on the bar come and go, reflecting transient fashions. But the essential function of the pub – and what people need from it – tends to remains the same.

ABOVE: The Castle at Edge Hill, Warwickshire, mixes traditional architectural detailing with a high degree of comfort and welcome.

OPPOSITE BOTTOM LEFT: Although The Royal Standard of England, in Beaconsfield, is not far out of London, its relaxed pace of life feels like a world away.

OPPOSITE TOP: The Fleece Inn, Evesham, Worcestershire, is a popular and archetypal country pub.

OPPOSITE BOTTOM RIGHT: An early example of the 'beer engine', drawing beer up from the cellar to the delight of weary 19th-century bar staff.

THE GEORGE INN ♜ 🏛

High St, Norton St Philip, Bath, Somerset BA2 7LH
www.georgeinnnsp.co.uk

When you're researching old inns, your perception of time alters. You run back and forth through the centuries, starting to think of the 18th century as relatively recent. You get used to reading comments like, 'You must come and see this charming ancient inn, which has stood here for centuries,' and then you realize this one was written by someone in 1524, and your head explodes.

The George in Norton St Philip was purpose-built as an inn in the 14th or 15th century, originally catering for merchants coming to a wool fair organized by the local Carthusian monks. It's carried on the same basic functions ever since, and today it attracts tourists, families enjoying Sunday lunch together, and nervous boyfriends and girlfriends brought out to meet possible future in-laws for the first time.

You can tell how old the George is from the size of its rooms. Once, back when our sense of scale and ambition was more modest, they would have seemed large and grand. Today they seem shrunken.

Pubs that survive have to evolve, and this often means a constantly shifting floor plan. But when you build a pub out of stone and make its walls as thick as these, it's a bit trickier than normal to knock all the rooms through into one because that happens to be the current fashion. The rooms in The George Inn have remained relatively stable, their characters becoming fixed over the centuries.

The signs of remoulding and renovation are everywhere (visual and chemical analysis during recent renovation works revealed 15 different types of plaster on the top floor alone) but the identity of the pub, the character of it, is anchored in space and time. There are some places where you can tell that a pub or restaurant is simply not meant to be.

Different operators come and go, bringing new concepts with them and leaving broken dreams when they go. The George is the opposite: it's a fixed point of pub-ness. It tells you that there has always been a pub on this spot, and that there always will be.

The galleried courtyard is so old that it's sunken and softened, the stone worn away. From the front, you can see what looks like newer, Tudor-style upper floors built on top of a medieval base. Parts of it look quite unformed, like something more primeval that will eventually evolve into a pub.

Like all the best pubs, there's a simple acknowledgement here of its incredible survival. It neither hides nor trumpets its history. There's a book for sale that will give you all the detail behind the tall, mullioned windows, the carved oak trusses of the 15th-century roof, the complexity of the patchwork structure of the building, if that's what you're after. You could probably find a member of staff who would be happy to tell you the stories behind the ghosts who regularly appear in the local press and Trip Advisor reviews. Or you could just enjoy it like you would any other pub. The beer is crystal clear. The service is calm and unhurried. The buzz in the bar is lively but subtle.

There are coats on the backs of many chairs, this being the first day that, by consensus around the bar, is 'definitely autumn'. The room is lit with candles as the sky darkens before 7pm for the first time in months, and raindrops hit the tiny, leaded windowpanes.

The beer glows in the candlelight, If the ghosts are restive, I bet they're just jealous that they had to make do with murky ale from pewter tankards when sat here, instead of the bright copper ale we drink now while looking out of the same windows, at the same rain.

OPPOSITE TOP: The exterior of The George Inn clearly shows the addition of new layers over the centuries.

OPPOSITE BOTTOM: In the main bar, the George evolves as slowly as it possibly can.

ARCHITECTURALLY INTERESTING PUBS

PUBS ARE PEOPLE'S PALACES. When they're doing well, they work because we long to be in them, dreaming of beer o'clock and our chance to escape from work to somewhere we'd rather be, where we feel at our best. This air of aspiration and celebration means some pubs have been the grandest buildings of their day.

But, at the same time, pubs can be unpretentious, open and democratic spaces, so there is often a degree of understatement in some pubs, a rejection of showing off.

With such a long and rich history, and with such diversity in their fortunes, pubs today represent a glorious cocktail of architectural styles and quirks rarely seen in other types of building, and in themselves, they tell the history of everyone's hopes and dreams.

Arguably the showiest pub in history was the Victorian gin palace. The interiors of those that survive are often listed, and they can still create the same sense of wonder now that they did back then, when they gave people a brief chance to experience the kind of grand surroundings that celebrated themselves and elevated those within them. Belfast's Crown Liquor Saloon (page 224) and The Salisbury in North London (page 149) remain as monuments to an age when going to the pub was first marketed as an experience rather than a functional thing, with mosaics, frosted and etched glass, marble pillars and huge globe lamps dazzling and delighting customers.

In some ways, the JD Wetherspoon chain is the heir to this tradition. Many Wetherspoon's pubs exist in converted spaces, grand buildings of their day that are no longer useful or cost-effective to the banks, legal firms or cinema owners that built or owned them. Love them or hate them, Wetherspoon's has helped preserve fine buildings, from neo-classical to art deco, in many of our towns and cities.

Out of the city centre, it's the old coaching inn that evokes lost glory, its courtyards and old stone reminding us of a Dickensian or TV costume drama idyll that was never quite as glamorous as the old buildings make it look.

On busier, more modern A-roads, we still see examples of the 1930s roadhouse, built to cater for an era between the mass adoption of the motorcar and the arrival of modern attitudes and regulations around driving under the influence. Modernist and sometimes brutal in their architecture, they were derided when they first appeared, but are now as revered as the gin palaces.

An interesting architectural style is a big help in keeping pubs open. CAMRA (the Campaign for Real Ale) has done an outstanding job of compiling a national inventory of historic pub interiors that draws attention to individual bar designs, like the magnificent main bar in the Garden Gate at Hunslet, Leeds (page 6) or the bonkers eccentricity of The Black Friar in London (page 136). This can't guarantee a pub will stay open, but it helps attract the interest of bodies such as English Heritage who celebrate and promote the best there is.

Away from glamour and eccentricity, simple alehouses hold their own appeal. If you look very hard, you can still find places in the countryside where pubs survive that are no more than someone's front room. But these establishments are dying, as proprietors age and their children opt for other careers.

Single-room pubs such as The Evening Star in Brighton (page 121) and The Pebbles Tavern in Somerset (page 108), or The Halfway House in Langport (page 106), with its spartan farmhouse feel, still evoke a modest, functional aesthetic where little is there that doesn't need to be. And yet these buildings and spaces fill us with joy of a different kind.

OPPOSITE TOP: Nottingham's Ye Olde Trip to Jerusalem probably doesn't live up to the claim of being England's oldest pub, but it's a fascinating space nonetheless.

OPPOSITE BOTTOM: The Royal Bank of England in London's financial district. Why can't all banks be put to use like this?

OPPOSITE TOP: Stripped-back chic at The Oxford Bar in Edinburgh.

OPPOSITE BOTTOM LEFT: The Royal Standard of England in Beaconsfield doesn't quite get away with its impersonation of a medieval church.

OPPOSITE BOTTOM MIDDLE: Attention to detail outside Manchester's Peveril of the Peak...

OPPOSITE BOTTOM RIGHT: ...and inside Liverpool's magnificent Philharmonic Dining Rooms.

ABOVE: Lovingly preserved 'snob screens' at the Lamb, Central London, evoke a bygone age of pub etiquette.

This, too, is being reinvented for the 21st century. The exposed heating vents and bare brick of bars like BrewDog (page 31) may have been born from a simple lack of budget, but they suggest a no-frills authenticity.

Between these two extremes, the traditional British pub follows a timeless aesthetic that makes us feel at home, but also 'out somewhere special' at the same time. Apart from those chain pubs where corporate owners have missed the point, pubs may follow similar basic rules, but every single one emerges as slightly different – just like the many and varied people who drink in them.

THE PHILHARMONIC DINING ROOMS ♜ ♒

36 Hope Street, Liverpool L1 9BX
www.nicholsonspubs.co.uk

There's a scene in Shakespeare's *King Lear* where the king's two scheming elder daughters cynically bring down and humiliate their father, after his ill-thought-through decision to divide his kingdom between them.

He'd imagined a life as King Emeritus, touring with his entourage, enjoying his retirement while his daughters did the day job. But entourages are expensive, and the daughters confront their father to ask if he really needs 100 soldiers getting drunk and tearing up the place. They embark on a reverse haggle: do you really need 100? What about 50? Why not 25? Until one of them delivers the devastating killer blow.

'What need one?'

'Oh, reason not the NEED!' explodes Lear. Of course, he doesn't actually need a 100 soldiers, but he deserves them, just as our monarch now doesn't need Horse Guards and soldiers in bearskins and red tunics. It's not about the need; it's about the pomp. The sisters know this, of course: they're not trying to strip Lear of his protection, but they are taking away his dignity.

Thirty years after I first studied King Lear and understood the power and seduction of literature for the first time, I'm standing at a pub urinal made of pink marble, staring up at a pink marble cistern. This cistern rests on a huge iron bracket which is, in turn, bolted into a beautiful mural. It's outrageous that a pub bog is so beautiful. So beautiful, in fact, that these urinals are Grade II listed by English Heritage. There is absolutely no need for this pub – or any pub – to have such stunning urinals.

'Oh, reason not the need!'

'The Phil' claims to be 'the most ornate pub in Britain', and I'm not going to argue. Built in the age of the Victorian gin palace, when pubs provided a glamorous alternative to the squalor in which many people lived, the level of detail, care and delicacy in every aspect of the architecture is simply absurd. The main door has gates across it that wouldn't look out of place on a royal palace. Gilt, chandeliers, stained glass, heavy velvet curtains, carvings and rich mahogany panelling erupt over the top wherever you look. The floors are mainly mosaic. The ceilings are dense with cornicing. When John Lennon was asked if there were any downsides to fame, he replied, 'Not being able to have a pint in the Phil.'

The Philharmonic is magnificent. It is, easily, the most architecturally striking pub in Britain.

The only problem is that, if a pub like this is owned by a large corporation that sees it as just one of many outlets in a portfolio, that recognizes its worth but doesn't respect the contract the pub originally made with people, the most stunning pub you've ever seen can be something of a disappointment.

When I visit the Phil, the service is surly and disinterested. The lighting is all wrong, too bright and industrial. Speakers blare out music more suited to a nightclub, loud enough to kill any conversation.

It may seem bizarre to be critical of a pub that I've chosen to represent the very best of pubs. But the thing is, despite the way it's currently being run, the Phil remains one of those pubs that you simply must visit if you love pubs. The negatives are significant, but they're still outweighed by the positives. You simply have to come and see this pub.

The people who run the place know this. They know people will still flock here even if they don't make it what it could and should be. They know they don't need to try.

Oh, reason not the need!

HUB OF THE COMMUNITY PUBS

THE MEDIEVAL ALEHOUSE was one of the simplest business ideas ever. You make beer that's so good your neighbours want to buy it from you rather than brew their own. When they come to collect it, they find other neighbours are already there, and stick around for a chat over a beer. We've been doing the same thing in pubs ever since.

Orwell talked about 'atmosphere' as the main draw of the perfect pub. In every piece of market research I've seen since I started working around beer and pubs, people who have never read Orwell's essay still say 'my type of atmosphere' or 'my type of people' are the main reasons they choose the pubs they visit (with price occasionally becoming a consideration during lean times).

That's why, if you ask someone who goes to the same pub regularly, their 'local' may not necessarily be the nearest pub to their house. It's the nearest pub that calls to them, even if it's a little further away. Once there, they feel not just a sense of belonging, but also a sense of ownership of, the space.

Even as a visitor from out of town, you can easily spot a community pub. There'll often be postcards from around the world pinned behind the bar, because when the regulars go on holiday, they can't wait to show off to their mates back home. In a community pub like The Royal Oak in Meavy (page 108), the regulars sit along a bench in the same poses as the photographs above their heads show them as their younger selves.

Perhaps the most celebrated aspect of the community pub is the special seats. In The Coopers Tavern in Burton (page 174), it's obvious which are the special seats and who is allowed to sit in them. In other places, it's not so easy. Tales abound in pub folklore of strangers entering community pubs to be told they can't sit on that stool because it's 'Clive's stool'. Eventually the stranger might ask if Clive is due in at any point soon, only to be told that he won't because Clive has been dead for two years, but that's still his stool.

Throughout most of the 20th century, the community pub competed with the working men's club, where membership, management by committee and a regular programme of entertainment bound tight geographical communities even closer together.

But as Britain's manufacturing base has disappeared and our sense of geographical community has atomized, the working men's club is disappearing. The community pub, too, is more under threat than any other – research shows that the rate of permanent closures in suburban pubs is far higher than either urban or rural pubs.

Wetherspoon's pubs today increasingly fill a gap left by working men's clubs and community pubs. Older drinkers retreat here as their familiar haunts are gentrified and the prices are pushed up. 'Spoon's' may have its faults, but in many towns and cities it caters for a far broader mix of the local population than any other pub.

There are other shoots of hope for fans of the community pub. Over the last decade or so, the micropub movement has gathered pace, converting small shops into alehouses that focus on good beer, good conversation and nothing more, with landlords opening the doors when they feel like it, and catering specifically for 'my kind of people', whoever they might be in that particular spot.

And so we end up back where we began: with the remarkably clever idea of getting together with people you like and having a chat over great beer. Of course, it's not always that simple. But it's an idea I find impossible to imagine ever going out of date over the next few centuries.

OPPOSITE TOP LEFT: 'Of course I'm old enough to drink. I'm 24 in dog years.'

OPPOSITE MIDDLE LEFT: It's old-school party time every Sunday at London's Grafton Arms.

OPPOSITE TOP RIGHT: Barter is bouncing back in rural community pubs.

OPPOSITE BOTTOM: Welcome to The Driftwood Spars in St Agnes, Cornwall. You weren't planning on leaving any time soon, were you?

BARTER BOARD

HOME GROWN PRODUCE
IN EXCHANGE FOR BEER

* BABY BEETS
* LETTUCE
* RADISH

* CABBAGE
* GARDEN HERBS
* CHARD

SING ALONG SUNDAY

Gather round the piano for a
good old fashioned knees-up!

From 7.30pm

THE TALBOT INN 👥🍺🍴

Towngate, Mapplewell, Barnsley, South Yorkshire S75 6AS
www.thetalbotmapplewell.co.uk

We all have the pub in which we first learned to drink. Mine was the Talbot in Mapplewell, the former pit village where I grew up.

I still have no idea whether you choose your local or it chooses you. I certainly had to walk past two other pubs to get to the Talbot, pubs that, to this day, I would never even consider entering. I have no idea why. The Talbot was our local and that was that.

I think we started going there for two reasons: the Wednesday night pub quiz, which as A-level students, we excelled at, and the fact that we could get served beer without being asked to prove our ages when we were still only 16 years old – something that is now illegal.

You could argue that drinking a small amount of alcohol in a pub, closely supervised by adults, is a good way to learn how to drink responsibly. In fact it is legal for 16 and 17 year-olds to drink beer, wine or cider in licensed premises with a meal in the UK, so long as they don't buy it themselves, and are with an adult. This is quite a different scenario to a group of unsupervised teenagers sending one 18 year-old into an off-licence to buy alcohol that's then drunk on park benches. It's the difference between alcohol as an initiation rite to adulthood, and getting drunk as children.

The Talbot was – and remains – a true community pub, attracting people of all ages from the surrounding streets. Such pubs are self-governing, benignly anarchic states. Everyone who drinks there enjoys the easy-going mood and recognizes that, for it to survive, everyone needs to behave themselves. When, in former times, you could order your first pint at 16, you were elated that you'd 'got away with it'. But the older drinkers were watching you. So, as long as you behaved yourselves while you were drinking in the pub, you were learning its codes and unwritten laws. Make a fool of yourself, and you were quickly barred.

A man in a research focus group once told me his own story about this coming of age rite. In his pub (which wasn't The Talbot, but remains so in my imagination) there was a carpeted part of the bar and a plainer area with a linoleum floor. It was understood that, as a young person, you stood on the lino, sipping a soft drink, with the carpet reserved for the 'proper drinkers', the pub's nobility. Across this divide, fathers uncles and neighbours would observe their teenage children and relatives, not intervening, just keeping check.

One evening, one of the men on the carpet beckoned this guy over on the pretext of asking a question to settle a dispute. But this was just an excuse. "Well, now you're here, you might as well have a drink." He looked back at his friends, still standing on the lino. He was the first to graduate to the carpet, and never went back, drinking with the grown-ups until one by one his friends were also deemed worthy.

Today The Talbot looks the same as it always did, although it's changed hands several times. It certainly no longer serves 16 year olds. It's now essentially the brewery tap for the Two Roses Brewery, which stands on the site of the long-gone carpet factory, where my dad spent most of his life. The brewery was built there by an enterprising local after he was made redundant, just like my dad had been. The beers are excellent, and drinking them in the Talbot remains the perfect introduction to the world of beer and pubs for anyone - over legal drinking age of course.

The pits are all long gone, and the much-reduced local working men's club is just about hanging on. But on the rare occasions I still get back to Mapplewell, it seems like The Talbot is thriving, which means the world hasn't quite lost its head just yet.

OPPOSITE TOP: The Talbot Inn, Mapplewell. When I was a lad (and the pits were still open) this stone was black.

OPPOSITE BOTTOM LEFT: The secret answer to a trivia question: a Talbot was a breed of hunting dog.

OPPOSITE BOTTOM RIGHT: I'm not sure that Talbots hunted bulls though.

TALBOT INN
&
1776
Mapplewell

🎤 PUBS WITH LIVE ENTERTAINMENT

ALMOST ALL FORMS of popular entertainment – from theatre and music hall to stand-up comedy and popular music – can be traced back to the pub.

Long ago, travelling minstrels and groups of players (actors) would put on a show in a woodland clearing or natural hollow. When they came to towns and cities, they'd set up in the courtyard of an inn instead. The shape of the courtyard allowed the stage to be placed at one end, and the galleries around upper floors could be used for a chorus or important guests. The designs of the first purpose-built theatres in London, such as The Rose or Shakespeare's Globe, clearly echo inns such as The George Inn (page138) as they looked at that time.

Pubs of all shapes and sizes have always hired poets, singers and musicians to keep people drinking a little longer and happier. In the early 18th century, in the face of growing competition in densely populated areas, some pubs were rebuilt so the main hall had a stage at one end and long benches down the middle. These new venues, dubbed music halls, hosted singers, comedians and acrobats, who were the first real stars of light entertainment. Music hall, and its more formal offspring, variety theatre, were the home of the first singing stars to ever make records, and the first cinema stars ever to appear on screen. Stand-up comedy, wrestling, musicals and the earliest forms of what would later become pop music were born here.

Perhaps this is why such a relatively small country as the UK has always punched well above its weight in popular entertainment – it's always had the pub to nurture all kinds of acts.

By the 1950s and 1960s, the pub and its relative, the working men's club, were where pop groups honed their routine and learned to deal with appreciative, bored or even hostile audiences. By the mid-1970s, there was even a genre known as 'pub rock' – stripped down, punchy and working class acts such as Dr Feelgood, the 101ers and Elvis Costello paved the way for punk as they played venues such as The Ivy House (page 142).

The pub remains at the heart of popular music. Elbow is just one band that met in a pub and played their first gig in one. Huge stars such as The Libertines, Damon Albarn and, even Coldplay's Chris Martin occasionally play secret gigs in pubs just for the fun of it, while those on the first rung of fame still play gigs for as little as 50 quid ($70)or even a couple of pints.

And it's not just music – hundreds of comedy clubs, upstairs or in the back room of someone's local, still give many stand-up comedians their first try-out. In the late 1980s, a comic named Jim Moir created a surreal show during a residency upstairs in a South London pub that eventually transferred to TV as *Vic Reeves Big Night Out*, helping turn alternative comedy into the template for mainstream entertainment for the next 20 years or so.

But pubs remain different from the theatres and concert halls they spawned: they're more democratic, more open places. A good live entertainment pub will invariably have an open mic night to allow anyone to get up with their guitar, and if that's too intimidating, or you're just not good enough, the pub is also the home of karaoke.

Any pub can become a little theatre. Upstair spaces and back rooms that cater for overspill on a Saturday may play home to all sorts on a quiet week night, and you can now find literary readings and festivals, poetry workshops and amateur dramatics down your local. Your fellow punters may dream of being the stars of tomorrow. Thanks to the generous opportunity offered by pubs, one or two of them just might end up being so.

OPPOSITE TOP: Musicians gather at the Pebbles Tavern in Watchet, North Somerset.

OPPOSITE BOTTOM: Live entertainment is a huge part of the Ivy House in South London, cementing its place within the life of the local community.

THE DUBLIN CASTLE 🏰🎤

94 Parkway, London NW1 7AN
www.thedublincastle.com

Camden bleeds music. It's dirty and hollowed-out and not what it was, but as soon as you emerge from the tube you're immersed in ticket touts and haircuts. People run through traffic, enacting a kind of rebellion.

The pub we're weaving our way towards was originally one of four. The navvies (navigators) who built Britain's canals and railways were housed here – in the most rudimentary way – when they connected North London to the rest of the country and dug the first London Underground lines.

They came from England, Ireland, Scotland and Wales, and after working all day, they spilled onto Camden's streets to drink – and fight.

The solution was a gently enforced segregation. Four pubs – the Windsor Castle, Pembroke Castle, Edinboro *[sic]* Castle and Dublin Castle – divided Camden into regional zones.

If there were any justice, the four castles would still prevail. Perhaps, inevitably, it was the Windsor that threw in the towel. Someone with no romance in their soul renamed it N.W.1, and when that inevitably failed, it became a branch of a soulless chain restaurant. The Edinboro Castle survives, as does the Pembroke (attempting to drop the 'Castle' part). Both are now sanitized gastropubs.

The Dublin Castle followed a beautifully alternative trajectory. In the late 1950s, Alo Conlon came to London from Ireland and earned a reputation as a fearless tunneller. He made enough money digging to invest in The Dublin Castle, and turned it into a live music venue. Its reputation was made in the late 1970s when seven young local lads turned up asking for a gig, claiming to be a jazz band. After that first Madness gig, Alo offered them a weekly residency. Since then, the pub has hosted bands including Blur and Arctic Monkeys. Amy Winehouse loved playing here so much

she'd sometimes help behind the bar.

Alo passed away in 2009, but his family still run the pub his way, and Suggs and the boys still pop in for a pint. Four nights a week, three bands still play in the back room.

On a late October Wednesday, the place is packed. There's a reckless energy that's reminiscent of the 1980s pub. The jostling at the bar is sharper than I'm used to these days. I think, 'Oh yes, that's what music venues are like,' and then catch myself and wonder why. Music may have been corporatized and sanitized now, but here at the grassroots it still wears rebellious clothes.

Men in suits, older ladies in black two-pieces and people whose parents used to love Madness all file into the back room to listen to a band that sounds like a cross between The Jam and Mumford & Sons.

Instead of following, I get a seat in one of the battered red faux-leather banquettes, choose a selection from the bespoke Dublin Castle compilations on the old CD jukebox, and put my drink down on one of the narrow tables with shiny golden tops that surely haven't changed since the 1970s. If Tarantino had been English, *Pulp Fiction* would have been shot in here.

The band now channels some kind of car crash between The Wurzels and King Kurt, and seem to be singing a song called 'Where's my ****** lunch you ******* ****'. One of them is probably Nigel from accounts, playing to workmates and relatives who don't really go to gigs any more, but have come tonight to support him as he lives his dream.

It's a brilliant dream, far better than the vampiric lust for fame that drives TV reality shows. This dream is simply about standing up on the stage that Suggs and Amy stood on, and playing your bleedin' heart out.

OPPOSITE TOP: The stage on which a journey to global stardom begins. Or a journey to working in accounts. But, once or twice, stardom, definitely.

OPPOSITE BOTTOM LEFT: Big brands give money to venues like The Dublin Castle in the hope that it will make them seem cool.

OPPOSITE BOTTOM RIGHT: The exterior of The Dublin Castle, Parkway, is a Camden Town institution.

🌳 COUNTRY PUBS

WHEN GEORGE ORWELL DEFINED his perfect pub in *The Moon Under Water*, he was careful to point out that he was talking about the urban pub, and that the country pub is quite different. But while his template for the town and city pub remains famous to anyone who takes an interest in pubs, we never get to find out what his rural equivalent was.

Just like London's Moon Under Water, it's probable that if Orwell had spelled out his country version, we would still recognize much of it today – maybe even more so than the city one. Things change more slowly in the countryside. Land tends not to get 'developed' as quickly. It's less likely that the pub will get squeezed out by rising rents, or bombed during wars, or zoned for alternative use. Of course, there are other dangers that threaten their existence (e.g. absent second-home owners), but country pubs tend to last longer and change less often than their urban equivalents.

The quintessential country pub is probably what many people imagine the British pub to be. It has a low, thatched roof and white walls, a spacious beer garden, and possibly ivy or trellises of honeysuckle growing around the door. Inside it's all low, beamed ceilings, ancient fireplaces and horse brasses on the walls. Sunday is the busiest day of the week because everyone comes along for the roast or, its more decadent cousin, the carvery.

There are, of course, many country pubs like this. It's a cliché, but it's a beautiful one. But there's a lot more to ye olde country inn than horse brasses and tankards of ale. (Not that there necessarily needs to be.)

The oldest surviving country pubs were invariably inns giving shelter to all kinds of travellers, from shepherds driving their sheep down from the hills to market, to merchants and nobles riding in stagecoaches. Centuries later, the arrival of the motor car reinvented them as destinations in their own right rather than pitstops on the way to somewhere else. You always know when you're close to a great one like The Crown Inn at Woolhope (page 178) or the Strines Inn in the Peak District (page 212), because in the middle of not very much at all you're suddenly among a jam of cars fighting for parking spaces.

But these grand old buildings are not the only types of country pub. There are also those that serve small communities rather than motorists, cyclists and bikers. For these places, times are tough. Younger generations move away to the cities, and city people buy up the houses as second homes, which they use only a few times a year. Even those living there all year round increasingly use country villages as dormitories, commuting into cities every day, and spending less time in their immediate community than they do at work.

All this means that even beautiful old pubs cradled by stunning green countryside are increasingly struggling. When the final pub closes its doors in villages like this, there's no longer a community, just a collection of houses standing near to one other.

Pub is the Hub was founded in 2001 to help save pubs in places like this. It encourages communities to buy their pubs as cooperatives when pub companies wrongly deem them no longer viable. They help pubs take on other functions that the village may also have lost. The Blue Bell Inn in Halkyn (page 244), for example, remains open all day, every day, in a quiet North Welsh village because it's now also the post office.

With increased penalties for drink driving – and much keener awareness of its dangers – country pubs struggle much harder to survive on drink sales than they once did, so many reinvented themselves as food pubs. A pub is a great place for an ambitious chef to work

OPPOSITE TOP LEFT: Take your coat off once you're inside The Clachaig Inn, or you won't feel the benefit.

OPPOSITE MIDDLE LEFT: It's amazing what you find in the garden of Devon's Rugglestone Inn.

OPPOSITE TOP RIGHT: The new landlord of The Rose & Crown in Huish Episcopi, Somerset, simply couldn't figure out what the big hole in the wall was for.

OPPOSITE BOTTOM: At the Wasdale Head, you have to adjust swiftly to Lake District Time.

out his or her craft, because there's little hype or expectation to start with. But when the pub makes its mark, people will drive great distances and book weeks in advance to get a table. Choose well, and you're close to wonderful ingredients and have little local competition. Around 20 pubs in the UK now have Michelin stars, and these are almost exclusively rural pubs.

Country pubs are in fact just as varied as urban pubs. A Lake District pub catering for climbers and walkers is different in every way from a 1930s roadhouse in Surrey.

But what country pubs all have in common is a wonderful change of pace from city life. Visitors from town behave differently, even drink differently, from the way they do back home. For these incomers, the country pub is the perfect example of somewhere that's not just a place to go for a drink, but a place to simply *be*.

ABOVE: The picture-perfect Rugglestone Inn, Devon, features the country-pub essentials of stonework, stunning views and wisteria-clad walls.

OPPOSITE TOP: A warm, glowing welcome awaits at The Hatchet Inn in rural Hampshire.

OPPOSITE BOTTOM: In Hinxton, Cambridgeshire, The Red Lion demonstrates the trap it uses to snare people and cause them to abandon whatever plans they had and settle in for the day.

THE TAN HILL INN 🏰🔨🌳❗

Reeth, Richmond, Swaledale, North Yorkshire DL11 6ED
www.tanhillinn.com

The Tan Hill Inn claims to be 'near Reeth', in North Yorkshire. This is an outrageous lie: the Tan Hill Inn isn't near anywhere. I suppose Reeth is the closest place on the map that has a name, but it's still a decent drive away.

When I look back at my photos days after my visit to the Tan Hill Inn, I briefly wonder if I've been on a trip to the Falkland Islands and suffered amnesia about it. Then I recognize that I'm looking at Great Britain's highest pub. It's an easy mistake to make, with the tall flagpole flying the Union Jack outside, the bunker-like hulk of the building, the brown and gold late summer heather and the craggy rocks that surely must also pass as Britain's wildest beer garden.

We reach the pub by driving up Arkengarthdale, which is perhaps the most northern-sounding word in the entire world. We're right on the tops of the moors, and as the sun eventually burns the mist from the tops, leaving clouds in the valleys below, we can see for miles and smell burning peat.

When we finally arrive, groups of cyclists are mounting up for the next leg of what can only be a gruelling journey. A bright orange vehicle on caterpillar tracks – like you might expect to see at an Antarctic research station – sits parked next to the pub. The Pennine Way crosses the narrow road at this point, and some walkers enquire about camping. 'Aye, just pitch round the back, under the rocks. That way you'll be out of the worst of the wind,' says the barman.

The Tan Hill Inn is obviously Britain's highest pub (528metres/1732 feet above sea level). It's not just that this fact is stated everywhere you look; it's the building itself, the way it's built. It doesn't seek shelter like the campers. It stands proud, daring the elements to bring it on. I realize there are two main types of country pub: twee, beautiful places with thatched roofs and pretty gardens, and places like this. Thatch wouldn't last two minutes up here. Instead, it's all about thick, hard stone. Even the roof tiles look like heavy slabs. Inside, the stone walls are naked and stark. The floor is made of stone flags. And the bar is built from the same stone. This pub is going nowhere.

Signs behind the bar warn that the staff are mad, due to altitude sickness. Another sign promises (warns?) that, 'Everyone staying [overnight] gets a full English breakfast.' Whether you want one or not, presumably.

The beer is good, honest, traditional Yorkshire bitter, and the food comes in backpacker's portions. For those of us travelling by car, a pie or a Yorkshire pudding filled with mash and a giant Cumberland sausage form the only meal we'll need all day.

The Tan Hill Inn is a famous pub, and it can be easy to lapse into clichés and talk about the many celebrity guests and TV appearances the pub has enjoyed. A pub sign on the wall for The Slaughtered Lamb, the pub from the film *An American Werewolf in London,* leads many to believe the movie was filmed here, which it wasn't. But the comparison is too entertaining to resist. Ted Moult definitely did appear in an ad for Everest Double Glazing that was shot here though. There's a barn that hosts regular live entertainment. In 2010, the indie band British Sea Power hosted their own music festival here. Mark Ronson and Arctic Monkeys have also played. But this fame has not dimmed the charm of a pub that knows how attractive it is, and manages to be boastful yet unfazed by its fame, like any good northerner.

In 2009, the barn saw a great deal of action when the crowd that arrived to celebrate New Year's Eve were snowed in for three days. I can't help but envy them.

OPPOSITE TOP: The Tan Hill Inn cunningly intercepts walkers hoping to complete the Pennine Way.

OPPOSITE BOTTOM LEFT: It's Britain's highest pub, you know.

OPPOSITE BOTTOM RIGHT: The Tan Hill Inn's response to rush-hour traffic.

⚓ COASTAL PUBS

There's an idea in social anthropology and psychology about 'liminal' spaces and states of being. It relates to the idea of being on a threshold between two states or places. These could be mental states or physical spaces, and it's an idea that underlies all sorts of fantastical fiction about different worlds or dimensions, from *Alice in Wonderland* to Harry Potter's platform 9¾.

Anthropologists and sociologists have written about how the coast – and, more specifically, the seaside – is a liminal space. I'm sure the average holidaymaker in Blackpool or Brighton would scoff at such a pretentious idea. But while doing so, that person will be drinking more, eating more, wearing less and caring less than they ever would in their normal lives, behaving in an entirely different way not only from how they would behave at home, but also how they'd behave in public on a different kind of holiday such as a countryside retreat or city break. The coast does something to our brains. It frees us from our inhibitions. On the cusp between land and sea, normal rules don't always apply.

Throw pubs into this mix, and things get very interesting indeed. Pubs everywhere also create different spaces where we lower our guard and relax, where many of us can be more confident and outgoing than we are elsewhere. So coastal pubs, combining as they do different kinds of magic, have the potential to take us to another level.

The appeal of a sea view is obvious, and sipping a pint while watching the crashing waves is a superlative experience. But there's much more to it than simply the view – the way in which a great coastal pub responds to its location is an important part of the mix.

Coastal pubs have a greater potential for romance – in the broadest sense of the word. Decorations – props if you like – such as paintings of tall ships, fishing nets, old ships' wheels and lanterns, reproductions of posters about wanted smugglers and auctions from shipwrecks, make us dream of different times, fantasize about a life on the ocean that has no bearing on reality, either now or then. Few pubs are more disappointing than the seaside pub that looks like it could be anywhere else.

In good coastal pubs we relax in a different way. We settle in for a longer, steadier time. These pubs are often lighter and airier than the comfortably dark and cosy haunts you find in towns and cities. Walls are often whitewashed to reflect the light from the sea. There's more wood involved, with planks making up the floor and sometimes the walls, evoking the sense of being aboard a ship.

Like country pubs – but perhaps even more so – coastal pubs are more exposed to the elements than pubs anywhere else. Even when you visit them in the height of summer, places like The Lochside Hotel in Islay (page 240) or The Square and Compass in Devon (page 114) are so solidly built you can almost feel the lash of the storm on the sunniest of days. The brutal chill never quite seems to leave the thick, solid stone walls.

But get down to the harbour and onto the beach on those perfect summer days, and the opposite is also true: here, pubs open themselves up to the sun. Most punters drink outside, the alcohol almost an excuse that facilitates the more contemplative experience of drinking in the view. The Driftwood Spars in Cornwall (page 101), The Anchor Inn in North Norfolk (page 156) and even Thameside pubs such as Rotherhithe's Mayflower (page 144) send your thoughts out into the distance.

Any good pub untethers us from the day to day. A great coastal pub goes further, setting you free, so you never know where you might end up.

OPPOSITE TOP: The Driftwood Spars on the North Cornwall coast has a pleasing whitewashed exterior, nautical style.

OPPOSITE BOTTOM: In Whitstable, Kent, The Old Neptune sits happily right on the beach itself.

THE TY COCH INN

Porthdinllaen, Pwllheli, Gwynedd LL53 6DB
www.tycoch.co.uk

The harbour at Porthdinllaen is a vague sketch: a low, rocky wall curving out from the shore just far enough to offer some protection for the tiny fishing vessels bobbing at anchor. Looking out from the shore, the view is of the Snowdonia and Yr Eifl mountains rather than the sea. We're on a peninsula sticking out from a peninsula; eastern facing, protected from the worst of the sea by the spit of land behind it.

'Ty Coch' is Welsh for 'Red House'. (North Wales has always been very practical.) The Ty Coch Inn was built in 1823 from the red bricks carried as ballast by ships coming in from the Netherlands, when the harbour was much busier. Originally a vicarage, the Ty Coch was turned into an inn catering for shipbuilders by the vicar's housekeeper when he moved out of the place in 1842.

The inn is now painted brick red, its name clearly stencilled on the sides and roof of the building. I imagine that hanging pub signs don't fare too well against the worst of the weather here. But today, at the very tail end of a typically non-committal British summer, we get one last chance to enjoy the beach.

Apart from the pub and the harbour, Porthdinllaen consists of about a dozen houses along a short quayside above the beach. A narrow road leads here across the golf course that occupies the mini-peninsula, but only residents are allowed to drive down it. For everyone else, it's a walk across the golf course or along the beach from the nearby village of Morfa Nefyn. You have to drive along the whole of the North Wales coast and down past Anglesey, or across Snowdonia, to get even that far. The sense of isolation and remoteness gives the whole village a romantic air and a sense that normal rules don't apply.

One step away from the beach, the Ty Coch engages with the sea in all its guises. It's not only the ships instruments and storm lanterns that adorn the walls and ceilings. Well-thumbed guidebooks to coastal footpaths and seashore flora and fauna hang from the walls by string. Posters advertise coastal wildlife cruises and longboats for sale. Collection points and memorabilia demonstrate a strong link with the Royal National Lifeboat Association. Today the sea has that wouldn't-hurt-a-fly shimmer to it, but there are photos on the walls showing the pub being submerged by waves, the whole quayside under water.

Everyone seems to know that this is the last weekend of summer. Drinkers with sun-kissed hair, fleeces and windcheaters, shorts and bare feet walk slowly into the pub and up to the bar, before taking their drinks back outside. Sand drifts and whirls across the floor.

And then I realize that I'm the only person in the pub that's drinking.

I've missed the point of this place. While the weather remains like this, the beach *is* the pub. About a hundred people – families, couples, of all ages and walks of life – are doing the same thing: sitting on the sea wall, or on the terrace full of tables or on the beach itself, staring out to sea, drink in hand, quietly contemplating. It's extraordinary to see so many people being so silent for so long.

The only interruption happens when a man proposes to his girlfriend down by the shore. I work out what's happened when she hugs him tight, and their friends produce a bottle of champagne and glasses from a cool bag and toast them. They get out mobile phones and turn to the pub. There's a webcam installed in one of the upper windows (you should check it out), and the happy couple face their friends watching at home and raise their glasses.

The sea, so innocent now, is a light ripple of applause on the shingle.

OPPOSITE TOP: CO328 was certain he was going to make it to the pub this time. So near, and yet so far. Never mind, he could wait until the next high tide.

OPPOSITE BOTTOM: The harbour village of Porthdinllaen. Yes, that really is all of it.

🚆 RAILWAY PUBS

EVERY TOWN WITH A RAILWAY station has a pub nearby. Sometimes, when I'm staring from the train window at a town I've never set foot in, I'm overcome with the urge to alight and see what the Station Tavern or the Railway Arms is like.

The main reason I don't do this (apart from wanting to get where I'm going in reasonable time) is that I'm fairly sure I'd be disappointed by what I find.

The typical pub relies largely on its regulars for custom – people who come in often, drink the same thing and help to build the unique culture of the place.

The railway pub does something quite different: it caters for those who are passing through, on their way to somewhere else. Too often, this means the railway pub can get away with the lowest standards of service. It doesn't matter if people feel let down or even ripped off; they've got a train to catch, and you're probably not going to see them again.

This is a tragedy. Seen another way, the railway pub should be capable of creating a uniquely charged atmosphere.

We enter a different state when travelling, a slightly altered reality. This manifests itself in half-joking assertions that the money you spend in Duty Free isn't really money, or the calories you consume on holiday don't count. Train travel can – or should – be every bit as romantic as air or sea travel.

When we're waiting for a train (at least one that isn't part of our daily commute), we're going on a little adventure, and there's at least a small charge of possibility – the poignancy of leaving, or the anticipation of arriving. Sitting in the station waiting to board should be an exciting experience, and the pub should take advantage of that.

Som pubs that are actually *in* stations – on the platforms or even inside old signal boxes – do succeed in capturing this. They're helped if the building they occupy dates from the Victorian era, when rail travel really was a thrilling experience. Vast ceilings and tall mirrors make us feel we're already somewhere special, and remind us of a time of vision, ambition and purpose.

Sadly, Britain's Network Rail seems not to care about any of this. Here and there, pub operators who care about railways are managing to restore some of these buildings to their former glory and give pubs back that special purpose. But it can be difficult.

One of the greatest recent successes is The Parcel Yard in King's Cross (page 144). At a time when many say it's not worth investing money in pubs, The Parcel Yard is a grand gesture by Fuller's Brewery. Architecturally stunning, it is a palace to the history of railways, a superb food destination and a great pub too.

Just down the road is the Euston Tap, a craft beer bar inside a tiny station gatehouse that's on a completely different scale, but just as audacious in its own way.

The North of England seems to have fared better in keeping decent station platform pubs than the rest of the country, with The York Tap (page 215) a stunning restoration, and the Refreshment Rooms at Carnforth, near Lancaster, lovingly preserved since their time as the location for the film *Brief Encounter*.

Across the UK, train station platforms and concourses present one of the gloomiest shopping experiences in the country, with almost every stand and shop run by the same lumpen franchise conglomerate. Those pubs that still operate outside this company's clutches, and which are done well, offer a glorious break from stifling conformity and robotic service. They may not have to put any effort into getting custom, but do so anyway.

OPPOSITE TOP LEFT: The striking interior of the Euston Tap is barely larger than a front room.

OPPOSITE MIDDLE LEFT: Sitting proudly near the entrance to London's Euston station, the exterior of The Euston Tap, makes it hard to resist the call of ale.

OPPOSITE TOP RIGHT: Great railway pubs gather their heritage around themselves and place it back on show for us to see.

OPPOSITE BOTTOM: The Parcel Yard in London's King's Cross Station, reminds us of bygone grandeur.

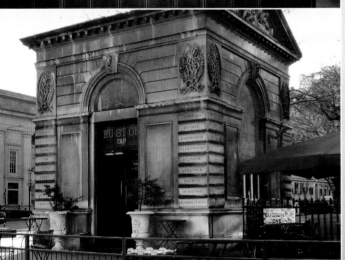

THE SHEFFIELD TAP 🏛 🏧 🍺

Platform 1B, Sheffield Station, Sheaf St, Sheffield, South Yorkshire S1 2BP
www.sheffieldtap.com

In some ways, Sheffield train station is one of the most civilized in Britain. Because the footbridge between the main road at the front of the station and the tram stop at the back also provides a vital thoroughfare to the city centre from a residential area on the other side, it's possibly the only remaining station of its size that hasn't installed ticket barriers.

Of course, East Midlands Trains hate this, paranoid that everyone moving through the station is a potential fare dodger, and seemingly uncaring that the absence of barriers makes things far more pleasant for the majority of fare-paying passengers too.

The policy also means that, for the time being at least, the former Edwardian Refreshment Room & Dining Rooms on Platform One can be accessed from both the platform and the front of the station.

This isn't the only feature of the Sheffield Tap that makes you feel like you've stepped back into an age where there was still some elegance and grandeur in rail travel.

When business partners Jamie Hawksworth and Jon Holdsworth rescued the building from decades of neglect, the building was derelict and roofless. The Grade II-listed interior had been heavily vandalized and left to rot. Jamie and Jon instigated a policy they describe as 'repair where possible and replicate as required'. A new roof was created by a number of local craftsmen using moulds taken from the original structure. The stunning mahogany bar was salvaged from the pieces that remained then rebuilt. Most of the original wall tiles were saved and restored.

Today, the Sheffield Tap lifts the spirits. Under the high ceilings, it feels sophisticated in a European way, if only because many European countries are better at preserving this kind of architecture than us British.

Until a few years ago, both locally brewed real ale and the glamorous dash of the steam engine felt like symbols of a bygone Britain that we could never have back. The old trains may be gone forever, but now there are more ale breweries in Britain than there have been since the golden age of steam. The Tap serves an astonishing array of them, in excellent condition, poured by knowledgeable staff who help you navigate unfamiliar brands without a hint of snobbery.

There's a rigorous passion in everything they do here. When the Tap first opened, I reviewed it and struggled to find one critical note, which I needed in order to prevent my piece from appearing sycophantic. Eventually I found the hand dryer in the male toilet, which was about as powerful as a pixie exhaling after a nice meal. When I returned a few months later, it had been replaced by something so powerful it almost blew the flesh from my bones.

Train travel may no longer be the adventure it once was, but it still richly deserves places like this. It should allow us space in which to contemplate life, detached from our normal, everyday surroundings.

When you walk into the Tap, you feel elevated. It recalls the days when important pubs were more pleasant places to spend time in than the houses we lived in, offering glamour and style to people who had precious little of that. Sheffield is a wonderful city, but it's not a city that's immediately easy on the eye. You have to get inside it to appreciate the energy and style born of its fierce northern pride. Perhaps the most delightful aspect of the most beautiful railway pub in the country, if not the world, is that it is here in Sheffield, one of the best cities for beer in Britain, and not in central London.

OPPOSITE TOP: The interior of the Sheffield Tap is both astonishing and elegant.

OPPOSITE BOTTOM LEFT: Not only is the interior beautiful, it also has a bar.

OPPOSITE BOTTOM RIGHT: Plenty of varied seating means you may linger longer than you intend to.

ECCENTRIC PUBS AND PUBS IN UNUSUAL LOCATIONS

A PENGUIN WALKS INTO A PUB. He goes to the counter and asks the barman, 'Have you seen my brother?' The barman replies, 'I don't know, what does he look like?'

There's a reason jokes like this always start with a man or a woman (or talking animal, or object, or abstract concept) entering a pub.

If it were a coffee shop or bakery or bank, it wouldn't work; it would just sound weird. Of course, it still sounds pretty unusual when we locate the joke in a pub, but here we suspend disbelief, because we know that pubs are quirky places where unusual things can happen, and we also know that pub humour frequently embraces the surreal. Often a degree of absurdity will be embedded into the pub's very fabric.

Some pubs are in odd or highly unlikely places. The Marisco Tavern (page 104) is on Lundy Island and can only be reached by the ferry and supply ship that sails there between three and five times a week, while Bristol's Apple (page 100) is a boat itself – a barge moored on a riverside wharf in the city centre.

Even in more conventional locations, the buildings that pubs inhabit can be odd. The Nutshell in Bury St Edmunds (page 164) is Britain's smallest pub, a sliver on the side of a larger building. Ye Olde Mitre in the heart of London (pages 76, 144) is impossible to find and was, for a long time, technically part of Cambridgeshire.

But pubs really start to show their character once you're inside. Pubs are traditionally decorated with household or functional objects: horse brasses and blacksmith's tools in coaching inns, old kitchen implements or beer memorabilia in urban pubs. Some pubs take this idea to its furthest reaches, creating interiors that qualify as outsider or folk art:

the unnervingly vast collection of branded tea mugs at The Blisland Inn, in Cornwall (page 100), the twin obsessions with mushrooms and angels at The Cartford Inn in Lancashire (page 196), or the *tour de force* of posh junk-shop clutter that covers every surface of the Canny Man's in Edinburgh (page 238) transcend the notion of collected junk and become something else, something that forces you to stop and contemplate life in all its jumbled, complicated magnificence.

Some of this stuff, along with claims of hauntings, or competitions, such as World Bog Snorkelling, Dwile Flonking or Nettle Eating Championships, makes for great tourist fodder and ensures a particular pub regularly features in newspaper top-ten lists of unusual pubs you must visit. Sometimes a claim feels a little forced, a cynical idea to get custom in an otherwise unremarkable pub. But often it's yet another feature of a pub that was already interesting, and may just be a logical extension of the landlord's passion. (Dwile Flonking may sound like an odd passion to have, but I assure you it's genuine.) The Bridge Inn at Topsham (page 100) doesn't feel contrived in its perfectly preserved Edwardian state, and while The Three Horseshoes in Norfolk (page 170) and The Albion Inn in Chester (page 194) may have been constructed retrospectively to evoke earlier eras, they've obviously been done with genuine and obsessive love.

That's just one aspect of how the best publicans imprint their personalities on a place. Some become legendary characters, showmen and women for whom the bar is a stage, with audiences travelling to see them perform. That The Red Lion in Histon, Cambridgeshire (page 166) and The Dispensary in Liverpool (page 195) are at

OPPOSITE TOP: The Butcher's Arms is where mobile phones come to die. Let me rephrase that: if mobile phones come to the Butcher's Arms, they die.

OPPOSITE BOTTOM LEFT: It's best not to stare too long at the ceiling of Edinburgh's Canny Man's.

OPPOSITE BOTTOM RIGHT: Every eccentic pub should have a resident bear. This one's in The Drover's Inn, near Loch Lomond, Scotland.

least as well known for the behaviour of their landlords as anything else, should not disguise the fact that these are superbly run businesses selling excellent beer.

Pubs don't fit neatly into prescribed boxes. Throughout history, they've sheltered us from the gaze of those who would like us to stay in line all the time and do as we're told. They liberate us from class and conformity. The quirky pub is an adult playground, where rules may apply, but are often arbitrary and made up on a whim. That's why a white horse can walk into a pub to be told it's got a whisky named after him[1] but if William Shakespeare follows him in, he's likely to be refused service[2].

1. 'What, Dobbin?'
2. Because he's Bard.

ABOVE LEFT: Despite what seems like a very clear sign here on the street, Ye Olde Mitre in London is still maddeningly difficult to find if you don't know where to look.

ABOVE RIGHT: The Three Horseshoes, Warham, Norfolk, close to the coast.

OPPOSITE: The singular main bar at the Red Lion, Histon, Cambridgeshire, features a huge range of bottled Belgian beers alongside a fine collection of cask ale.

THE PIG'S NOSE INN

East Prawle, Kingsbridge, Devon TQ7 2BY
www.pigsnoseinn.co.uk

The Pig's Nose Inn doesn't really exist. It was invented when George Orwell, Neil Gaiman and the late beer writer Michael Jackson sat down together and worked out their consensus vision of the rural equivalent of the city's Moon Under Water.

This is not true. But it might as well be.

The Pig's Nose is so good I'm reluctant to tell you where it is or how to get there. You'll have to find it for yourself, to prove yourself worthy. It's at the end of a winding road of tidal inlets crossed by exquisite bridges and boats playing lazily in the evening sun, in a tiny village where you pitch your tent in a field that slopes gently towards the top of a low cliff overlooking the sparkling sea.

With the tent up, you cross the village green with its minute shop and cafe, and enter what looks, from the outside, like a nondescript, grey little boozer.

Like Gaiman's World's End – the inn where travellers between realms shelter during reality storms in his *Sandman* series – the pub defies its external dimensions. It's far bigger inside than it is on the outside. You explore all evening and never see all of it. A curtained doorway leads into a tiny snug, which has windows on the outside wall opposite, and those windows look out onto more of the pub.

The inn has grown to absorb the other buildings around it. One of these is a small concert hall with a stage at the far end. One family sits in a row eating crisps, gazing at the space. A handwritten list pinned to the wall, and verified by cuttings from local newspapers, tells you that, in the past decade or so, this venue has hosted gigs by The Yardbirds, The Animals, Geno Washington, Dr Feelgood, Wishbone Ash, Curiosity Killed the Cat and Damon Albarn. You know this can't possibly be true, but the photos are there to prove it.

The beer in the Pig's Nose is, of course, served straight from the barrel behind a particularly low bar. This creates greater intimacy between staff and drinker, and every time you're served, it's with particularly lingering eye contact and a warm smile. The proprietor, who looks like the actor David Warner in his rakish prime, sits on a wooden chair in front of the barrels, chatting to customers as he constantly refills his own half-pint glass.

Other pubs may be decorated with a collection of sporting prints or horse brasses, but The Pig's Nose Inn turns utilitarian objects into outsider art. The walls and beams are plastered with pistols, model ships, keys, carpentry tools, dolls and figurines, bed pans, trumpets, lacrosse sticks, barometers, a swarm of butterflies, antlers, kettles, lamps and telescopes; the random detritus of our lives, being presented back to us.

After 10 o'clock, the energy ramps up. People come and go, then come back again. Many of them are unfeasibly tall. They all seem to know each other: the hippies and the red-trousered Audi driver; the campers; local farmers; the northern holidaymakers and the posh Londoners. They all create a sort of friction as they interact, creating a heat and a specific spell that jumps from person to person by proximity, until it covers the entire pub, making everyone the best versions of themselves that they can be.

The next morning, you find last night's barman chatting to a bunch of girls. He tells them he can't remember what time he finished work or went to bed, but that last night was 'A funny one. A bit quiet.'

And you think to yourself that if that – one of the best nights you've ever spent in a pub – was 'a bit quiet', you need to come back. If you can ever find it again.

OPPOSITE TOP: The gaffer holds court in The Pig's Nose Inn.

OPPOSITE BOTTOM LEFT: Is the price list meant to be this unnerving?

OPPOSITE BOTTOM RIGHT: It looks pretty small doesn't it? Inside, it's at least three times bigger.

ALES

OTTER (3·6)
DEVON (3·8)
EDDYSTONE (4·8)

CIDERS

SPARKLING
ASHRIDGE (4.5)
KATY (7.0!)
(MAKES YOU SMILE)

FARM
THATCHER'S
HERITAGE (4.9)

SOFT DRINKS

GINGER BEER · J20
LEMONADE · APPLETISE
ELDER FLOWER
JUICE: 1/-

GREAT BEER PUBS

BEER IS THE PERFECT DRINK for the pub. Pubs are places you want to linger in for a while. If you were to stay for two or three hours in a coffee shop, buying a new drink each time you finished the one in front of you, you'd be bouncing off the ceiling. If you were to make one drink last, it would soon be cold.

Stick around in a pub drinking wine or spirits, and you'll soon be worse for wear. Try it with soft drinks, and the volume will make your teeth itch and your stomach fizz.

Beer has co-evolved with the pub as a long, slow drink. Cask ale – what tourists think of as 'British beer' – has long been the spiritual partner of the Great British pub, usually lower in alcohol and less gassy than other beers, which means it can be drunk in bigger sizes than that of many other brewing nations. Cask ale is designed for 'the session', the slow curve of intoxication that you can keep track of and control, and finish early enough to still be able to do something useful if you need to.

Beer is so ubiquitous, it's something many drinkers – and pubs – take for granted. It's just there and always the same, with little thought paid as to how it should be kept and served, and none at all as to how an exciting range of beers can improve a pub.

Happily, this is now changing. There's a revolution in British brewing that shows no signs of abating, and the pubs that are part of it are regenerating the idea of what the British pub is all about. At the time of writing, the number of breweries in Britain has trebled since the millennium, and new ones are opening at the rate of three or four every week.

Good beer is not essential for a good pub. (There's at least one pub in this book where the beer was dreadful when I visited, but the food and the incredible atmosphere more than made up for this.) But overall, nearly every pub here serves beer that is decent. So those that

have the beer icon next to them are a cut above – the beer isn't just good, it's one of the main reasons to go here rather than another pub that may look nicer or feel like it has more of a buzz about it.

There are two main aspects to making beer truly special, evidence that a good publican understands that great beer is a truly artisanal product that should be treated with a good deal of care and respect.

The first is how the beer is kept. Cask ale is a living thing, with a slow, secondary fermentation going on in the cask in the cellar. Like many aspects of food and drink, it's easy to keep a cask adequately – getting the cellar temperature right and keeping the lines clean – but there's an art to getting the best out of it, judging precisely how long the beer needs to condition, when it's ready to serve and when it's past its best. Environmental factors influence these variables, and the best publicans get to know the quirks of both the beer and their cellar, and how they interrelate.

The second aspect is range: the art of judging how many beers should be on the bar – depending on how busy the pub is, more isn't always better. But size isn't the only thing that matters: a perfect range of beers has a mix of different styles and strengths, with familiar favourites, local heroes and new discoveries, permanent core beers and an ever-evolving mix of seasonals and guests.

And great beer no longer begins and ends with cask ale (if it ever did). The craft beer revolution means keg beers – so long regarded by real ale campaigners as 'cheap fizz' – as well as bottles, and even cans, now contain beers that have a different character from cask ale but are no less interesting.

Like I said, a good pub doesn't *have* to serve good beer, but it probably will. Someone who cares so much about their beer will probably

OPPOSITE TOP LEFT: An iconic pump clip for an iconic brand. When it was modernized, some fans would only drink it when served from this old-fashioned design.

OPPOSITE TOP RIGHT: The house beers at the Barrels, which is the brewery tap and former home of the wonderful Wye Valley brewery.

OPPOSITE MIDDLE LEFT: Passing the time of day at Brighton's Evening Star.

OPPOSITE BOTTOM LEFT: Some sound advice for the practical drinker.

OPPOSITE BOTTOM RIGHT: Pewter tankards and past trophies are a welcoming sight in any pub with great beer.

IF WE DON'T HAVE WHAT YOU DRINK, DRINK WHAT WE HAVE!

The bar with chalkboard labels:

WHEAT £4.4½/2.20 — WHEAT £4.4½/2.20 — STRONG HALF PINTS £3.80 — CASK £3.80 — CASK £3.20/1.60 — CASK £3.20/1.60 — CASK £3.20/1.60 — CRAFT £2.80/1.60 — LAGER £3.4½/1.60

BACCHUS FRAMBOZEN BELGIAN RASPBERRY 5.0%

WEIHENSTEPHANER GERMAN HEFE-WEIZEN 5.6%

VEDETT EXTRA WHITE BELGIAN WITBIER 4.7%

ANDERSON VALLEY HOP OTTIN' IPA 7.0%

ARBOR CHINOOK 6.5%

O'HANLON FLAGSHIP IPA 4.2%

PENZANCE POTION № 9 4.0%

ADDLESTONE'S CLOUDY CIDER 5.2%

CROMARTY HAPPY CHAPPY 4.1%

ORANJEBOOM 3.9%

IF WE DON'T HAVE WHAT YOU DRINK, DRINK WHAT WE HAVE!

be good at everything else that's needed to create the perfect pub.

You might find the occasional pub that feels like a private members' beer appreciation club, the members of which hang around the bar and get involved in stocking and ranging decisions. But now that well-kept, flavourful beer continues its ongoing journey from hobbyist niche to mainstream interest, it's becoming so much easier to find not just great beer, but a passionate advocate for it behind the bar, ready to introduce you to new worlds of flavour. The whole experience may even be as close to you as your local pub.

ABOVE: The bar at The Anderson near Inverness is an altar to great beer in all its forms, as well as housing an astonishing collection of single malt whiskies and beer.

OPPOSITE TOP: The Wenlock Arms, one of London's legendary beer houses, has been threatened with demolition, but has now been restored for the local community.

OPPOSITE BOTTOM LEFT: The brewery under The Bridge Tavern in Newcastle.

OPPOSITE BOTTOM, RIGHT: Refreshment, pure and simple, as presented in Gloucestershire's Salutation Inn.

THE BRIDGE BIER HUIS 👥🔧🌳⚓❗

2 Bank Parade, Burnley, Lancashire BB11 1UH
www.thebridgebierhuis.co.uk

In the early years of Britain's craft beer boom, my enthusiastic endorsement of interesting, flavourful beer from small-scale, passionate brewers would invariably be met with the same comment: 'Yeah, this fancy beer is OK for all your Shoreditch hipsters down in London, but it would never work in [insert the name of pretty much any town of your choice].'

I had two rebuttals to this. The first was to point out that London was pretty much the last major city in the UK to witness the growth of craft breweries, that craft beer leading lights BrewDog had started in Aberdeenshire, Thornbridge in the Peak District, and Dark Star in Brighton, and that the first 'craft beer bar' opened in Leeds in the late 1990s. The second was to simply smile and talk about The Bridge Bier Huis in Burnley.

The Bridge is in the centre of this grimy northern town that's much like Barnsley where I grew up. The pub sits next to a busy road intersection and a massive multistorey car park. It doesn't look like a great location for a pub, but it's central, always busy, and often full with Burnley FC fans on match days.

This is because, inside, it's a great pub. Most of it is one big, airy space, with a small snug off to the side. There are stools at the bar and tables scattered around, but it looks like it's accustomed to catering for large, standing crowds when the football is on TV.

In this respect, The Bridge is no different from hundreds of other pubs across the north. It's only when you get to the bar that you realize this place is extraordinary. The beer range consists of six cask ales and real ciders, and a great array of European beers on tap, from Belgian fruit beer to German smoked beer. The bottled range runs to over 40, lovingly compiled into a list that sits on tables and is promoted on chalkboards.

This is not the biggest, or most eclectic range of beers you'll ever see. But it's incredibly well chosen and spans all aspects of good beer, with traditional British ales, proper pilsner lagers, heady Belgian Trappist ales and the most celebrated modern craft brands all represented in some form. There's not a duff one in the entire selection. This isn't a case of someone contacting an importer or distributor and saying, 'Give me a craft beer range' – you can feel the personal touch.

And if you're surprised that a place like this should prosper in Burnley – or Barnsley or Halifax or anywhere else people may look down on as being not ready for craft beer – here's the secret of the Bridge's success. Publicans Simon Scott and Emma Harrison love their beer. They go on regular fact-finding trips to Belgium and other centres of beer excellence and return with their latest discoveries. And because they're good publicans in every respect – looking after the beers and promoting them effectively on the one hand, and building up great relationships with their regulars on the other – the punters in the Bridge are happy to try whatever Simon and Emma suggest, because they trust them. So on match day, you'll find the unlikely sight of Burnley FC fans sipping Trappist beers or American porters rather than downing pints.

The best beers in the world, well looked after, will find an audience anywhere. But good beer doesn't sell itself if people are unfamiliar with it. The Bridge Bier Huis is a perfect beer pub because it takes the exotic and unfamiliar, and makes it approachable and engaging to a clientele most of whom would never consider themselves to be beer geeks. In theory it's a template that's easy to copy. But if you don't love beer the way Simon and Emma do, you'll find it surprisingly difficult to carry off.

OPPOSITE TOP: The Bridge Bier Huis in the heart of Burnley, Lancashire.

OPPOSITE MIDDLE LEFT: The real ale pumps are present and correct, but the beer offering goes much further.

OPPOSITE BOTTOM LEFT: Beer can make you feel quite arty of a late afternoon...

OPPOSITE BOTTOM RIGHT: ... although you'd probably need to be sober to do this.

🍴 GREAT FOOD PUBS

FOR MOST PUBGOERS, there's something wonderfully soothing about the solidity of the Great British Pub Menu.

I had my first meal in a pub in the mid-1980s. The choice consisted of pie and chips, fish and chips, burger and chips, ham, egg and chips, possibly a Caesar salad (which, with its dressing, croutons and bacon, was more calorific than the chips) and steak and chips, if you were feeling posh.

Since this time, Britain has undergone a culinary revolution. The country has become a melting pot of different cuisines from around the world. Sushi, noodles, dim sum, Thai curry, American barbecue, tapas and Korean food have gone from esoteric novelties to mainstream high-street chains.

But go to the pub and you can almost guarantee that the old staples will still be the favourites on the menu. They may have been joined by an indifferent Chicken Tikka Masala or melancholy Spaghetti Carbonara, but if Marty McFly had travelled to the future from an English town rather than Middle America, pub cuisine is one aspect of 21st-century life that his 1985 self would have no doubt found reassuringly unchanged.

If you spend as much time in pubs as I do, this conservatism can be depressingly stifling. But there are reasons the basic pub menu template never changes. The pub is the second-most popular attraction for tourists from abroad after the Royal Family. When they arrive at the bar, they want traditional British beer and traditional British food. As for the Brits, with such a culinary smorgasbord open to them, when they choose to eat in pubs, we have to assume that this is the style of food they want at that time. Craft beer bars have adopted a variation on burger and chips inspired by American barbecue, and wings, pulled pork and Mac 'n Cheese are slowly

entering the mainstream, but the stodgy template remains consistent. People don't go to the pub for sashimi or ramen; they go to the pub for pub food.

The highlight of traditional pub fare is the Sunday roast. It's the dish everyone grew up with, and for many families, it was the one meal of the week when everyone ate together around the table. But the perfect home-cooked roast takes hours to prepare, more time than many families are prepared to sacrifice these days. The pub has taken up the slack, and this has become a key reason for its survival, the preservation of a uniquely British treasure. The aromas of roasting meat trigger a Proustian reaction that says, 'This is home, you're OK now.' A perfectly judged Yorkshire pudding or roast potato separates a kitchen team that knows and cares about what they're doing from the dead-eyed chain workers who throw pre-prepared, blast-frozen meals into the microwave. When you find a place that does a Sunday roast properly, the jungle drums beat loudly, and you have to reserve a table two days before if you want to be sure of a seat. For any pub with a competent kitchen, Mother's Day is possibly the busiest day of the year.

Of course, in some places there has been a dramatic reinvention. The first 'gastropub' is generally agreed to be the Eagle in Farringdon, London, which in 1991 came up with the idea of doing restaurant-standard food in a pub setting. It was swiftly copied. Today the gastropub can be immediately identified by its breathlessly excited-sounding chalkboard menus, mismatched furniture, posh wallpaper and the muted shades of Farrow & Ball paint.

The gastropub has been a mixed blessing. Some pubs have transformed into restaurants while still insisting they are pubs, even if you're not allowed to sit down in them without a reservation. Others have brought in the decor,

OPPOSITE TOP LEFT: Birmingham's Purecraft has a relentless dedication to pairing beer and food.

OPPOSITE MIDDLE LEFT: A blackboard is crowded with daily specials at The Lion & Lobster in Brighton.

OPPOSITE TOP RIGHT: The Fat Pig in Exeter has its own smokehouse, which is cool.

OPPOSITE BOTTOM: Mismatched tables and chairs create an informal dining area at The Tickell Arms in Whittlesford.

THE FAT PIG
FREEHOUSE

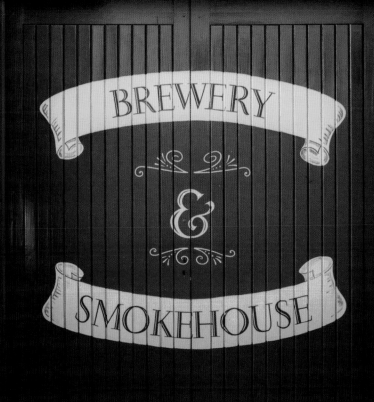

BREWERY

&

SMOKEHOUSE

big white plates and prices of gastropubs but continue to serve food that's inferior to what a competent cook could rustle up at home.

The best gastropubs tend to be those that hate having the term applied to them. They simply cook pub food to the highest possible standard, retaining a relaxed, unpretentious air around everything they do. Others have gone further than this and become wonderful restaurants. The Hand & Flowers in Marlow was a perfectly ordinary pub when chef Tom Kerridge took it over in 2005. In 2011, it became the first (and so far only) pub in Britain to be awarded two Michelin stars.

ABOVE LEFT: Mmm... sausage rolls and pork pies. Two reasons why I absolutely love The Southampton Arms in Kentish Town, North London.

TOP RIGHT: Sometimes, chefs have been known to use 'cook books', to help them decide what food to make.

BOTTOM RIGHT: At Worcestershire's Fleece Inn, the condiments wait in quivering anticipation of a top-notch meal.

FRIENDS OF HAM

Bar + Charcuterie

It's not listed here because it now definitely feels more like a restaurant than a pub (complete with its own shop and a beauty spa open to residents who stay over), but it is an incredible dining experience that still owes a great deal to the idea of the pub, and is better because of it.

The pubs listed in this book as food pubs are still pubs. You don't need to make a reservation to have a drink, and if you need to book ahead to eat, it's definitely worth it. As people choose to drink less generally, food is becoming increasingly important as a source of revenue that keeps pubs alive. And this emphasis can express itself in different ways. It's becoming more common now for pubs to have a decent range of bar food, filling the gap between a bag of crisps or nuts and a full meal. Orwell's Moon Under Water had a 'snack counter where you can get liver-sausage sandwiches, mussels (a speciality of the house), cheese, pickles and those large biscuits with caraway seeds in them which only seem to exist in public-houses.' It sounds a heck of a lot more appetizing than a tub of Pringles, and it's a mystery that such food ever went away. OK, maybe not the liver-sausage sandwiches. But the idea of a 'tapas-style' pub menu proves you can never keep a good idea down for long.

THE GURNARD'S HEAD 🐾 🎣 🌳 ⚓ ❗

Zennor, Ives, Cornwall TR26 3DE
www.gurnardshead.co.uk

Approach it from the wrong direction (as I inevitably did) and a trip to the Gurnard's Head can feel like an expedition to uncharted lands. Miles of winding single-lane roads twist and turn through the wind-blasted, dun-coloured desolation of the north Cornish coast, offering occasional glimpses of the sea, and then you round the crest of one hill and it's there, unmissable on account of it being painted bright mustard yellow, a safe haven in the wilderness.

As soon as we park we realize it's just off the main road if you come the other way, and there's a bus that stops outside every 20 minutes or so. But this moderates the sense of isolation only slightly.

The Gurnard's Head refers to itself carefully as a 'dining pub'. I always approach places like this wondering if I'm appropriately dressed, if I'm going to be glared at by the well-heeled country set in their mustard or bright red trousers. But such fears are usually unfounded, as they prove to be here. The main bar is as you'd expect the bar in any pub to be: warm and welcoming, with a small but carefully chosen range of beers. We can tell from the car park that the place is busy, but when we ask apologetically if there's a spare table for lunch, we're quickly seated in a kind of parlour room, between the bar and the main dining room, so our dog can sit with us while we eat.

The Gurnard's Head looks like a smart restaurant inside a modest (albeit mustard-coloured) stately home. But it feels like a pub all the way through. It's not just the relaxed and friendly approach of the staff, it's the philosophy that runs through everything. There's an inevitable tendency in top-flight food pubs that as they reach their peak, they're no longer places for locals to have a quiet drink; they're the preserve of people who can afford

and appreciate fine dining. Here, the prices are no more expensive than a typical pub menu, but the food is extraordinary.

Ray wings, crab claws and lobster are served imaginatively but unpretentiously. The green herb pancakes with fresh green herbs and cucumber salad is so simple, yet so different and so wonderful, it might have arrived from another planet.

The drinks list is unique, written by someone who adores what they do and wants to communicate their passion to the reader. As a piece of writing, it's worth exploring, even if you're just going to stick to water, as its account of the adventures involved in pulling together wine, sherry, beer, coffee and spirits from across Europe is fascinating. The wine list is structured according to instinctive categories created by the sommelier. 'The Tip of the Tongue' section offers bright, grassy wines from France, Australia and New Zealand. 'The Aristocrats' are made with Riesling and Chardonnay grapes, while 'Just Like Grace Kelly' is reserved for wines that are perfectly poised and have everything – the complete package – if you like.

It's not often a gastropub makes you want to hire a room and stay on, but then, this is not a gastropub as you might imagine it to be. It's a dining pub with rooms, one that offers special 'sleepover' packages for anyone who fancies changing their plans after lunch and settling in. And the pub makes you want to do exactly that. Having planned to stop for an hour or so, we long to move to the bar after our meal and curl up with one of the books from the shelf behind us.

Wonderful things are sometimes described as 'worth travelling to the ends of the earth for'. At the Gurnard's Head, I feel like we've done exactly that. And it was totally worth it.

OPPOSITE TOP: In its spare time The Gurnard's Head makes extra money as an improvised lighthouse.

OPPOSITE BOTTOM LEFT: Inside, painted stonework creates a cosy corner for dining.

OPPOSITE BOTTOM RIGHT: Rustic charm oozes out of this remote pub restaurant, with its nautical panelling and exposed stone walls.

4

Great

PUBS

PUB NATION

What's the British pub really like? That often depends on which part of Britain you're in.

PUBS ARE PLACES WHERE people come together not just to drink, but to *be*. They're shared community spaces and, as such, they're shaped by the communities of which they are a part. Sometimes they might differ because they serve everyone who lives in a geographical community or specific communities within one location. A pub that caters for everyone in a village will look quite different from one that aims its offering at young drinkers or craft beer enthusiasts.

But in an age of increasing conformity, it's comforting to discover that one of the biggest influences on what a pub feels like is where it is in the country. Sure, there are some basic rules that pubs follow in their look and feel, but beneath the surface, the character of pubs changes when you go from place to place.

The best pubs are those that, if you took them apart brick by brick and moved them to a different part of the country, wouldn't feel right. If you woke up in them and had no knowledge of how you got there, you'd be able to tell you were in Yorkshire, or the Lake District, or London, without looking outside.

Victorian gin palaces are grand wherever you go, but their glamour in London has a different shade from that in Lancashire. A country pub in Somerset has a different rhythm from one in the Yorkshire Dales. Old community pubs in Birmingham tell a different story from pubs built around the same time that serve a similar function in Belfast.

Some of this might be down to local building materials – the flint walls in Norfolk versus the granite of Glasgow. Part of it is the practical necessity of withstanding coastal winter storms rather than merely lighting up a narrow street and calling people down it. But much of it is an intangible expression of a region's character and outlook.

This is why touring Britain's pubs is the best way to get to know the country. Every city and large town have the same coffee shops and fast food joints, the same stationers and mobile phone shops. And yes, there are thousands of pubs that follow the same branded template, and in their managed uniformity resemble 'Ye Jolly Olde English Pub' that you might find in a mall in Tokyo or an airport in California. These places may look like British pubs, but they don't feel like pubs, because individuality cannot be replicated.

There are no generic pubs on the pages that follow. Where a pub does belong to a corporate chain, it's here because it has something that resists the branding template. Pubs are shaped by people and custom as much as by physical materials. The best thing about researching a book like this was to discover just how much variety there still is when you travel around the nation. The pub is a short cut to really getting a feel for a new town, city or village. Make it your first stop wherever you go, and you'll develop a rare understanding of what makes Britain tick.

OPPOSITE: The City Arms in Cardiff has all the ingredients of a great pub: good atmosphere, interesting people and a fine beer offering.

SOUTH WEST

With many more great pubs than it deserves given its small population, the generous coastline and slow, laid-back attitude down here help make pubs perfect.

GLOUCESTERSHIRE

WILTSHIRE

SOMERSET

DEVONSHIRE

DORSET

CORNWALL

BEERWOLF BOOKS ❗🍺

3 Bells Court, Falmouth, Cornwall TR11 3AZ
www.beerwolfbooks.com

Every new idea that is now accepted as common sense was once regarded as heresy. The first people to suggest that the earth was round, or that slavery was immoral, or that women deserved the vote, were dismissed as lunatics or heretics.

Many architectural styles that we now regard as classic were once seen as hideous modern carbuncles, from Sir Christopher Wren's St Paul's Cathedral in London to Victorian gin palaces or 1930s roadside inns.

Any idea or movement must weather derision in its early stages. Today, it's easy to dismiss anything from beards to craft beer as a hipster fad. Sure, it's easy to mock people who at times seem self-consciously retro and ironic. But in among the beards and tattoos are some great business ideas that will dominate for decades to come.

I have no idea whether the people who run Beerwolf are hipsters or not (they'd probably disown the word even if they are), but it's the kind of place that makes it easy to assume they are. You could walk in here and snort derisively at both the concept and the execution of a bookshop in a pub. Indeed, it would be easy to dismiss the idea – especially a bookshop with an arty, beatnik sensibility in a pub with a leaning towards craft beer – as posturing affectation. Or you could see it for what it really is – the possible future of the pub as we know it.

Sure, books aren't everyone's idea of a great time in the pub and I'm sure there'll always be a place for Sports TV, in a pub very different from this one. But Beerwolf reinvents the pub in the most wonderful way, and in so doing draws in an eclectic bunch of people that any pub would be happy to serve. Falmouth in the summer is a curious mix of tourists, students, artists and Bohemians. They're all in here, sharing the space with local real ale aficionados, young couples and weathered barflies.

The concept obviously has to be carried through correctly. As you cross the floor and enter the bookshop, there's a sign on an empty table answering any questions you might have.
'What are you?'
'We are a bookshop, in a pub.'
'Where do I pay for a book?'
'At the bar please.'
You are kindly asked to leave your drinks on a table that's provided, to protect the stock.

The shelves are an intriguing mix of new, secondhand and remaindered books, all displayed together, organized by subject. The selection leans towards art, culture and counter-culture. By the time we head to the bar for a pint, we have a pile of books to pay for.

The bar itself is noteworthy on its own, with a great international bottled beer selection, a healthy range of local cask ales and a craft beer range from further afield. If you fancy spending a day here reading your purchases, there's also a wide range of teas and a formidable coffee machine.

This welcoming scene is framed by red fairy lights and crêpe paper balls, Christmas-style decorations that, here amid the red vaulted ceilings, bare brick walls and bare floorboards, feel appropriately festive all year round.

A great pub is a place to spend time in, and an interesting range of books holds you here far longer than you planned. Several struggling rural pubs have incorporated post offices to keep them open. This is no different. The pub and the bookshop are two endangered institutions in Britain. Together, they're stronger.

Beerwolf is a wonderful space in the former home of Falmouth Working Men's Club. As one institution has faded, it has made way for two more threatened places to thrive.

OPPOSITE TOP: The most appealing bookshop cash till counter you are ever likely to see.

OPPOSITE BOTTOM LEFT: Pop your pint down here while you browse the bookshelves.

OPPOSITE BOTTOM RIGHT: Such a simple and stylish idea, bringing books and booze together in one place.

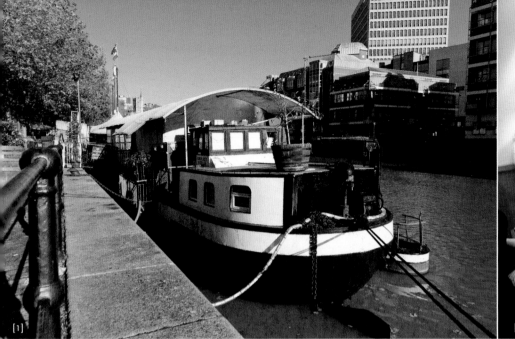

[1]

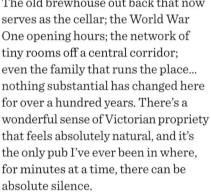

[2]

THE APPLE [1]

Welsh Back, Bristol BS1 4SB

www.applecider.co.uk

Sticking a truck load of strong ciders on a floating barge may sound like a recipe for disaster, but this unique concept works brilliantly (and safely), making the Apple one of the best cider pubs in the UK. The fact that it's on a barge gives it an open, free feel, a liberated, benignly anarchic air that suits the excellent range of ciders and makes going to the pub feel like a little adventure.

THE BARLEY MOW [2]

39 Barton Rd, Bristol BS2 0LF

www.barleymowbristol.com

As this is the flagship pub of the celebrated Bristol Beer Factory, the quality of the beer was never going to be in doubt. The Brewery's own range is complemented by craft beers from across the UK and around the world. The pub follows the usual spartan interior design template of craft beer bars, but with just enough quirky and homely touches to take the edges off and make it cosy.

THE BLISLAND INN

Blisland, Bodmin, Cornwall PL30 4JK

www.bodminmoor.co.uk

Like a farmhouse kitchen in which the beams have, for some reason, been decorated with real ale pump clips and an extensive collection of retro souvenir mugs, bearing logos for brands like Oxo, Fuji Film, Toblerone and Cup-A-Soup. The blackboards advertise an extensive range of Cornish real ales, ciders, fruit wines, and 'Polo shirts with large Buddha on the back'.

THE BOTTLE INN [3]

Marshwood, Bridport, Dorset DT6 5QJ

www.bottle-inn.net

As if hosting the World Nettle Eating Championships were not enough, the Bottle is also home to the Curry Bus – a 1961 Albion Nimbus converted into a takeaway curry kitchen. The original idea was for it to tour the area, but it broke down and stayed here. When it was repaired and moved on, people complained, so it came back. Oh, and the building is wonderful and the beer is amazing.

THE BRIDGE INN

Topsham, Exeter, Devon EX3 0QQ

www.cheffers.co.uk

The old brewhouse out back that now serves as the cellar; the World War One opening hours; the network of tiny rooms off a central corridor; even the family that runs the place… nothing substantial has changed here for over a hundred years. There's a wonderful sense of Victorian propriety that feels absolutely natural, and it's the only pub I've ever been in where, for minutes at a time, there can be absolute silence.

THE BUTCHER'S ARMS

Lime St, Eldersfield Gloucester GL19 4NX

www.thebutchersarms.net

There's only the sign on the road to distinguish this pub from a private dwelling, housed as it is in a couple of redbrick buildings set within immaculate gardens. Locals stand at the bar drinking cider or ales on stillage against the back wall, next to diners who have booked weeks in advance to enjoy Michelin-standard food in this country cottage.

[3]

[4]

THE CHRISTMAS STEPS

2 Christmas Steps, Bristol BS1 5BS

www.thechristmassteps.com

Located in a building that used to be a sugar factory and confectioners, this attractive pub blends modern trends and old world pub character quite beautifully. It's what a craft beer bar would have looked like if they'd existed in the Dickensian era.

THE CIDER BAR

99 East St, Newton Abbot, Devon TQ12 2LD

There are depressingly few traditional cider bars left in the UK – some estimates suggest as few as four – so it's a joy to see this one going strong. There's not much here: bare floors, a wood-panelled bar, with cider barrels piled high behind. That's it. But that's all you need.

THE DOLPHIN INN

14 The Barbican, Plymouth, Devon PL1 2LS

The Dolphin sits near Plymouth's inner harbour, where the fish market used to be, and retains the ribald air that such harbourside and market pubs tend to have. It's famous for being the haunt of artist Beryl Cook, who set several of her paintings here. It remains unfussy, a haven of traditional ale, and dares you to stick around until you get an eyeful of Cook's depictions.

THE DREWE ARMS

The Square, Drewsteignton, Exeter EX6 6QN

www.thedrewearmsinn.co.uk

When 'Auntie Mabel', landlady of the Drewe Arms, retired on her 99th birthday in 1994 after running the pub for 75 years, there were those who worried for its survival. It's still going strong under new owners, who may have changed a few more things than Mabel did (she presided over the introduction of running water and electricity and that was it), but still do their best to keep the pub frozen in time.

THE DRIFTWOOD SPARS

Trevaunance Rd, St Agnes, Cornwall TR5 0RT

www.driftwoodspars.co.uk

At the end of a road that runs from a small village down to the beach and a rugged cove, you couldn't get a more idyllic location. The pub has its own brewery just across the road, and a great selection of local craft beers and real ales. If there had been a pub in Enid Blyton's *Famous Five* novels, it would have been this one.

THE FAMOUS ROYAL NAVY VOLUNTEER

17–18 King Street, Bristol BS1 4EF

www.navyvolunteer.co.uk

'The Volley' pub and restaurant spreads over two houses in this famous Bristol drinking street. The pub half is a listed building dating back to 1665 and retains its weathered charm despite a smart refurbishment. One wall is dominated by a list of 20 beers on tap. The restaurant boasts locally sourced, seasonal food, and there's regular live entertainment.

THE FAT PIG [4]

2 John St, Exeter, Devon EX1 1BL

www.fatpig-exeter.co.uk

Hidden in a quiet street, this revamped old pub wears its new clothes well. A microbrewery in the cellar and a smoker out back ensure that the food and drink served here are always excellent and inventive.

THE BLUE ANCHOR ♖ ♟ 🍺

50 Coinagehall St, Helston, Cornwall TR13 8EL
www.spingoales.com

Entering the Blue Anchor is like walking into a picture of a pub that was taken many years before I was born.

We've all been to pubs that are largely unchanged physically over the decades, but this is more than that. First built as a monk's rest home in the 15th century, it became a pub after the dissolution of the monasteries and has remained one ever since. In the 19th century, it was so popular with local tin miners that their wages were paid in the bar.

It's not just the building that's been preserved; the whole place feels like it's still in, say, the 1930s. There's little sign of anything that's been added since then. There's no piped music or fruit machines. The furniture is antique.

As we arrive towards the end of a sunny afternoon, a group of elderly men, who have obviously been drinking here for hours – and decades – are making a great fuss of leaving. It's a process that must be completed gradually, by degrees. Stand up. Stoop down to tell a joke, rock back to gales of barking laughter. Pick up a flat cap. Put it down again. Trade insults with a barman. Put flat cap on. Break into a rousing rendition of *We'll Meet Again*, sustained until the whole pub has joined in. Pick up walking stick. Weather insults from drinking companions about lack of stamina. Begin walking to the door. Turn back. Return insults with interest. And so on. Rarely does pub banter make such satisfying spectator sport.

It might be something in the beer. For about 300 years, the Blue Anchor has been home to an in-house brewery, Spingo Ales. It's certainly the oldest brewery in Cornwall, and possibly the oldest surviving alehouse brewery in the country. The highlight is Special, a rich, sweet, ruby-coloured 6.5% ABV ale that justifies its name. A few sips of it make my head spin, so I go for a wander round the pub.

From the corridor where you enter, the pub looks as though it was once a smaller building with a bunch of outbuildings, and at some point, the alleyway between them has been roofed over to join them up. As you walk down this narrow corridor, doors lead off either side into inviting little rooms. There's a skittle alley that was once used as a stable. Trying to convey its special appeal, the pub's website informs readers of the fact that, 'The skittles and bowls are made of solid sycamore. The bowls are approximately 12 inches (30 centimetres) in diameter and weigh 4 pounds (1.8 kilogrammes) each.'

I want to sit and have a drink in each of these rooms. At the end is a beer garden with its own bar and a short set of steps leading up to the brewery. I wonder whether people have their favourite rooms that they always drink in, whether each room has a different personality, and whether people who drink in different rooms ever meet each other.

Back in the front bar, among ancient tables and chairs that look like they've been set for a medieval banquet, I find my wife in conversation with one of the elderly drinkers. His wife has appeared at his arm, gently trying to encourage him out of the pub, but he's telling his life story. I'm sure we're not the first tourists to hear it – nor even the first today.

'You can't progress without moving forward,' he says philosophically, and goes on to share his mixed feelings about the opening of a new JD Wetherspoon's in town. He's been drinking in the Blue Anchor for 60 years, and has no plans to change his allegiance any time soon. 'Things have got to change. But they'll never change this place because it has char'trrrr.'

This particular char'trrrr is absolutely right about that.

OPPOSITE TOP: The Blue Anchor, visibly resisting the march of time.

OPPOSITE BOTTOM LEFT: The pub has been brewing its own beer since the 17th century – one of only four ale houses to still do so.

OPPOSITE BOTTOM RIGHT: The bar at the Blue Anchor, packed with Spingo beers brewed a mere 10m (30ft) away from the customers.

THE GLOUCESTER OLD SPOT [1]

Piffs Elm, Tewkesbury Road, Cheltenham, Gloucestershire GL51 9SY

www.thegloucesteroldspot.co.uk

This sprawling pub a few miles out of Cheltenham is one of those places that, while still very much a pub, has such a reputation for its food that it makes it very difficult to get a seat on a Sunday afternoon. The unfussy farmhouse feel and relaxed service in the face of endless custom makes it the perfect place to relax with the papers after perfectly cooked roast beef accompanied by awesome homemade horseradish sauce.

THE GROVE INN

The Grove Inn, Kings Nympton, North Devon EX37 9ST

www.thegroveinn.co.uk

This old thatched pub in the middle of a tiny village has a good range of local cask ales and a reputation for excellent food based on the fact that the pub works closely with local food suppliers. You also can't fail to appreciate a huge collection of bookmarks hanging from the beams in the main bar, like bunting made by someone having a breakdown.

HAND BEER BAR [2]

3 Old Brewery Yard, High Street, Falmouth, Cornwall TR11 2BY

This place takes the blueprint of craft beer bars, as established by Leeds' North Bar (the boss used to work there) and popularized by the BrewDog chain, and softens the edges a little. The beer selection is thoughtful and adventurous, but the low leather chesterfields, snug yard outside and work by local artists on the walls combine to create a more relaxed vibe than you sometimes get in similar places.

HAWTHORNES

8–12 Northload St, Glastonbury BA6 9JJ

www.hawthornshotel.com

The town of Glastonbury is unlike any other you'll ever visit, a jumble sale cornucopia of spirituality where the Middle Ages and the new age meet. All bets are off, and you should expect anything in its pubs. For example, you'd never expect to find a backstreet boozer that does a comprehensive selection of some of the best and most authentic curries in the UK, soundtracked by a phenomenal live blues jam that creates an atmosphere you never want to leave. But here it is.

THE KINGS ARMS [3]

Paul, Penzance, Cornwall TR19 6TZ

www.thekingsarmspaul.com

Popular with locals and tourists alike, the Kings Arms has banned fruit machines and televisions to help preserve the kind of atmosphere most people want in a quiet old village near the coast. Inside it's bare, almost spartan, yet still manages to feel warm and welcoming to both locals and the wild-eyed summer tourists who endure gridlock traffic to get here. Also offers bed & breakfast for tired travellers and a bicycle lock-up for the many cycle tourers who pass by.

THE LAMB & FOUNTAIN

57 Castle St, Frome, Somerset BA11 3BW

Still known to locals as 'Mother's' after the landlady who ran the place for 40 years, this is another pub that appeals because it is casually unchanged rather than carefully preserved. Now well into her nineties, Mother has retired from working the bar but is still the official licensee. The Elizabethan icehouse in the cellar is possibly linked to a semi-mythical maze of tunnels beneath Frome.

THE MARISCO TAVERN [4]

High Street, Lundy Island, Bristol Channel EX39 2LY

www.landmarktrust.org.uk

If you fancy a pint at the Marisco, you need to prepare yourself for a two-hour boat trip out to the middle of the Bristol Channel. It is, of course, an enchanting place once you get there, isolated and unique. If you miss the boat back to the mainland, you could be stuck there for a few days, but the pub never closes (although it does stop serving alcohol outside the usual hours) and there'll be a part of you that's glad you did.

THE NEW INN

14 Long St, Cerne Abbas, Dorset DT2 7JF

www.thenewinncerneabbas.co.uk

This 16th-century coaching inn manages to shine as one of the most beautiful buildings in a village regarded as one of the prettiest in England. Thoughtfully refurbished, it's certainly no museum, but it does combine the best of ancient and modern design. It's mainly all about food and accommodation rather than beer, but it manages to retain an atmosphere that is relaxed and 'pubby' at the same time.

THE OLD GREEN TREE

12 Green St, Bath, Avon BA1 2JZ

There's a Dickensian feel to this 17th-century tavern standing in the middle of a terrace, with its lattice of small frosted windowpanes almost shrinking back from its neighbours. Inside, the walls are wood panelled, and the three small rooms always seem to offer up a corner even when the place is full. Dedicated to great cask ale and food, you're unlikely to encounter a fruit machine or a juke box in this historic pub.

[1]

[1]

[3]

[4]

[2]

[4]

THE HALFWAY HOUSE 👥 🌳 🍺 🍎 🔲

Pitney Hill, Langport, Somerset TA10 9AB
www.thehalfwayhouse.co.uk

When I was first brought to the Halfway, it was love at first sight – or rather, first sniff. There are fireplaces at either end burning split logs, and the smell of wood smoke hits you as you walk through the door, defining the space and filling it with rustic incense.

Back here with my notebook a couple of years later in early August, the fires still burn low, curled up like dozing cats, managing to create atmosphere more than heat. A pile of logs is stacked three feet high in the corner, just in front of what seems to be a perfectly good radiator. Candles burn low on the bar.

The furniture in the Halfway is basic and practical, and yet it's the next thing you notice after the wood smoke. The long tables are a mix of scrubbed farmhouse kitchen pine and rough-hewn affairs made from old floorboards. These are lined by old church pews up against the wall and benches opposite, which give the place a mess-hall feel.

Where tables don't fit in the space, other stuff is squeezed in. A low, leather chesterfield sofa sits under a row of coat-hooks covered in waxed Barbour jackets and a chalkboard advertising apple and rhubarb crumble, chocolate cheesecake and Bakewell tart. The whitewashed stone walls ebb and flow beneath the low, sagging beams of the ceiling. And then there's the floor of naked stone flags; heavy, ancient, worn smooth and polished with the passage of time.

This all combines to create a woozy amnesia. You zone out, your thoughts drift away to a good place, and when you come to, for a few seconds, you have no idea what's outside, where in the country you are, or what day or time it is, because none of that matters. Pubs like this cradle you, returning you to a toddler state, removing all cares.

Whenever I tell anyone that I'm travelling through the West Country to visit its best pubs, without fail they ask me if I've been to the Halfway near Langport. When I tell them I have, they often struggle to hide their disappointment. This is a pub you want to introduce people to, to take them to, so you can vicariously share their delight.

The person who did introduce me to the Halfway is my friend Bill, with whom I wrote a book about cider. We came here ostensibly to sample the ciders, which are listed on a blackboard and served direct from the stillage in a room out back. There are hardly any drinks displayed on the bar itself. I've no idea why, but this lack of overt display only adds to the Halfway's appeal.

I say we came 'ostensibly' to sample the ciders, because it soon became clear that wasn't really the point. You come to the Halfway to be at the Halfway. People in the pub trade often talk about the number of 'chimney pots' in the vicinity of a pub when assessing its commercial viability, and there are precious few of those visible from the front door. But the Halfway has a very large car park, and then an overspill car park. As its name suggests, it's in between places. Bill and his family will often walk here on a Sunday, and various members of his family have worked behind the bar. The Halfway doesn't sit in a sizeable community, so it creates a community around itself.

The Halfway gives the impression that it simply opens its doors and waits for people to come and visit. But running a pub just isn't that simple any more. People will no longer casually wander in unless there are good reasons to do so. Like so many pursuits, it's only when it's done with this much skill and intuition that managing and running a pub is able to give the illusion of being completely effortless.

DRAUGHT CIDER
4.8 ASHTON PRESS 3.10
4.8 THATCHERS GOLD 3.30
4.8 MALLETS 3.30
BOTTLED CIDER
6.0 Burrow Hill (LOCAL) 3.40
6.0 HARRY'S CIDER 3.40
6.5 (VERY LOCAL) HARRY'S MEDIUM 3.60

HECK'S
SWEET
2.70

THE PEBBLES TAVERN [1]

24 Market Street, Watchet, Somerset, TA23 0AN
www.pebblestavern.co.uk

This long, narrow, gaily painted pub is a treasure-trove of great cider and beer, created by a musicial couple who did what they felt was right, and proved to have a natural instinct. The regular live music sessions have enabled it to create a solid community of locals and tourists alike – one evening here and you'll soon become part of the family. It feels like a tiny indoor music festival, with a similar spirit of abandon and adventure, as much as it does a pub.

THE ROSE & CROWN (ELI'S) [2]

Huish Episcopi, Langport, Somerset TA10 9QT

When someone first tells you about Eli's, it sounds too good to be true: the fabled 17th-century country pub where there's no bar, only a parlour room with casks against the wall from which locals help themselves. And a separate skittle alley. Surely it closed years ago? But, no, it's still there, pretty much unchanged since Eli (the grandfather of the current generation) ran it a century and a half ago.

THE ROYAL OAK [3]

The Village Green, Meavy, Devon PL20 6PJ
www.royaloakinn.org.uk

This is one of those country pubs where a row of seasoned locals line up along the back wall of the parlour, holding court. The wall behind the regulars is full of photos showing them over the years, sitting where they are now, as if they themselves were creating the folklore and feeling of the place. They stop talking when strangers walk in, then turn to give them a hearty welcome.

THE RUGGLESTONE INN

Widecombe in the Moor, Newton Abbot, Devon TQ13 7TF
www.rugglestoneinn.co.uk

Nestled in the heart of Dartmoor, this is one of those pubs that you fantasize about stumbling across when you're starting to regret heading out for a walk in the hills. Originally a cottage, it was converted to an inn in 1832. The locals are as friendly as the staff, which is just as well given how crowded this cosy little pub can get.

THE SANDFORD PARK ALEHOUSE

20 High St, Cheltenham, Gloucestershire GL50 1DZ
www.spalehouse.co.uk

This grade II-listed building feels like a Georgian townhouse that's been converted to a light, airy pub. It's owned and run by beer lovers and has created a huge stir since it opened in 2013. The beer selection is as good as anywhere I've seen. Cheltenham is one of those towns where people tell you a 'craft beer' concept definitely wouldn't work. The Sandford Park alehouse is a pub that proves it can work anywhere.

THE SEVEN STARS

1 The Moor, Town Centre, Falmouth, Cornwall TR11 3QA

Mobile phones are not just banned in this ancient pub; they're nailed to the walls as a warning to any potentially connected visitors, hidden among the hundreds of key rings that form the main theme of the decor. But you'd be mad to gaze at your screen in a pub like this. Ancient, unchanging, it's a space in which you should simply order a drink, then sit and have a quiet think in the fairy-lit dusk.

THE SHIP INN

Pentewan, St Austell, Cornwall PL26 6BX
www.theshipinnpentewan.co.uk

How could you possibly improve a pub on the coast that has delightful views overlooking the harbour, a great selection of local ales and decent food, sunny tables in summer and roaring fires in the winter? The only thing that would make it even better would be a charity pig race in August. Oh, hang on – turns out they're already doing that too.

THE SLOOP INN [4]

Bantham, Kingsbridge, Devon TQ7 3AJ
www.thesloop.co.uk

Down a single lane road, this pub is in the kind of place people tell you doesn't exist any more – a single row of houses, a pub, and a famous beach two hundred yards away. The pub itself has the salty, fresh brightness you hope for in coastal pubs, complete with dog bowls, comfy sofas, superb freshly caught seafood throughout the menu and even one bar made from an old wooden lifeboat.

SMALL BAR [5]

31 King St, Bristol BS1 4DZ
www.smallbarbristol.com

The format of the hip craft beer bar is so consistent as to be almost clichéd, but Small Bar makes increasingly familiar elements feel fresh and different again. The 25 craft beers are served only in third-, half- or two thirds-pint (170ml-, 285ml- or 340ml-) measures, and include several from the in-house brewery. The distressed, reclaimed industrial decor is done with charm and warmth. The old Stella Artois font that now dispenses water is a nice touch too.

[2]

[4]

[5]

THE SALUTATION INN 👥 🍺 🍎

Ham, Berkeley, Gloucestershire GL13 9QH
www.the-sally-at-ham.com

A common refrain in any institution people care about is, 'You just don't see the likes of old Barry these days. This new generation just isn't the same. When the old characters go, who'll replace them? They just don't make them like that any more.'

People have of course been saying this about workplaces, pubs and bastions of light entertainment for centuries. Yet somehow, new characters do emerge. Often they're like baby pigeons – you never see them until they're fully grown – and then it seems instantly like they've been there forever.

At the time of writing, The Salutation Inn is the Best Pub in Britain – as far as CAMRA (the Campaign for Real Ale) is concerned, anyway. It won this award chiefly on the basis of the quality and range of the real ales and ciders it stocks – an important aspect on which to judge a pub, but not the only one.

What makes the Sally's achievement so remarkable is that it comes less than two years after the new landlord, Peter Tiley, pulled his first pint here.

Pete and his wife Clare are just settling into their early 30s and Pete gave up a job in the city to come to this tiny village and run the pub. His lack of experience simply doesn't seem to have mattered, as he discovered an instinctive grasp of what makes great pubs work (backed up, it has to be said, with the energy and determination of youth, and the willingness to work insanely long hours).

I first visit the Sally on Apple Day, the increasingly popular autumnal celebration of the apple harvest and, more broadly, of local diversity in food and drink. From the outside, the pub is not much to look at – a simple, utilitarian building – which means all its charm must come from what the publican actually does with it.

In the yard outside, a local morris dancing troop entertains families, many of whom have driven here for the event. A hog roast by the main door does a roaring trade. Mums, dads, kids and dogs are all equally entranced by the proceedings.

Later, I'll be presenting a talk and tutored tasting about cider, because Pete wrote and asked me if I would. I need to decide what ciders to use, so Pete shows me around his cramped, tiny cellar (actually a room behind, rather than below, the bar).

I'm amazed that he can serve so much beer and cider of such good quality from such a cramped, restricted space. I'm also surprised at some of the choices of beers, with a range of challenging brews I would more readily expect to see in a London craft beer bar than a traditional country pub.

'The locals will try them, and even though they're more expensive, they'll go for the stronger ones because that's value for money – you're getting more alcohol than in traditional ales, so they accept it,' he explains.

Talking to the regulars after my tasting event, I find there's more to it than that. They regard Pete as an expert. He may be half their age, and he may only have been here for five minutes, but he's the guv'nor. The gaffer. He is *their* publican. 'If he says it's good, well you have to give it a try, don't you? The lad's usually right.'

This is how great pubs work, and this is why the best pubs can no more be cloned than the people who run them. Like any pub of its type, the Sally is an extension, a representation, an aspect of Peter Tiley's character – because he has plenty of character and displays his character so well.

Occasionally, they do still make them like that you know.

THE ST KEW INN [1]

St Kew, Bodmin, Cornwall PL30 3HB

www.stkewinn.co.uk

The St Kew Inn could well be an accident black spot. Reached via an endless succession of narrow, winding country lanes through a wooded valley, the tendency is for you to brake your car reflexively and say, 'Let's go in here,' because it looks like your dream country pub. It actually is.

THE STAR

23 Vineyards, Bath, Avon BA1 5NA

www.abbeyales.co.uk/www.star-inn-bath.co.uk

One of the oldest pubs in Bath, The Star has served generations of drinkers. The senior members tend to sit on a long bench against one wall, known as Death Row for its formality and for the age of its inhabitants. Like so many venerable pubs, The Star has had a few scares of its own, narrowly surviving wartime bombs and the march of large pub companies.

THE STAR INN

Crowlas, Cornwall TR20 8DX

The home of the Penzance Brewery is a no-nonsense community boozer on a very busy main road. Inside, shelves of trophies for the pub darts and pool teams compete with the awards for the beers brewed out back, which line the walls. The regulars propping up the bar all day will be happy to help you choose an ale.

THE URBAN STANDARD [2]

35 Gloucester Rd, Bristol BS7 8AD

www.theurbanstandard.co.uk

For a certain generation, this pub closes the loop between childhood and adult playgrounds. Once an amusement arcade, it's now a stripped back, industrial-influenced craft beer bar softened by the rediscovery of pretty thistle-patterned tiles, probably dating from when the building was a 'toy and fancy warehouse' in 1890, and by well-chosen, really quite modern pieces of art.

THE WARREN HOUSE INN

Postbridge, Devon PL20 6TA

www.warrenhouseinn.co.uk

Outside Britain's third highest pub, you can tell it's summer because the rain is only slanted at 45 degrees rather than being completely horizontal. People enter with glazed expressions, hair plastered to their skulls, to be welcomed by two matronly barmaids and a fire that has famously been kept alight continuously for centuries.

THE WYNDHAM ARMS

27 Estcourt Rd, Salisbury, Wiltshire SP1 3AS

www.hopback.co.uk

This elegant redbrick Victorian pub is the birthplace of the Hop Back Brewery, one of the first and, indeed, best of the new wave of British microbreweries. But the pub would still be noteworthy even if that were not the case. It's simple, clean and well kept, with a homely welcome that makes perfect sense when you learn it was originally built as a private dwelling.

WOODS [3]

4 Bank Square, Dulverton, Somerset TA22 9BU

www.woodsdulverton.co.uk

Incredibly, this former bakery has only been a pub since 2004. In little over a decade, it's created a seemingly permanent pub ambience, its weathered timbers opening cracks and fissures into which people have jammed notes and coins, ready to watch with amusement as sneaky visitors try to pry them out. Its wine and beer lists are superlative too.

Also Try...

THE BRIDGE INN

20 Bridge St, Dulverton, Somerset TA22 9HJ

www.thebridgeinndulverton.com

THE EBRINGTON ARMS

Chipping Campden, Gloucestershire GL55 6NH

www.theebringtonarms.co.uk

THE JOURNEYS END

Ringmore, Devon TQ7 4HL

www.thejourneysendinn.co.uk

THE STAR INN

1 Fore St, St Just, Cornwall TR19 7LL

www.thestarinn-stjust.co.uk

THE TROUT INN [4]

Faringdon Road, Lechlade, Gloucestershire GL7 3HA

www.thetroutinn.com

THE SQUARE AND COMPASS

Worth Matravers, Swanage, Dorset BH19 3LF
www.squareandcompasspub.co.uk

Perched up here on the limestone cliffs above the Jurassic Coast, it's all about the stone.

The heavy walls of the Square and Compass are so thick, and its roof so low, it feels like an ancient dwarven hall. Built to withstand the ravages of a coastal winter, the place feels like it wouldn't fare too badly against anything up to a nuclear attack.

Originally built as a pair of stone cottages, the Square and Compass has been a pub since 1793. A stonemason took over in 1830 and named it after his tools. The Newman family acquired it in 1907 and have run it ever since, with the current generation taking over in 1994. Four years later, current landlord Charlie turned the end room into a museum of stonemasonry and local fossils. This may not seem an obvious attraction for a pub to have, but it's one that draws almost every pub visitor for a proper look.

In a beer garden that slopes gently down towards the cliff tops, the 10ft (3m) wide tables and 8in (20cm) thick benches are hewn from massive hunks of stone, as if Stonehenge itself has been remodelled as a party venue for those hardy enough to withstand the biting wind.

When we arrive, the area is being put to good use: the annual stone carving festival is in full swing. Someone has left a hunk of limestone by the side of the pub, halfway through cutting away all the parts that are not the sculpture within. A stage of scaffolding poles and boards has been erected on top of beer barrels beside the pub's main entrance. Inside, the sounds of fiddles and guitars comes from behind a thick, closed door.

You can tell the place wasn't originally designed as a pub. The layout of the rooms hasn't been changed (good luck trying with these walls) and it simply doesn't work as a pub at all. Or rather, it shouldn't. But in places like this, wonder, curiosity and respect override confusion, and everyone just works it out. The queue for the bar stretches down the narrow corridor to the front door. But no, that's not quite right, because there is no bar. The queue starts at what was originally the kitchen door, which stands open with rows of casks sitting in the room beyond. Servers come to the door to take your order, and you stand there, not knowing what to do with your limbs, until they return with your drinks.

There's another serving hatch a little further along the central corridor between rooms. As the corridor is only really wide enough for one person, anyone standing here to be served creates an interesting field exercise in the English pursuit of politeness.

With a drink finally secured, you can go and look at the stone museum, or try to get a seat in one of the other rooms. With just one sitting room available today (the other one being closed for band rehearsals), space is at a premium, and groups of strangers sit snugly on the benches along the walls.

When no one is speaking, the atmosphere is reverential. People absorb the surroundings: simply being here is a special occasion. But drinkers don't remain strangers for long. Bunched together, hunkered down behind the walls, an atmosphere of cheery conviviality builds as pleasantries turn into conversations, and conversations turn to laughter.

As each new group arrives, it takes them a little while to catch up. The occasional brief visitor acts as though they've stumbled into a private party and tries not to look embarrassed as they turn to leave. But anyone who finds a seat eventually thaws. Whether they've been frozen by the elements or ossified by the black magic of modern existence, the Square and Compass returns them to life.

SOUTH EAST

It's easy to dismiss the south east of England as London's affluent commuter belt. But when you start to look at its pubs, they reveal the variety of communities within these rolling green hills.

THE BLACK DOG ! 🍺 🍎

66 High St, Whitstable, Kent CT5 1BB

For every single action there's an equal and opposite reaction.

It's true in physics, and it's true in society. Every trend has its own counter-trend. And as we read about the doom and gloom of pub closures, there are currents flowing the other way that prove the death of the pub is greatly exaggerated.

The most dramatic of these is the rise of the 'micropub'. Many micropub founders are motivated by the need to take a stance against what they see as the stranglehold on the British pub market by big chains.

The original idea is attributed to Martyn Hillier, who converted an off-licence into a one-room pub, The Butcher's Arms in Herne Bay, Kent, in 2005. Hillier inspired so many other people to follow suit that in 2012 he was able to co-found the Micropub Association, which defines a micropub as 'a small freehouse which listens to its customers, mainly serves cask ales, promotes conversation, shuns all forms of electronic entertainment and dabbles in traditional pub snacks'.

It's a gloriously loose and subjective definition, a statement of belief and intent as much as a description. It cuts to the very core of what a traditional pub is all about, revitalizing the basic idea of the alehouse. The last time I visited Whitstable, the site of The Black Dog was apparently a delicatessen. I have no idea it's there until I'm walking past it, and as soon as I look up through the window, I'm drawn in by my 'good pub radar', an instinct that says the place is unmissable.

Inside, the space looks nothing like a pub. But it *feels* like one. The room is long and narrow, with high-seated benches down each wall, and slim wooden tables leaving space to walk down the middle to the bar.

The bar itself is so small only one person can stand comfortably behind it – a second server stands at the side asking politely if anyone is waiting to be served. While there are real ale hand pumps on the bar, these are for display only, advertising what beers are currently on. All drinks are served from a temperature-controlled back room that doubles up as the pub's cellar. When you place your order, the bar person disappears to the back room to get it.

This system works well because of a clever design feature. There's an antique wooden back bar, richly varnished, with arches that probably held shelves of spirits in the structure's previous home. There are no shelves here (and no spirits) but where you would expect mirrors to be against the wall, there are windows through to the cellar, so you get a good view of your beer being poured directly from a rack of casks at the back.

When the affable, unfailingly polite bloke behind the bar comes back with a pint, he takes time with every single customer to share his thoughts on the beer and the brewery. This is clearly a labour of love for him, and I eventually learn that he's usually in here as a customer – he's helping out today because the owner is ill.

Mid-afternoon, there isn't a spare seat in the place, and I'm perching my drink on a narrow ledge along the wall that leads back to the kitchen sink, where the glasses are washed, and the single toilet at the rear of the building.

What I love about this particular micropub is that, despite the cramped space and sacrifices that must be made, it still feels luxurious. The walls are a deep shade of green and the space is lit by chandeliers. If alehouses began life as the front rooms of people's homes, this place continues the tradition in a very stylish way – an Edwardian sitting room as a pub. All in all, that's pretty special for what was once a disused shop.

OPPOSITE: The owners of The Black Dog have turned a shop into a tiny pub that feels like it's been here forever – the true meaning of the words 'property development'.

[3]

[3]

[1]

THE BEAR INN [1]

6 Alfred St, Oxford OX1 4EH

www.bearoxford.co.uk

Possibly the oldest pub in Oxford (claiming a lineage back as far as 1242), this is certainly the most charming. The walls and ceilings are covered with glass cases full of cuttings from ties, carefully labelled, most of them signifying some kind of club membership. They were originally offered in return for halves of beer from the landlord, who came up with the idea in 1952. The collection is now a bit silly, but can be unexpectedly moving too.

THE BLACK BOY [2]

1 Wharf Hill, Winchester, Hampshire, SO23 9NP

www.theblackboypub.com

There are pubs that have walls decorated with a selection of quirky ephemera, and then there's The Black Boy. Resembling a junk shop more than a pub, and feeling like some kind of folk museum, on your first visit you simply wander around and stare at the walls and ceiling. The stuffed giraffe is particularly arresting.

THE BOOT

4 Market Place, St Albans, Hertfordshire AL3 5DG

www.thebootstalbans.com

This building is so old, the ceiling isn't just low, it actually slopes in different directions wherever you look, and then the upright beams and edges of the walls all join in, like an optical illusion. Cosy and dark during the day, The Boot is rocking on Friday and Saturday nights, with all manner of humankind. This ancient pub is at the heart of St Albans, and the Sunday roast dinner is also quite a draw.

THE BUTCHER'S ARMS [3]

29A Herne St, Herne Bay, Kent CT6 7HL

www.micropub.co.uk

Martyn Hillier began a quiet revolution when he converted this former butcher's shop from an off-licence into a tiny pub. It's his gaff, his rules, with opening hours that suit his schedule and beers he enjoys drinking. He's a true pioneer of pub preservation and has managed to reinvent the core idea of what pubs should be, in reaction to their creeping network of corporatization.

THE CHAPEL

44/46 Albion Street Broadstairs, Kent CT9 1EU

www.thechapel-broadstairs.com

This former church is either a bookshop in a pub, or a pub in a bookshop. The books are secondhand and gloriously random and esoteric – you have no hope of finding a specific title you've been looking for, only of finding something you had no idea you wanted until it falls into your hands. You'll also find a great selection of Kentish ale, cider, perry and wine being served seven days a week.

THE EVENING STAR [4]

55-56 Surrey St, Brighton, East Sussex BN1 3PB

www.darkstarbrewing.co.uk

A simple one-room bar and one of the most utilitarian pubs I've seen, The Evening Star was almost a micropub years before the concept was invented. The Dark Star Brewery began life in the cellar here back in 1994 with a minuscule brewing kit, and the pub remains the best place to try their excellent beers, as well as a great range of craft beers from around the world, presented with zero pretension.

THE HATCHET INN ♜ 👥 🌳 🍴

Lower Chute, Andover, Hampshire SP11 9DX
www.thehatchetinn.co.uk

Britain is full of pubs that know they don't have to try too hard to attract custom.

If you're lucky enough to have a 13th-century coaching inn in a beautiful part of the country, you know that tourists will flock to you. So long as the food is hot and the beer is cold, you can turn a profit without having to worry about things like friendly service, home cooking or a carefully kept range of ales. I've lost count of the number of establishments I've encountered that look like your dream pub on the web, only to find that, when you get there, they are soulless shells, businesses run by big companies who care nothing about the importance of a personal, individual touch, or the broader meaning of what a good pub should be about.

We encounter The Hatchet Inn while looking for an alternative to a motorway service station on a long journey home. It comes highly recommended and looks utterly stunning. I cross my fingers.

Ten minutes' drive off the M3 near Andover, the satnav guides us into a cluster of small villages known as the Chutes. Surrounded by thatched roofs and whitewashed walls, the pub is a palatial variation on the theme. The low ceilings and tiny windows, which you have to stoop to see out of, encourage the quiet reverence you always find in ancient buildings.

We seem to be the only customers – we're a little early for lunch – but it still takes a while to get served. The barmaid is on the phone. She hands it to an octogenarian man sitting on the other side of the bar and takes our order.

'Are we still on hold, George?' she calls over her shoulder as she pours our pints.

George grunts and nods. And then starts – there's someone on the other end of the line.

The barmaid excuses herself and takes back the phone. 'What's your postcode, George?'

George gives it.

'I'm on hold again, George. Daniel is just sorting out a time to come and visit tomorrow.'

'Who's Daniel?' asks George.

'He's the man who has to sort out your claim. Oh, he's gone. I'll just take these people's food order and then I'll call the people back who are going to help you.'

We place our food order and take our perfectly kept pints of locally brewed golden ale to a table in a tiny room that just about accommodates the four of us. It feels like camping in the middle of the pub, cosy and adventurous.

The barmaid gets the woman she needs to speak to, and asks George for his postcode once again. She relays the information back over the phone. 'I'm calling on behalf of someone,' she explains. 'He's staying with us for a few days.' George is asked for his postcode yet again. Then, 'I'm on hold again. Oh, they say they'll call you back, George.'

The landlord of the pub comes into the room. 'What size waist are you, George?'

'Not sure. I think 42.'

'OK, we'll sort you out.'

We finish our pints and steak and ale pies and are on our way again before we find out who it is that needs to come and see George and why, or the circumstances that mean he is staying at the pub for a few days and borrowing the landlord's clothes. But it's an exchange that says so much about the difference between the essence of a great pub and the reality of faceless modern commerce. We've just witnessed a perfect little play that demonstrates why pubs built in the 13th century still endure, while brands that claim to be personal and caring in their advertising campaigns come and go on a regular basis.

THE FIVE BELLS

Baydon Rd, Wickham, Newbury, Berkshire
RG20 8HH

www.fivebellswickham.co.uk

This beautiful thatched pub was rescued and refurbished in 2012 after years of neglect, and now offers the best of beer, both old and new, in the delightful Berkshire countryside. The microbrewery out back ensures a mix of traditional real ales and modern craft beers, as well as more than 30 bottled Belgian ales, all kept in excellent condition and served with real dedication and passion.

THE FOX GOES FREE [1]

Charlton, Nr Goodwood, West Sussex
PO18 0HU

www.thefoxgoesfree.com

This elegant, flint-walled, 400-year-old country pub was the venue for the first-ever meeting of the Women's Institute, organized by landlady Mrs Laishley. A ten-minute stroll from the Goodwood racecourse, it's a classy country retreat that caters for well-heeled racegoers and local farmers alike, retaining an unpretentious charm whether you fancy a pint and a game of darts in the public bar or prefer to sit down to a more formal meal in the restaurant.

THE LAMB & FLAG

12 St Giles', Oxford OX1 3JS

A pub like this could only really exist in a city like Oxford. The back part is medieval, the middle is Elizabethan and the front is Georgian. It's owned by St John's College, and some of the profit is used to provide scholarships for graduate students. Patronized by students and academics alike, the pub has an atmosphere that's as eccentric as some of its regular patrons.

THE LEWES ARMS

Mount Place, Lewes, East Sussex BN7 1YH

www.lewesarms.co.uk

Don't pick a fight with the people of Lewes. When former owners, Greene King, took the town's Harveys Ale off the bar here, the locals picketed the pub for a year. They're friendly enough if you don't upset them though. The Lewes Arms hosts pea throwing, pantomime and dwile flonking, a sport for which, according to those who play it, 'the rules are impenetrable and the result is always contested'.

THE LIFEBOAT

1 Market St, Margate, Kent CT9 1EU

www.facebook.com/The-Lifeboat-Ale-And-Cider-House-Margate

There's a feel of the 1940s to this delightful little pub in the rapidly regenerating Old Town. It's plain and simple, warm and cosy, with ale from the cask, cider from boxes piled behind the bar, and simple meat, cheese and seafood dishes on the menu. The stillage for the casks is a rack in the centre of the pub, literally putting beer at the heart of the place.

THE LION & LOBSTER [2]

24 Sillwood St, Brighton, East Sussex BN1 2PS

www.thelionandlobster.co.uk

My wife and I stumbled across this pub by accident late one night, and spent the hour before closing time gazing at the eclectic collection of pictures covering the walls. The place is careworn without being tatty, faded but not threadbare. A couple of streets away are rows of chain bars that attract large hordes of people on hen and stag dos on a regular basis. It's therefore no surprise to learn that, among Brighton residents, The Lion & Lobster is known as 'the antidote'.

THE MONTEFIORE ARMS

1 Trinity Place, Ramsgate, Kent CT11 7HJ

www.montefiorearms.co.uk

This pub has long had a reputation as one of the best beer pubs in Thanet, and in 2014 that was cemented when Eddie Gadd of the Ramsgate Brewery took over the lease. Gadd's beers share space with the best from Kent and Sussex microbreweries, and the pub conforms to its own natural rhythms, not trying too hard and succeeding quite wonderfully.

THE ODD ONE OUT

28 Mersea Rd, Colchester, Essex CO2 7ET

Another pub where time appears to have stopped. Here, it seems as though the Oddie is unaware of any trend or movement happening outside its doors. Its appeal seems to be spread entirely by word of mouth, among people who want a quiet pint and nothing more to go with it than a cheese roll and a bit of a chat. A pub that has a culture all of its own, one that involves stepping back in time by around 50 years.

THE OLD NEPTUNE

Marine Terrace, Whitstable, Kent CT5 1EJ

www.neppy.co.uk

An outpost between sea and land, the Neptune is surrounded by shingle beach, with the sea just yards away. Inside it's all worn, varnished wood befitting a building that was rebuilt entirely in 1897 after another storm lashing. Even when the weather's fine, it feels like you're sheltering from a storm, because people keep bursting through the door in that relieved way we do when getting out of the rain. As it gets more crowded, people laugh with relief that they're here, and the noise pitch starts to get ever higher.

[1]

[1]

[2]

THE SNOWDROP 👥 🎣 ! 🍺 🍴

119 South St, Lewes, East Sussex BN7 2BU
www.thesnowdropinn.com

If there's one problem with the giddy rise of the craft beer bar, it's wrapped up in the subtle shift from 'pub' to 'bar'.

There's always a place for bars alongside pubs, and for a licensed premises to switch from one to the other. But there's a stifling uniformity to the new craft beer destination, especially in the south of England. If you want to sell craft beer, it seems you absolutely must strip out any soft furnishings, ideally back to the bare brick. Naked filament lightbulbs, old, mismatched furniture and an industrial or distressed look are as mandatory in the new craft beer bars as harsh striplights, stinking toilets and banners advertising Sky Sports and John Smiths Smoothflow for £1.99 ($2.80) a pint were in the pubs they've replaced.

I don't dislike this look. But when there are more than a handful of people in the place, the total lack of sound insulation fills the room with loud echoes and makes it impossible to hear anyone sitting more than a foot away. And the uniformity of it – the lack of variation from the template in a scene that's supposed to be all about creativity and expression – gets depressing.

That's why The Snowdrop is such a delight. It's a craft beer bar that looks nothing like a craft beer bar. (It's also a gastropub that looks nothing like a gastropub.) There's a wonderfully idiosyncratic vision at work here, in a pub that looks like the result of a malfunctioning experiment when someone tried to teleport a fairy-tale cottage, a 19th-century carpenter's workshop and an old but lovingly preserved canal boat at the same time. I know, it looks wrong on paper. But it looks bloody wonderful in reality.

I once did a reading at The Snowdrop, from a book about India Pale Ale and its historic sea voyage. When I arrived, the room was decked with homemade ship's bunting, fishing nets,

Union Jacks and a portrait of Queen Victoria. Food had been prepared to match each of the beers I presented for tasting.

This obsessive attention to detail is in everything owners Tony and Dom do. The food is sourced from local farmers, and they rear their own pigs in collaboration with a nearby smallholder. They've even created a magazine celebrating local food.

The year after my book launch, I was invited back to do an event at The Snowdrop's annual Beer Expo. Curated by a local brewer, the beer list was as individual as the pub, referring to current craft beer trends but not slavishly following them, with a mix of old and new breweries, and some imports I've never seen anywhere else in the UK.

One of the activities of the weekend was the Snowdrop's second Pro-Am Scotch Egg-making competition, which I was invited to judge. The entries had been so numerous and varied in Year One that this year they were divided into three categories: traditional, vegetarian and 'experimental'. If dreams came true, that last category would have been won by the Full English Breakfast Scotch Egg, but on the day, the baked beans proved to be its undoing.

This is what happens when talented, creative people pour everything into a pub – the local community responds in kind. And when your local community is as creative and quirky as the town of Lewes, and you're in tune with it to the degree The Snowdrop is, the ideas just bounce back and forth and feed each other, pulling the essence of what makes a great pub into wonderful new shapes.

There should be more craft beer bars that look like this. And more traditional pubs that sell such an exciting and well-kept range of beers. And more of everything in between. Surely that's not too much to ask?

OPPOSITE TOP: The ebullience of The Snowdrop simply cannot be contained by a mere building.

OPPOSITE BOTTOM: Indoors, The Snowdrop has the kind of pub interior you'd expect to find in a fairy-tale.

YE OLDE FIGHTING COCKS [1]

16 Abbey Mill Lane, St Albans, Hertfordshire
AL3 4HE

www.yeoldefightingcocks.co.uk

This contender for the 'Oldest Pub in Britain' title bases its claim on its foundations, which have been there since 743. The modern building, while much newer, is still fascinating, with its octagon-shaped bar area and very low, beamed ceiling. This alone makes it worth a visit, because other aspects of the pub feel like an aggressive marketing campaign aimed at tourists.

YE OLDE REINE DEER INN [2]

47 Parsons Street, Banbury, Oxfordshire,
OX16 5NA

www.ye-olde-reinedeer-inn-banbury.co.uk

The highlight of this cosy, town-centre pub, first built in 1570, is the stunning Globe Room, thought to be the HQ used by Oliver Cromwell when planning attacks on Banbury Castle.

THE RED LION

Snargate, Greatstone-on-Sea, Kent, TN29 9UQ

www.goachers.com/pubs/the-red-lion

A survivor from the 16th century, the Red Lion has been in the same family for over a century, with half of that under the watchful eye of one legendary landlady. Its location on the remote and otherworldly edge of Romney Marsh makes the welcome all the warmer, but take note of the traditional (i.e. limited) opening hours before setting off to find it.

THE ROEBUCK INN [3]

Lewes Rd, Lewes, East Sussex BN8 6BG

www.theroebuckinn.pub

Recently taken over by Tony and Dom from the nearby Snowdrop Inn, the Roebuck has been lavished with the same loving care and intimate attention to detail. There's a steampunk vibe to the detail, with exposed copper pipes, dials and clocks around the place. This would be a dreadful idea if it were in the wrong hands, but here it's done very well.

THE ROYAL STANDARD OF ENGLAND [4]

Forty Green, Beaconsfield, Buckinghamshire
HP9 1XS

www.rsoe.co.uk

One of the contenders for the oldest pub in Britain, this place claims to have been here for 900 years. It certainly looks the part, with some beams and bricks definitely showing serious age. But it's listed here because it doesn't only rely on history; it creates a great pub experience.

THE STAR

17 Church St, Godalming, Surrey GU7 1EL

This ancient building, once a bakery, was converted into an alehouse in 1832. Having built up a great reputation for beer, more recently the landlord has focused on developing his cider offering, which has been recognized as one of the best in the south east, well worth travelling for. Knowledgeable staff and paddles of sample measures make it a cider explorer's dream.

THE TURF TAVERN

4–5 Bath Place, Oxford OX1 3SU

www.turftavern-oxford.co.uk

Possibly the most famous of Oxford's pubs, the Turf is a sprawling student haunt with a hell of a pedigree: not only did Bill Clinton 'not inhale' during his time as a Rhodes Scholar here, but also former Australian Prime Minister Bob Hawke set the world record for downing a yard of ale (11 seconds), which he technically still holds, as Guinness no longer recognize feats of drinking prowess.

Also Try...

THE EAGLE AND CHILD

49 St Giles, Oxford OX1 3LU

www.nicholsonspubs.co.uk

THE OLD CROWN

83 Thames St, Weybridge, Surrey KT13 8LP

www.theoldcrownweybridge.co.uk

THE ORANGE TREE

6 Lower Anchor St, Chelmsford, Essex CM2 0AS

www.the-ot.com

THE RISING SUN

144 Ongar Rd, Brentwood, Essex CM15 9DJ

www.rising-sun-brentwood.co.uk

THE SPORTSMAN

Faversham Road, Seasalter, Whitstable,
Kent CT5 4BP

www.thesportsmanseasalter.co.uk

THE THATCHERS ARMS

Hall Road, Mount Bures, Essex CO8 5AT

www.thatchersarms.co.uk

THE FORAGERS @ THE VERULAM ARMS 🍴

41 Lower Dagnall St, St Albans, Hertfordshire AL3 4QE
www.the-foragers.com

Verulamium was a Roman city that stood in the south west of what is now St Albans. It was destroyed, and the stone was plundered to build medieval St Albans, much of which still survives, and bits of Roman stuff still keep being unearthed. Ancient and modern rub shoulders comfortably here.

I think that's why the Verulam Arms, taking its name from the vanished city, works so well in St Albans and might be less impressive somewhere else. If it were in London, it would be too self-conscious, too wilful and too full of dead-eyed cynics. Here it just fits, and relaxes, and can be itself.

The Verulam Arms is a modest corner pub joining redbrick terraces. It should be a quiet community boozer, and surely was for much of its history. But open the door now and you're surprised to find a light, airy gastropub, complete with Farrow & Ball shades on the walls, refectory-style furniture and shelves of cookbooks.

Beyond the basics, The Verulam Arms has a nice twist. A stack of laminated sheets hangs by each table. I initially think it's the menu, but it's not quite. It's a guide to the foraging the pub uses to create its food and drink. It goes into detail about each ingredient sourced from nearby fields or woodland: the spicy wild garlic that's dried and sold at the bar in garlic salt; the sharp, citrussy wood sorrel that garnishes the fish dishes, and the rainbow-coloured Scarletina Bolete mushrooms that... well, I don't know what they do with them, but they look really cool.

Framed photos of the team foraging or cooking in the woods hang on the walls, alongside art that reflects on our relationship with nature. Blackboards announce the next dates – two Saturdays a month – when you can meet here for a lunchtime pint before being taken out by the team to their foraging sites and shown what to look for.

The menu doesn't rely entirely on foraged materials, of course, but it's permeated by the same spirit of being close to the land. There's gin-cured salmon, 'Bruce the Hunter's game terrine', and pan-seared pigeon breasts with pickled berries and chocolate oil. The burger is made with venison and beef, and is apparently cooked to a Roman recipe.

The drinks haven't been forgotten. There's a well-chosen range of craft beers on the bar. Each font has a brown parcel label attached to it with string, and on each label are three carefully chosen words to describe the flavour. On the back bar, a massive Victorian apothecary-style glass jar with a small tap at the bottom dispenses homemade hedgerow sloe gin. Wild forest liqueurs are made with foraged herbs such as ground ivy, mugwort and yarrow. Woodruff and Douglas fir needles are made into syrups. All are available to buy to take home.

Turning to the final page in the stack of laminates, I learn that if you eat here in a party of four or more between Monday and Thursday, the pub will supply free taxis home to most nearby postcodes – a civilized way to attract custom from all over the city.

On their website, the foragers' manifesto talks about how 'not so very long ago, human life depended upon a relationship with the natural world that has been almost lost today'. I love the idea of a modern gastro/craft beer pub that ticks all the boxes of contemporary trends here in St Albans – a city that reveres and cannibalizes its past to move forward – reviving and recapturing ancient practices for a world that needs them back.

'We want to keep tradition alive,' continues the website. 'We want to survive the winter.'

OPPOSITE TOP: A carefully restored bar, painted in obligatory Farrow & Ball colours, doesn't detract from the foodie welcome of this friendly pub.

OPPOSITE BOTTOM LEFT: In a quiet residential street, The Verulam Arms announces itself on the street corner with a traditional pub sign.

OPPOSITE BOTTOM RIGHT: Once a street corner local, now a foodie destination offering foraged ingredients, wild cocktails and weekly food-gathering walks for pubgoers.

THE
VERULAM ARMS

MEDIOCRIA FIRMA

GREAT PUBS IN
LONDON

The capital's pub scene is as busy and vibrant as you'd expect. But its pubs also reveal the city's rich history, and reflect its diversity. Truly, all human life is here.

1: **The Antelope** *(page 136)*, 87 Maple Rd, Surbiton, Surrey KT6 4AW

2: **The Auld Shillelagh** *(page 136)*, 105 Stoke Newington Church St, London N16 0UD

3: **The Black Friar** *(page 136)*, 174 Queen Victoria St, London EC4V 4EG

4: **The Black Lion** *(page 136)*, 59-61 High St, London E13 0AD

5: **The Bull** *(page 136)*, 13 North Hill, Highgate, London N6 4AB

6: **The Chesham Arms** *(page 136)*, 15 Mehetabel Rd, London E9 6DU

7: **The Coach & Horses** *(page 134)*, 29 Greek St, Soho, London W1D 5DH

8: **The Cock Tavern** *(page 137)*, 315 Mare St, Hackney, London E8 1EJ

9: **The Compton Arms** *(page 137)*, 4 Compton Avenue, London N1 2XD

10: **The Dog & Bell** *(page 137)*, 116 Prince St, London SE8 3JD

11: **The Draft House** *(page 137)*, 206–208 Tower Bridge Rd, London SE1 2UP

12: **The Dublin Castle** *(page 58)*, 94 Parkway, London NW1 7AN

13: **The Eagle Ale House** *(page 137)*, 104 Chatham Rd, London SW11 6HG

14: **The George Inn** *(page 138)*, 77 Borough High St, Southwark, London SE1 1NH

15: **The Grafton** *(page 137)*, 20 Prince of Wales Rd, London NW5 3LG

16: **The Grange** *(page 141)*, Warwick Rd, Ealing, London W5 3XH

17: **The Grapes** *(page 141)*, 76 Narrow St, Limehouse, London E14 8BP

18: **The Grenadier** *(page 141)*, 18 Wilton Row, Belgrave Square, London SW1X 7NR

19: **The Hand & Shears** *(page 141)*, 1 Middle St, Cloth Fair, London EC1A 7JA

20: **The Hand in Hand** *(page 141)*, Crooked Billet, Wimbledon Common, London SW19 4RQ

21: **The Harp** *(page 141)*, 47 Chandos Place, London WC2N 4HS

22: **The Hermits Cave** *(page 141)*, 28 Camberwell Church St, Southwark, London SE5 8QU

23: **The Hope** *(page 141)*, 48 West St, Carshalton, Surrey SM5 2PR

24: **The Ivy House** *(page 142)*, 40 Stuart Rd, Nunhead, London SE15 3BE

25: **The Lamb** *(page 141)*, 94 Lambs Conduit St, Bloomsbury, London WC1N 3LZ

26: **The Lamb & Flag** *(page 144)*, 33 Rose St, Covent Garden, London WC2E 9EB

27: **The Mayflower** *(page 144)*, 117 Rotherhithe St, London SE16 4NF

28: **Ye Olde Mitre** *(page 144)*, 1 Ely Court, Ely Place, London EC1N 6SJ

29: **The Parcel Yard** *(page 144)*, King's Cross Station, London N1C 4AH

30: **The Pelton Arms** *(page 145)*, 23-25 Pelton Rd, London SE10 9PQ

31: **The Prospect of Whitby** *(page 145)*, 57 Wapping Wall, London E1W 3SH

32: **The Rake** *(page 145)*, 14a Winchester Walk, Borough Market, London SE1 9AG

33: **The Ranelagh** *(page 145)*, 82 Bounds Green Rd, London N11 2EU

34: **The Salisbury** *(page 149)*, The Salisbury Hotel, 1 Grand Parade, Green Lanes, London N4 1JX

35: **The Seven Stars** *(page 146)*, 53-54 Carey St, London WC2A 2JB

36: **The Snooty Fox** *(page 149)*, 75 Grosvenor Avenue, Canonbury, London N5 2NN

37: **The Southampton Arms** *(page 149)*, 139 Highgate Rd, London NW5 1LE

38: **The Spaniard's Inn** *(page 149)*, Spaniards Rd, Hampstead, London NW3 7JJ

39: **The Stag's Head** *(page 150)*, 55 Orsman Rd, London N1 5RA

40: **The Trafalgar Tavern** *(page 149)*, Park Row, Greenwich, London SE10 9NW

41: **The Wenlock Arms** *(page 149)*, 26 Wenlock Rd, London N1 7TA

42: **The White Horse** *(page 149)*, 1–3 Parson's Green, London SW6 4UL

43: **The Windsor Castle** *(page 149)*, 114 Campden Hill Rd, London W8 7AR

ISLINGTON

CAMDEN

HACKNEY

WESTMINSTER

TOWER HAMLETS

CITY

NEWHAM

KENSINGTON
& CHELSEA

SOUTHWARK

HAMMERSMITH
& FULHAM

GREENWICH

LAMBETH

LEWISHAM

WANDSWORTH

THE COACH & HORSES ♜ 👥 ❗

29 Greek St, Soho, London W1D 5DH
www.thecoachandhorsessoho.co.uk

The pubs of Soho are steeped in legend. For much of the 20th century, this square mile in the heart of London was louche, seedy and decadently glamorous. The people who drank here were a mix of artists, poets, writers, pop stars, actors, and those who mistakenly believed they were. Wannabes and has-beens mingled at the bar with talents that only seemed to burn brighter with booze, even if they ended up fading away before their time.

Norman Balon was landlord of the Coach & Horses for 50 years before retiring in 2006. Opinions differ as to whether the man whose autobiography was titled *You're Barred, You Bastards!* really was the rudest publican in London, or whether it was just that the staff of *Private Eye* magazine, together with the other writers who made up the core of his regular clientele of legendary drinkers, were on hand to record his every utterance.

The most famous of Norman's regulars was Jeffrey Bernard, journalist and alcoholic, who detailed his misadventures in a column for *The Spectator* magazine called 'Low Life'. The 1989 play *Jeffrey Bernard Is Unwell*, named after the line that ran where his column should have been when he was too inebriated or hung over to write it, is set in The Coach & Horses. In the play, Bernard has been locked in overnight, and uses the occasion to tell the audience the stories of his drinking life.

Today, the sign outside and the title across the (fully vegetarian and vegan) menu refers to 'Norman's Coach & Horses', and the place is often touted as Soho's most famous pub. The walls are full of *Private Eye* cartoons invariably depicting Norman barring someone, or a punter popping his head around the door to ask, 'Jeff been in?'

If this seems like self-reverence, it should be said that these cartoons were here when Norman was still behind the bar. I began drinking in The Coach & Horses – occasionally – in the late 1990s, and found Norman to be perfectly pleasant, if a little imposing. As I look around it today, it's hard to spot anything that's changed since I first came here. There's WiFi now, and some different beers on the bar, but the ratty carpet and worn tables are the same. The whole place glows orange, thanks to the untouched 1960s Truman's Brewery pale wood, illuminated by a collection of lamps under twee pink shades. There's no music and no games machines, just the quiet hum of refrigerators in the background.

Some punters try to keep the Bohemian spirit alive at a time when Soho's individuality is being bulldozed into chain-brand conformity, along with the rest of Central London. People whose clothes and haircuts look slightly wrong sit reading battered paperbacks, occasionally muttering to themselves. Others stand at the bar, attempting to engage long-suffering staff in conversation with lines like, 'I haven't been back here since old Balon ran the place,' or 'My friend met Terence Stamp in here once.'

Groups of tourists approach the bar nervously, as if they expect to be shouted at, and become the audience for the rambling anecdotes that follow these opening gambits. Others enter nervously, clutching guidebooks which they peer at, confused and betrayed, before making a hasty exit.

Bohemia has gone, and in the cold light of day the lives of people like Jeffrey Bernard look sad rather than glorious. But strip all that away, and The Coach & Horses is an unlikely treat in the middle of London: a quiet, relaxed boozer, a place to escape the frenetic madness outside. I always pop in when I'm near, even though Jeffrey is long gone.

OPPOSITE TOP: Still bearing elements of a traditional 1960s Truman's pub interior, all orange wood and red detailing, this pub wears its history with pride.

OPPOSITE BOTTOM: The Coach & Horses is one of a dwindling number of Soho drinking institutions, steeped in literary history and media folklore.

THE ANTELOPE

87 Maple Rd, Surbiton, Surrey KT6 4AW

www.theantelope.co.uk

With 18 beers and five ciders on tap, plus an impressive array of bottles, this is the best beer pub for miles around. The regular, diverse clientele, who create a gentle buzz throughout the day, prove it's not just East London hipsters who love craft beer. There's even a microbrewery – the Big Smoke Brew Co – out back, providing three regular, permanent beers for the bar.

THE AULD SHILLELAGH

105 Stoke Newington Church Street, London N16 0UD

www.theauldshillelagh.co.uk

There are Irish pubs, and Irish theme pubs – and they're quite different. To be authentically Irish, you don't have to be in Ireland. As the Auld Shillelagh demonstrates, you just have to be run by, and for, Irish regulars with a minimum of fuss, occasional live music, the indefinable *craic* and the eternal hiss of the Guinness tap.

THE BLACK FRIAR [1]

174 Queen Victoria St, London EC4V 4EG

www.nicholsonspubs.co.uk/
theblackfriarblackfriarslondon

Proving that the appeal of a 'theme pub' depends entirely on the theme chosen, this place was inspired by the Dominican friary that used to stand here. It's completely over the top, heavily stylized and utterly wonderful – quite unlike any other pub. I'd love to have a pint here of whatever the designers were on when they conceived it.

THE BLACK LION

59-61 High St, London E13 0AD

www.blacklionplaistow.co.uk

The low wooden beams and Tudor-style walls of this ancient coaching inn evoke the era when Dick Turpin supposedly stabled his horse here in the outbuildings. But the Black Lion is a resolutely contemporary East End pub, rammed when West Ham are at home. It's one of actor Ray Winstone's favourite pubs, and Bobby Moore drank here – what more can be said?

THE BULL [2]

13 North Hill, London N6 4AB

thebullhighgate.co.uk

This elegant, upmarket pub combines food as good as any gastropub, beers as good as any craft beer bar (several from the pub's own brewery), a welcome as warm as any community boozer, and a packed programme of events in the opulent upstairs room. It's impossible to imagine it as the run-down, exhausted, empty place it was until a few short years ago.

THE CHESHAM ARMS

15 Mehetabel Rd, London E9 6DU

cheshamarms.com

This mid-terrace Victorian pub was recently saved by committed community action during a closure that lasted exactly a thousand days. The interior is completely remodelled, though you'd never guess it. The impeccable beer selection draws largely from local breweries in Hackney. The Chesham reasserts the importance of the pub as the heart of a local community.

THE COCK TAVERN

315 Mare St, London E8 1EJ

www.thecocktavern.co.uk

The sister pub to The Southampton Arms in Kentish Town, The Cock is gloriously spartan, with old furniture, bare floors and old-fashioned hand pumps on the bar. A traditional alehouse reinvented for the craft beer generation, it always stays the right side of the line between old-school authenticity and trying too hard.

THE COMPTON ARMS

4 Compton Avenue, London N1 2XD

www.thecomptonarms.co.uk

'Only two minutes from a bus stop, but it is on a side street, and drunks and rowdies never seem to find their way there... Its clientele consists mostly of "regulars" who occupy the same chair every evening and go there for conversation as much as for the beer.' Was Orwell talking about the Compton in his famous essay? He was certainly a regular visitor here, and it's changed little since then.

THE DOG & BELL

116 Prince St, London SE8 3JD

My mate Chris once walked in here soaked from rain and defeated by work. The barman looked at him, said, 'There's a man who needs a pint of London Pride,' and the beer was on the bar before Chris had got there. His money was waved away. They don't offer free pints to just anyone, but this backstreet boozer understands and caters for all its varied, ever-changing cast of regulars.

THE DRAFT HOUSE

206-208 Tower Bridge Rd, London SE1 2UP

www.drafthouse.co.uk

The Draft House chain is spreading across London, offering carefully chosen beers from around the world in fresh, modern surroundings with the quirkiness and warmth that identifies a pub rather than a bar. Tower Bridge is the flagship bar, always buzzing and friendly, with the decor of a teenage gang hut. The foot-long long pork scratchings alone make a visit to this establishment absolutely essential.

THE EAGLE ALE HOUSE

104 Chatham Rd, London SW11 6HG

www.eaglealehouse.co.uk

This area of South London has famously been dubbed 'Nappy Valley' thanks to its influx of affluent families. The chain-pub refurbishments that seek to attract them seem to drain the soul of a place with every lick of Farrow & Ball paint. Those who drink in the Eagle see it as a last bastion of pubby independence and authenticity – and excellent beer, of course.

THE GRAFTON [3]

20 Prince of Wales Rd, London NW5 3LG

thegraftonnw5.co.uk

A smart, revamped pub whose old-fashioned features have been retained and new ones added sensitively. Events such as 'bring your own vinyl' and a Sunday night 'sing-a-long' don't feel forced, and the 'street meets pub' themed menu delivers decent pub food. Cool but not pretentious or pricey, the Grafton is a traditional local, smartly updated for the 21st century pubgoer.

THE GEORGE INN ♜ 🏛

77 Borough High St, London SE1 1NH
www.george-southwark.co.uk

If I tell you that this humble volume about the British pub is a little under 70,000 words long, and that I've written a book about the George Inn alone that is over 90,000 words long, you might appreciate how difficult it is to capture the enigma of this ancient, unique pub.

The George is full of paradoxes. You could work in Southwark for years and be completely unaware of its existence, yet there are people who travel halfway across the world to see it. It has strong associations with Geoffrey Chaucer, William Shakespeare and Charles Dickens – the three most famous and important figures in English literature – yet they all preferred the inns that once stood either side of the George, when this white street consisted of inns just like it. In its heyday, the George was the least famous of the magnificent coaching inns that once defined this part of South London, but it is the only one that has survived.

The stories behind these odd facts are the ones that are too long to be told here, so let's look at some of the more straightforward aspects of London's most interesting pub.

There's been an inn on the site of the George since at least Chaucer's time, but back then it was known as the Syrcote. It gradually shed its old name and acquired its new one by the middle of the 15th century, and appears on the oldest surviving map of Southwark, drawn around 1542, as The George.

It was modified and enlarged over the centuries, burned to the ground twice in the 1660s, and the current inn dates back to 1677, after the rebuilding necessitated by the last of these fires. So depending on how you define a pub, the building itself is nearly three and a half centuries old, but the ongoing business concern that is today known as The George Inn is over 600 years old.

The building as it stands represents about 20 per cent of the George in its prime. Part of the reason it survives in its reduced state is that when its vast stables and warehouses were no longer needed, they were sold off bit by bit, allowing the pub itself to survive.

What remains is still majestic. When tourists find the narrow passageway from Borough High Street that leads into what was once the inn's first great courtyard, then a railway goods yard, and is now a cobbled space overlooked by offices and a tacky bar, as well as the George itself, they often gasp. You just don't see architecture like this any more, the elegant galleries facing down onto the cobbles, the ancient beams sagging a little, much like a deflating balloon on the morning after a great party.

The George is as grouchy and cantankerous and forgetful as any senior citizen. Most first-time visitors enter the door nearest the yard entrance, and stand in the old taproom looking around with growing confusion until they realize that, while there are people drinking in here, there's no bar, and they have to go back outside and enter the next door along to buy a drink. Once they've located the main bar, they can walk for close to another hundred yards through room after room, where wood-panelled walls hang with fragments of the inns past.

But the George continues to succeed because it wears its past lightly. It was regarded as a tourist attraction when many others in London were still newly built, but it has never let its status go to its head. Yes, it's ancient, but it's no museum or theme park. It simply continues to do what it has done for centuries: providing shelter and sustenance to those who come to London looking for fame and fortune, the bright lights and the big city.

OPPOSITE: London's last surviving galleried coaching inn draws gasp of admiration from tourists who wander down a narrow alley to find it.

[1]

[3]

[2]

THE GRANGE

Warwick Rd, London W5 3XH

www.grangeealing.co.uk

The Grange uses its vast space to create something that feels almost like a country club on the edge of Ealing Common, except that it's a club that anyone can enter. It's a space to stretch out in and relax with the weekend papers, reading to create an appetite for meals of a quality that would not be out of place in a decent West End restaurant.

THE GRAPES

76 Narrow St, London E14 8BP

www.thegrapes.co.uk

A narrow sliver in a fat block of redevelopment, The Grapes shouldn't have survived until now. That it did is largely thanks to the actor Ian McKellen, who bought the place to save it – Gandalf's staff now hangs proprietorially behind the bar. The deck at the back of the pub hangs over the Thames and overlooks an Antony Gormley sculpture standing 10yds (9m) out, gazing pensively downriver. At sunset, this deck is often crowded with people and blissful, like a miniature Ibiza bar.

THE GRENADIER [1]

18 Wilton Row, London SW1X 7NR

taylor-walker.co.uk

The first ten times I visited The Grenadier, I had to be guided through the maze of grim passages that lead from Knightsbridge, Narnia-like, to this quiet mews. The pub was once the Officers' Mess for The First Royal Regiment of Foot Guards, and a red guard box still stands outside. It rewards those diligent enough to find it with arguably the finest Bloody Mary in London, and stories of the ghost of a guardsman who was beaten to death for cheating at cards.

THE HAND & SHEARS

1 Middle St, London EC1A 7JA

www.thehandandshears.co.uk

The beautifully preserved interior doesn't draw attention to its exquisite partitions, wooden panelling and lacquered fireplaces. It just carries on doing what it's done, in some form, since the 12th century, dispensing decent beer with no-nonsense bar snacks to soak it up. Once patronized by Tudor tailors and drapers, who gave it its current name, it's now a secluded haven from the Barbican's concrete bustle. The survival of pubs like this in areas like this becomes more remarkable with every passing year.

THE HAND IN HAND

Crooked Billet, London SW19 4RQ

www.thehandinhandwimbledon.co.uk

Given its setting, the green outside and the proximity to a certain tennis tournament, this place could easily have become the preserve of people who want a meal and a glass of wine but find real pubs a bit scary. It hasn't – the pub is still one of the local CAMRA's favourites – and that's a real feat of great business judgement. The poker night on Mondays is a particularly nice touch in keeping the place real.

THE HARP [2]

47 Chandos Place, London WC2N 4HS

www.harpcoventgarden.com

The pump clips of past guest ales overlap and completely cover the panelling above the bar. The beautiful stained glass on the back bar – partially lit and easily missed – and the walls crowded with random portraits encourage a contemplative mood. But the place is always so jolly it often feels like stumbling into a party, with punters spontaneously starting up conversations with their neighbours.

THE HERMITS CAVE

28 Camberwell Church St, London SE5 8QU

Ostensibly an Irish pub, the Hermits Cave (no apostrophe needed, apparently) is popular with the local community in this area; people of all ages, races and walks of life. The bar curves gently, echoing the attractive curve at the front of this corner building. Along it, people order from a curious and eclectic array of drinks, and put the world to rights. Sometimes given indifferent reviews by tourists, it's passionately defended by locals. These include elderly residents and students from the nearby art college, who rub along together quite nicely.

THE HOPE

48 West St, Carshalton, Surrey SM5 2PR

hopecarshalton.co.uk

When this pub was threatened with closure in 2010, a group of real ale-loving locals successfully put together a bid to buy it. So in terms of sheer, unbridled enthusiasm for all things ale, The Hope is unmatched. The ever-changing, expertly sourced range of cask ales is complemented by a great selection of bottled beers from around the world, all served without the snobbery some might expect from such dedicated beer geeks.

THE LAMB [3]

94 Lambs Conduit St, London WC1N 3LZ

www.youngs.co.uk/pubs/lamb

The Lamb is famous for having preserved its beautiful etched-glass Victorian snug screens. The small, private compartments these screens create were once notorious for allowing illicit behaviour in London pubs, but here, today, they give The Lamb a quiet, almost regal air. When I'm asked to film news stories for TV about the pub, we often end up here.

THE IVY HOUSE 👥 🎤 🍺

40 Stuart Rd, London SE15 3BE
www.ivyhousenunhead.com

In *The Moon Under Water*, Orwell raged against 'the puritanical nonsense of excluding children – and therefore, to some extent, women – from pubs that has turned these places into mere boozing-shops instead of the family gathering-places that they ought to be'.

On a sunny August afternoon, as an earnest conversation at the bar becomes a little too loud after one daytime pint too many, a pair of children on their school holidays run in, transgressing. 'You again!' laughs the barmaid, and she chases them out, joining in the game, laughingly telling them they're barred – at least until they come back in with their parents in tow.

Orwell wasn't the first to want to champion pubs as a hub for everyone in the community. In the 1930s, in the face of dwindling numbers of pubgoers, the campaign for the 'Improved Public House' encouraged the building of pubs with larger rooms and better facilities for the whole family to hang out in.

In response, Nunhead's Newlands Tavern, owned by Truman's Brewery, was rebuilt to include two spacious bars and a wonderful concert hall that recalled early Victorian music halls. It held dances and parties, none more memorable than the one celebrating VE Day, almost a year after the pub was narrowly missed by the V1 rocket that destroyed much of the street around it.

By the 1970s, the pub was a grittier affair, the concert hall a key venue on the 'pub rock' circuit that gave birth to punk. Artists such as Joe Strummer, Elvis Costello and Dr Feelgood blew the roof off this intimate venue.

It was still a popular pub in 2012 (having been renamed The Ivy House in the 1990s) when owners Enterprise Inns evicted the tenants with only a week's notice and announced their intention to sell it for redevelopment into modern flats.

What followed was a pioneering example of community action. London's pubs tend to be busier than those in remote and rural parts of the country, yet pubs in London are more likely to face closure than any other region in the UK, simply because, even if a pub is making huge, six-figure annual profits, there's often immediate gain in selling it for housing.

The locals of the Ivy House, with the support of CAMRA (the Campaign for Real Ale), managed to get the largely unchanged interior a Grade II listing. They were the first in London to have their pub declared an 'Asset of Community Value' under the provisions of the new Localism Act, and thanks to this, were able to successfully buy what became the UK's first cooperatively owned pub.

I sit against a wall, smiling at background music that would have been popular when the building was new. The small stage, with its ornate moulding and gold lamé curtains, once again hosts bands on the circuit, sometimes punching well above its weight. Flyers for these gigs mingle with magazines and posters for other community information and news on a table and noticeboards by the bar. The preserved golden lettering for Truman's beers from the 1930s contrasts with and contextualizes the extensive range of modern cask ales and craft beers – including some from the newly resurrected Truman's brewery.

Like the rest of London, housing is in short supply and high demand. But it's pubs like this that make an area worth living in, rather than simply sleeping in and commuting into town from. While we must reluctantly accept that monetary value counts for more than anything else these days, The Ivy House is a powerful reminder that money is not the only measure of worth in a community.

THE LAMB & FLAG [1]

33 Rose St, Covent Garden, London WC2E 9EB

lambandflagcoventgarden.co.uk

With its wooden slatted walls and a front that opens up almost completely to the outside, you imagine you can step outside the Lamb onto a shingle beach. Instead, you are met by a small courtyard, formed in the space of a crooked alley between busy Garrick Street and Floral Street. Halfway along this alley, pub regulars secretly escape from the unending tourist craziness of Covent Garden.

THE MAYFLOWER

117 Rotherhithe St, London SE16 4NF

www.mayflowerpub.co.uk

'Customers please be aware, feet and belongings may get wet at high tide.'

The width and solidity of the door onto the deck, on which this notice is hung, give credence to the warning. You can see the tidal Thames surging in through the slats beneath your feet, hear the waves shushing and smell the fresh sea tang. Blankets are available, and are often needed, as you settle down to enjoy London's best pub cheese selection.

YE OLDE MITRE [2]

1 Ely Court, London EC1N 6SJ

yeoldemitreholborn.co.uk

Despite being clearly signposted from Hatton Garden, this pub can be maddeningly difficult to find. But it's worth the effort. In business since 1547 (rebuilt in 1772), historically it's within the Diocese of Ely, part of Cambridgeshire, and there are legends of jewel thieves escaping here because London's police had no jurisdiction. It still feels like escaping to another world.

THE PARCEL YARD

King's Cross Station, London N1C 4AH

www.parcelyard.co.uk

A stunning reinvention of a Grade 1-listed building that was once – you guessed it – the parcel offices for King's Cross station. Now a vast palace to beer, food and railway memorabilia, it's been redone so lovingly that even if you have no interest in trains when you arrive, you'll be a geek by the time you eventually leave. This place is an emphatic vote of confidence in the future of the pub.

THE PELTON ARMS [3]

23–25 Pelton Rd, London SE10 9PQ

www.peltonarms.com

Red-shaded lamps illuminate these rust-coloured walls with a warm, bordello glow. Here and there, homely touches such as vases of flowers and standard lamps smooth the edges and soothe the soul. The geezer in the sharp mod clothes who runs the pub quiz needs to be cloned for any London pub under threat of closure as a matter of the utmost urgency.

THE PROSPECT OF WHITBY [4]

57 Wapping Wall, London E1W 3SH

www.taylor-walker.co.uk

Dating back to 1520, the Prospect of Whitby claims to be London's oldest surviving riverside pub. Now owned by a large pub company and polished up to attract tourists, it's as much at home on the new Thames of endless, soulless apartments as it was in the days of the docks. But the ghosts of the smugglers, pirates and robbers who used to drink here are not far away.

THE RAKE

14a Winchester Walk, London SE1 9AG

www.facebook.com/The-Rake

This former market-worker's cafe may not actually be the smallest pub in London, but it's certainly the most unlikely. An astonishingly wide range of beers is supplied by Utobeer, which also runs the excellent beer stall in the nearby Borough Market. The space is tiny, the toilets are dreadful, and the best place is to stand is outside by the bins. It absolutely shouldn't work, but it totally does – this place is a mecca for the capital's beer writers and bloggers, as well as visiting brewers from further afield.

THE RANELAGH

82 Bounds Green Rd, London N11 2EU

www.theranelaghn11.co.uk

London is lucky to have an ever-increasing number of Victorian-built pubs that, having lost their way, have recently been sympathetically reinvented for a less intense, more leisurely age of pub-going. With 20 beers on tap, a famous Sunday lunch, a pile of board games and a massive beer garden, The Ranelagh is a perfect example of why these old institutions remain relevant today.

THE SEVEN STARS ! 🍺 🍴

53-54 Carey St, London WC2A 2JB
www.facebook.com/The-Seven-Stars

If you're on the hunt for interesting pubs, then somewhere with a landlady who goes by the name of Roxy Beaujolais and a pub cat who lives on the bar top and sports an Elizabethan ruff, is bound to attract your attention.

Happily, every detail lives up to the headlines.

Reviews of The Seven Stars talk about how difficult it is to get a seat in this popular hideaway just behind London's law courts, where lawyers order 'champagne to celebrate their victories or whisky to drown their sorrows', and where the action usually spills onto the street outside, beneath bounteous hanging baskets that trail flowers through your hair.

If you do want a seat, it's best to go mid-afternoon when it's quieter, though not entirely deserted. People in suits often sneak in for a quick glass of claret on the premise of needing to discuss an urgent procedural point away from the office. Others, for whom career advancement is no longer a concern, simply settle in for the day.

The green-checked plastic tablecloths remind me of a Soho Italian restaurant. In fact, the whole place feels like an eastern outpost of Greek Street or Frith Street, where Roxy once ran the front-of-house at legendary jazz club Ronnie Scott's. If The Seven Stars were in Soho, where it belongs, it would attract a more self-conscious clientele. It doesn't really fit in this part of the city at all, and that makes it much more appealing, a delightful aberration, as a pub like this should be.

In her varied career, Roxy has worked as a TV chef, and she still oversees the food here. It's a simple menu that changes daily, depending on what she fancies cooking. My wife orders Napoli sausages with mash, which changes its mind and becomes a wonderful salad of potatoes, dill, pickles and mustard by the time it arrives.

We're also tempted by the roast beef dish. 'What's it served with?' asks my wife.

'Bread,' is the surprisingly cryptic reply.

The pub is a museum to itself, its area and its clientele. The interior was designed by Roxy's architect husband, who is so good at his job you'd never guess an architect had been anywhere near it during the past 100 years or so. The walls feature posters for forgotten legal-themed comedies with titles like 'A Pair of Briefs', and a collection of stunning black-and-white portrait photography, much of it featuring Roxy herself.

The wall behind your back as you enter and face the bar is full of pictures of Tom Paine, the first pub cat, who reigned here from Roxy's arrival in 2000 until his passing in 2011. His dapper selection of ruffs, sourced by Roxy from the Westminster Abbey Choir School, made him a local celebrity. When asked by visitors if the cat's attire was a flea collar, Roxy was fond of replying, 'No, darling, it's show business.'

Tom Paine the cat was succeeded by a former stray, called Ray Brown. By all accounts he didn't live up to his predecessor's reputation as a 'weapon of mouse destruction'. He preferred to sit on the bar, being fed from an ashtray. He too is now departed, but there'll be a new ruff-wearer in place by the time you read this book.

The Seven Stars is a refuge for the demi monde that still lurks within an increasingly corporatized, blanded-out London. It's a place that makes me want to drink red wine during the day instead of beer. It is, as Roxy once described it to a magazine, 'A home for the bewildered.' I can think of no better mission statement for the idea of the pub.

OPPOSITE TOP: The Seven Stars, Holborn, dressed to impress with an exterior of colourful hanging baskets. A welcoming sight.

OPPOSITE BOTTOM LEFT: The menu at this Holborn institution is gloriously esoteric...

OPPOSITE BOTTOM RIGHT: ...but not as esoteric as the pub cat, whose choirboy collar is handed down through generations of 'weapons of mouse destruction'.

[2]

[2]

[1]

[3]

[4]

[5]

THE SALISBURY

1 Grand Parade, London N4 1JX

www.remarkablerestaurants.co.uk

Originally built as a hotel, restaurant and public house, the Grade II-listed Salisbury is a classic Victorian gin palace. For some, 'palace' was a term of sarcastic derision. Today, the rejuvenated Salisbury's fluted columns, high ceilings, frosted glass and decorated mirrors make it feel like a true palace but for ordinary folk – a palace with a juke box, a Sunday roast and a pub quiz, which are all regally excellent.

THE SNOOTY FOX [1]

75 Grosvenor Avenue, London N5 2NN

www.snootyfoxlondon.co.uk

Being a curved building on a street corner gives the Snooty a curious shape, all angles and odd bits here and there, which create the foundation of its charm. This is a pub that celebrates great music as much as wonderful food and drink, with DJs, music-themed beers and – a rarity nowadays – a jukebox full of old 45s.

THE SOUTHAMPTON ARMS [2]

139 Highgate Rd, London NW5 1LE

www.thesouthamptonarms.co.uk

Sister and forerunner to Hackney's Cock Tavern, this was a complete original when it (re)opened in 2009. Its style of decor has now been copied so widely by the new wave of craft beer bars, to the dismay of the owners, it has started a new trend in pub style. 'BEER. CIDER. MEAT.' reads the painted sign on the wall outside, stealing hearts in three simple words.

THE SPANIARD'S INN

Spaniards Rd, London NW3 7JJ

www.thespaniardshampstead.co.uk

This feels like a sleepy country pub yet is to be found in the heart of affluent North London, so is therefore always packed. One of London's oldest pubs, The Spaniard's makes a strong claim to have hosted everyone from Dick Turpin to Charles Dickens in the past. Today's celebrities may not have the same legendary status, but you often find familiar TV faces settling down for the wonderful Sunday roast, together with dogs and children.

THE TRAFALGAR TAVERN [3]

Park Row, London SE10 9NW

www.trafalgartavern.co.uk

Nineteenth-century taverns turned the idea of the pub into something much grander. Downstairs the Trafalgar looks like an ordinary, if sizeable, pub. Upstairs, it's a palace, with outrageously high ceilings and tall windows opening out onto balconies over the Thames. Dickens set a wedding breakfast here in *Our Mutual Friend,* and I can confirm from personal experience that it's a great place to get married.

THE WENLOCK ARMS [4]

26 Wenlock Rd, London N1 7TA

www.wenlockarms.com

This London real ale institution was under threat of closure a while back, but emerged stronger and better after redevelopment, retaining its no-nonsense basic pub appeal but smartened up for the modern beer scene. It is what it is: sturdily independent and unpretentious, like all great pubs should be, serving both cask ales and real ciders.

THE WHITE HORSE [5]

1–3 Parson's Green, London SW6 4UL

www.whitehorsesw6.com

The 'Sloaney Pony' is known to thousands of locals as a gastropub that offers superlative food and wine in opulent surroundings, and a place where if you shout 'Jemima' in a posh drawl, half the women will turn around. Curiously, the pub is also considered to be one of the very best beer pubs on the planet by beer fans and brewers. What a brilliant collision.

THE WINDSOR CASTLE

114 Campden Hill Rd, London W8 7AR

www.thewindsorcastlekensington.co.uk

Hidden in a narrow lane between Notting Hill and Kensington High Street, this old coaching inn has defied the huge change in the area and appears unaltered for centuries. It can be a bit too much if the well-heeled locals are out in large numbers, but it's worth seeking out at quieter times, especially for its brilliant beer garden.

Also Try...

THE BIRDCAGE

80 Columbia Rd, London E2 7QB

www.drafthouse.co.uk

THE CHARLES LAMB

16 Elia St, London N1 8DE

www.thecharleslambpub.com

CRAFT BEER CO

82 Leather Lane, London EC1N 7TR

www.thecraftbeerco.com

THE EUSTON TAP

190 Euston Rd, London NW1 2EF

www.eustontap.com

THE STAG'S HEAD 👥 🔨 🍺

55 Orsman Rd, London N1 5RA
stagsheadhoxton.com

What do you do if you're a local community boozer and the community moves on?

In theory, the answer is straightforward. The reason pubs have survived for so long is that they reflect the communities that focus around them. As the community evolves, so does the pub. The quiet boozer that becomes a theme pub then a gastropub that reverts to being a traditional community boozer fortified by craft beer is simply reflecting the hopes and aspirations of its time, moving with the times.

But this simple economic pragmatism becomes a little more complicated in urban communities experiencing rapid gentrification. Here, the incomers have money to spend, and the local pubs need that money to survive. Usually, this means a reinvention that says goodbye to the old regulars who have propped up the bar for decades – either by gently easing them out, replacing Foster's with a craft brewed Pilsner that costs a quid ($1.40) a pint more, or in some cases, actually telling them their custom is no longer welcome. These lifetime drinkers inevitably find themselves corralled into the nearest Wetherspoon's, or stop going to the pub altogether. No one feels good about it, but it has to be done. Or so the commercial logic goes, anyway.

We stumble across a wonderful exception to this rule on a gentle afternoon pub-crawl between two familiar haunts. We're taking a short cut down a street I've never been on before, when we're caught short and need an urgent loo break. The Stag's Head is the only place we can see. It looks forbidding from the outside, but we're desperate, so we decide to have a quick half while we use the facilities, and get out as quickly as possible. We end up staying for the rest of the day.

The Nag's Head is an old Truman's Brewery pub that has been meticulously preserved.

The golden wood panelling glows in the soft light. A battered piano, clearly still used, sits inside the door, its top strewn with gig flyers.

We first notice something unusual when we look at the bar: craft brews from small London breweries sit side by side with Stella Artois and Foster's. The stools at the bar are occupied by a group of East End likely lads who look as if they've been sitting there since the 1970s. As they move to allow my wife through to the toilets, one of them says, in proper old-fashioned cockney patois, 'Ow roight, Treacle?'

But when we move into the back room, we find the new generation of East Londoners lounging on furniture that is mismatched and random, seemingly by age rather than contrivance. While the new owners, who took over in 2011, have gone to great pains to preserve or even restore original fittings to this Victorian pub, they've also brought the pub into the 21st century. It runs regular gigs and club nights, the evidence of which is strewn around the walls. Being in here on a cold, grey Sunday afternoon, it's like being in both a nightclub during the hours before it opens and the most traditional of London boozers at exactly the same time.

Given the right space and the right attitude, you don't have to adopt a scorched earth policy towards the past in order to bring in the new. When it's natural like this, rather than forced, when it's authentic rather than contrived, a self-consciously old-fashioned boozer is equally relevant to a new generation in search of retro cool, and the older generation who remember it from the first time around. And this reminds us that the very best pubs are egalitarian, bringing generations together, for the benefit of all. Which, you have to admit, is an unexpected bonus when all you were looking for was a quick toilet break.

OPPOSITE TOP LEFT: Frosted glass panels offered interesting architectural details while providing privacy from one section of the pub to another in Victorian times.

OPPOSITE TOP RIGHT: A basic interior can be the essence of a great pub.

OPPOSITE BOTTOM: The Stag's Head is simple but, at the same time, a cool, retro hangout for young drinkers. The style of the pub comes full circle in this place.

EAST ENGLAND

This is the heart of English barley growing country, and barley makes beer. Beer is in the soul of the region, and the rolling, flat fields and fens are dotted with pubs where you can both savour it and pay tribute to it.

1: **The Adam and Eve** *(page 156)*, 17 Bishopgate, Norwich NR3 1RZ

2: **The Anchor Inn** *(page 156)*, The Street, Morston, Norfolk NR25 7AA

3: **The Anchor** *(page 156)*, Walberswick, Suffolk 1P18 6AU

4: **The Brewery Tap** *(page 157)*, 80 Westgate, Peterborough, Cambridgeshire PE1 2AA

5: **The Butt & Oyster** *(page 157)*, Pin Mill, Ipswich, Suffolk IP9 1JW

6: **The Cambridge Blue** *(page 157)*, 85–87 Gwydir St, Cambridge CB1 2LG

7: **The Crown Inn** *(page 161)*, The Green, East Rudham, Norfolk PE31 8RD

8: **The Dabbling Duck** *(page 161)*, 11 Abbey Rd, Great Massingham, Norfolk PE32 2HN

9: **The Dove Street Inn** *(page 161)*, 76 St. Helen's St, Ipswich, Suffolk IP4 2LA

10: **The Eagle** *(page 161)*, 8 Bene't Street, Cambridge CB2 3QN

11: **The Earle Arms** *(page 158)*, The Green, Heydon, Norwich NR11 6AD

12: **The Elm Tree** *(page 161)*, 16a Orchard St, Cambridge CB1 1JT

13: **The Fat Cat** *(page 161)*, 49 West End Street, Norwich NR2 4NA

14: **The Kitchener Arms** *(page 161)*, Brockford Station, Wetheringsett, near Stowmarket, Suffolk IP14 5PW

15: **The Live and Let Live** *(page 161)*, 40 Mawson Road, Cambridge CB1 2EA

16: **The Lord Nelson Inn** *(page 161)*, East Street, Southwold, Suffolk IP18 6EJ

17: **The Murderers and The Gardeners Arms** *(page 154)*, 2–8 Timber Hill, Norwich NR1 3LB

18: **The Nutshell** *(page 164)*, The Traverse, Bury St Edmunds, Suffolk IP33 1BJ

19: **Pint Shop** *(page 164)*, 10 Peas Hill, Cambridge CB2 3PN

20: **The Queen's Head** *(page 164)*, 7 Cross St, Eye, Suffolk IP23 7AB

21: **The Queen's Head** *(page 162)*, Fowlmere Rd, Newton, Cambridgeshire CB22 7PG

22: **The Red Lion** *(page 166)*, 27 High St, Histon, Cambridgeshire CB24 9JD

23: **The Red Lion** *(page 164)*, 32 High St, Hinxton, Cambridgeshire CB10 1QY

24: **The Rose** *(page 164)*, 235 Queens Rd, Norwich, Norfolk NR1 3EA

25: **The Rose and Crown** *(page 164)*, Old Church Rd, Snettisham, Norfolk PE31 7LX

26: **The Signal Box Inn** *(page 169)*, Lakeside Station, Kings Road, Cleethorpes, Lincolnshire DN35 0AG

27: **The Station Hotel** *(page 169)*, Station Rd, Framlingham, Suffolk IP13 9EE

28: **The Struggler's Inn** *(page 169)*, 83 Westgate, Lincoln LN1 3BG

29: **The Three Horseshoes** *(page 170)*, The Street, Warham, Norfolk NR23 1NL

30: **The Tickell Arms** *(page 169)*, North Rd, Whittlesford, Cambridgeshire CB22 4NZ

31: **The Tobie Norris** *(page 169)*, 12 St Paul's St, Stamford, Lincolnshire PE9 2BE

32: **The Victoria** *(page 169)*, Earl Soham, Suffolk IP13 7RL

33: **The White Horse** *(page 169)*, The Street, Neatishead, Norwich NR12 8AD

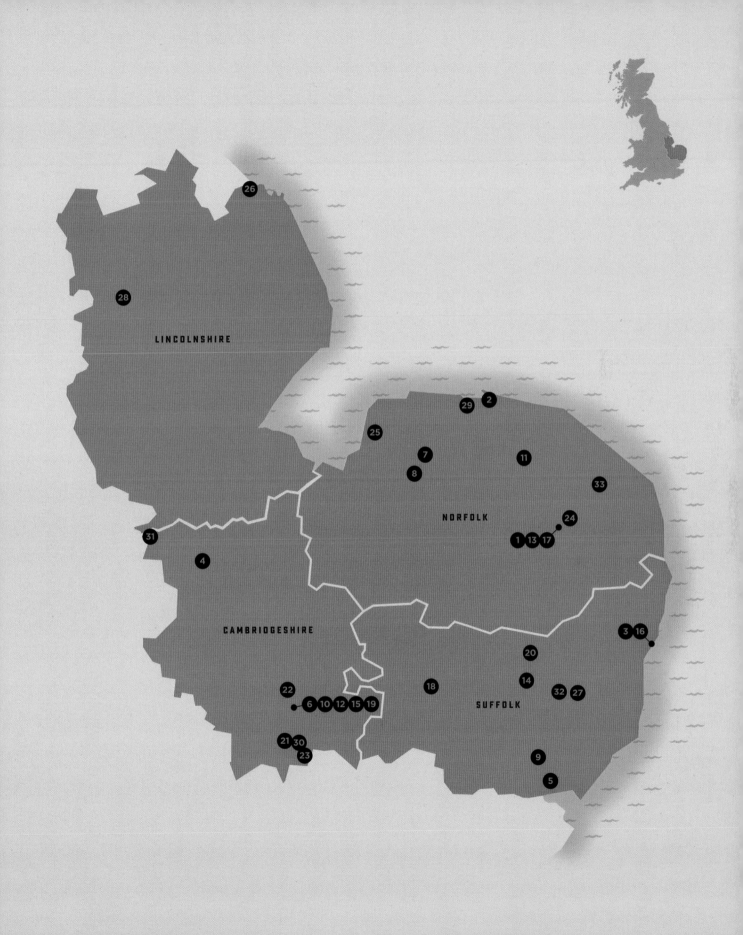

LINCOLNSHIRE

NORFOLK

CAMBRIDGESHIRE

SUFFOLK

THE MURDERERS AND THE GARDENERS ARMS 🏰 🏛 👥 🔨 ❗ 🍺

2–8 Timber Hill, Norwich NR1 3LB
www.themurderers.co.uk

The Murderers *almost* has the lot.

If it were in a village on a remote coastal clifftop and had just a little more energy in its menu, it would tick every criterion we use in this book to describe great pubs. That fantasy might seem like a tenuous stretch, but the Murderers also has all the bits that fall between the gaps in any system of classification, which, when you apply it to something as complex as the pub, is always going to come up short.

The Murderers is two pubs knocked into one, which gives it more scope to appeal to everyone who walks by. Apart from the headline stuff, it's a sports pub with screens everywhere that explode into life when there's a big Champions League match on. It's a geek's pub, a haven for sun-shy devotees to debate whether Spiderman or Captain America is the truest representation of the American Dream, without fear of ridicule. It's a locals' pub, where geezers who want to sink a few Stellas can throw their shoulders back and plant their feet wide apart. It's a tourist pub, with a physical vibe you could describe as Dickensian, so long as you specify that it's a twisting, shadowy haunt more suited to Fagin or Magwitch rather than the fantasized coaching inns of Pickwick.

And then there's the name. In June 1895, the landlady's daughter was murdered by her estranged husband following an argument the previous evening when she was seen walking into the pub with another man. They don't go quite so far as to say the pub is haunted by the girl's ghost. They don't need to.

Google 'the Murderers', and you're most likely to find it mentioned in connection with its commitment to real ale. Some publicans pay lip service to beer. Others dutifully do the best they can. For others still, it becomes an obsession, the beer quality demanding a commitment beyond anything that would be reasonable to ask from an employee.

Murderers landlord Phil Cutter is clearly obsessed by beer. As well as keeping a perfect cellar all year round, he hosts two beer festivals a year featuring around 60 ales over a period of ten days. Phil is also one of the founder members and co-chairs of the Norwich City of Ale initiative. When this first happened in 2011, some beer aficionados smirked at the idea of Norwich becoming the foremost beer city in the UK. That title is still up for debate (with Sheffield and London, to name but two, having strong counter-bids), but over the course of a few years, Norwich has started to stake a serious claim to rival many other beer cities of excellence.

Go into some celebrated real ale pubs, and if you don't know exactly what you want, or if you haven't been there before, you immediately feel like one of Jack Black's record store customers in the film *High Fidelity*. The pub trade refers to places like this as 'real ale shrines', the choice of words surely conveying an idea that, while they represent the top of their game, they're really only of interest to the dedicated and the devout.

As its awards attest, the Murderers pub is one of the foremost real ale shrines in the UK. Yet despite its passion for brewing tradition, it's not exclusive. The very best real ale pubs are those that delight the most ardent fan without alienating lager or wine or Coke drinkers who have come in only to watch the game or the band, just like everyone else. Whether you're here because of Wenger or the webslinger, mediated history or massive hops, chips or cheesy alliteration – you feel like you belong in the Murderers.

Comforting thought, isn't it?

OPPOSITE TOP: Part of the warren that makes up these two pubs in one.

OPPOSITE BOTTOM LEFT: 'It wasn't me, guv. I wasn't even here.'

OPPOSITE BOTTOM RIGHT: The Murderers. Or is it the Gardeners Arms?

THE ADAM AND EVE [1]

17 Bishopgate, Norwich NR3 1RZ

Norwich's oldest pub is a cranky, split-level warren that obeys its own rules of time and space. The nearby law courts keep it perpetually busy. A fat lawyer in braces who's spent the afternoon here shouts at the barmaid when she presents his bill. This doesn't go down well. After he leaves the barmaid says sympathetically, 'Still, you've got to think about what it's like for them, the people they have to talk to. The people I have to talk to are bad enough.' Well said.

THE ANCHOR INN [2]

The Street, Morston, Norfolk NR25 7AA
www.morstonanchor.co.uk

Possibly the only pub with its own separate counter to book seal-watching boat trips, The Anchor Inn is almost a museum to the local fishing industry, and is famous for the quality of its seafood. The old wooden panelling has been smoothed by so many backs at rest that it resembles driftwood, and the pictures and decorations almost succeeed in evoking a saltwater tang in the air. As nautical pubs go, this has it all.

THE ANCHOR [3]

Walberswick, Suffolk 1P18 6AU
www.anchoratwalberswick.com

Mark Dorber is a legend on the pub scene and one of the world's leading authorities on beer. He also happens to be married to a very talented chef. So when Mark and Sophie took over The Anchor a decade ago, it quickly became an important food and drink destination while somehow retaining the quiet charm of a small village community boozer. This is a dazzling showcase of best practice in how to run a truly interesting pub.

THE BREWERY TAP 🍺

80 Westgate, Peterborough, PE1 2AA

www.thebrewery-tap.com

The home of the much-celebrated Oakham Ales has something for everyone. Oakham has a great reputation for both traditional cask ales and more modern craft styles, and the Tap offers a comfortable environment to enjoy them in. But it also happens to be a big, city-centre late-night venue. As such, it raises the bar dramatically for a much-maligned style of pub, showing what's possible with a bit of imagination.

THE BUTT & OYSTER [4] 🏰 🍴 🍺 🍴

Pin Mill, Ipswich, Suffolk IP9 1JW

www.debeninns.co.uk/buttandoyster

Riverside pubs have a habit of disappointing the romantic: their location often means they don't bother trying too hard to be as special as they should be. The Butt & Oyster, though, is the riverside pub you hardly dare to dream about: all barges, yachts, fishermen and a fresh seasalt whiff in the air from the adjacent tidal, and appropriately named, River Orwell. Here you'll find a true *Wind in the Willows* waterside idyll.

THE CAMBRIDGE BLUE 🍺 🍎

85–87 Gwydir Street, Cambridge CB1 2LG

www.the-cambridgeblue.co.uk

Looking like a modest terraced house from the front, the Blue goes back an unfeasibly long way, first as a railway-tunnel-sized pub, and then as a Narnia-sized beer garden. You may never discover this though, as the sight that greets you as soon as you enter, blocking out the actual bar, is an array of fridges crammed with hundreds of Belgian beers that stops you in your tracks and makes you want to stay all night.

THE EARLE ARMS

The Green, Heydon. Norwich NR11 6AD
www.earlearms.vpweb.co.uk

The hardest time to decide whether or not a pub has 'atmosphere' is when you're the only people in it.

The atmosphere of a pub is made up of several components: the people who drink there, the serving staff, the landlord, the circumstances, and the physical place itself. Is it possible for you to still feel the atmosphere if the people aren't there?

I think so. A good publican puts their stamp on a place so authoritatively that the fabric, fixtures and fittings are an extension of their personality. As for the punters, yes they're important, but different spaces make people behave in different ways: people who might create a great atmosphere in one pub might sit quietly and solemnly in another.

Some of it is in the way the space is shaped, the *feng shui* of the furniture, the height of the ceiling, the brightness or naturalness of the lighting, and the volume or absence of music.

But some of it is the accumulation of what's happened over time. The atmosphere of a pub is in the fabric, like the nicotine stains on the ceiling before the 2007 smoking ban, or the grooves worn in old seats by a million bottoms.

This is perhaps why it's easier to pick up atmosphere in old pubs, and why we complain that when a pub is gutted and renovated, it has 'lost its character'.

We arrive in the beautiful, privately owned village of Heydon at around 5pm on a sunny afternoon to discover that the pub doesn't open till six. A middle-aged couple on a bench outside watch us get out of the car, check the opening times by the locked door, get in the car and drive away again, barely suppressing the amusement of regulars in the know.

When we return an hour later, we're the only two customers in the pub. The two serving staff are very pleasant and capable,

but they're very much employees, working in the place but not really shaping how it feels.

So it's all down to the building itself. And all on its own, it delivers. It manages to tell us that it is a pub with great character, that ever since it was built as a coaching inn in the 16th century, it has been showing people a great time (apart from the night Oliver Cromwell allegedly stayed here – this really isn't his kind of place).

Illuminated almost entirely by candlelight, it's dark and gloomy, even on a regal summer's evening outside. The candleholders over the fireplace are Georgian wigs of congealed wax, spattering onto the blood-red ancient floor tiles below.

The redbrick bar in one corner looks like a recent addition, and I wonder how long this place has had a bar rather than the ancient set-up of bringing beer up directly from the cellar below. Not so long, I reckon.

The heavy door ooooooooohs like Frankie Howerd as more drinkers arrive, eyeing our table enviously. There's plenty of room but we clearly have the best spot, in the corner next to an alcove that was once a toilet, or maybe a priest hole, and now serves no purpose other than to house a baleful-looking taxidermy fox.

There's a restaurant next door, and most people who enter are trying to make reservations rather than simply buy a drink. The menu looks amazing – all freshly caught fish from the nearby Norfolk coast and game with intriguing sauces.

But, sadly, we have to leave. The loud door seems to whine, 'Don't go', and the fox looks more annoyed than ever as a lady jumps into my seat even before I've lifted my bag. Outside, it seems the pub is busier than I thought – the regulars are all sitting by the door, soaking up the sun, still regarding us with silent amusement.

OPPOSITE TOP: The Earle Arms, on the edge of the green in the privately owned village of Heydon.

OPPOSITE BOTTOM: If you look closely, somewhere in this picture is a stuffed mouse sitting in a rocking chair.

[1]
[1]

[2]

[2]

[3]

[4]

THE CROWN INN

The Green, East Rudham, Norfolk PE31 8RD

www.crowninnnorfolk.co.uk

A gentrifying refurb could have robbed this old building of all its character, but it hasn't. The main space is a smart dining room, but at the back there's a cosy, low-ceilinged lounge and an open staircase up to a library in the loft. A seasonal menu – including four different asparagus dishes at the time of our visit – shows why The Crown Inn has been named Norfolk Food Pub of the Year.

THE DABBLING DUCK [1]

11 Abbey Road, Great Massingham, Norfolk PE32 2HN

www.thedabblingduck.co.uk

The village of Great Massingham presents an English idyll: a village green, ancient church and, thanks to a campaign by the locals to save it, a perfect pub. Previously two cottages now knocked through, this gastropub is full of welcoming touches. I especially love the bar top, carved from a massive piece of wood – the rich grain twists around the taps, its edges curving in and out to embrace the punters leaning against it.

THE DOVE STREET INN

76 St Helen's St, Ipswich, Suffolk IP4 2LA

www.dovestreetinn.co.uk

One of the best things about pubs is, that in order to excel, they don't have to go upmarket, fancy or 'premium'. They just have to do the basics really, really well. The Dove has been named the best at what it does by every organization that cares for at least the past ten years. It's merely a nice, plain, straightforward pub that sells great beer kept in perfect condition, and makes you feel happy to be there. Simple really.

THE EAGLE [2]

8 Bene't Street, Cambridge CB2 3QN

www.eagle-cambridge.co.uk

This 17th-century coaching inn still retains the wonderfully rambling warren of its original plan. World War Two pilots stationed at local airfields burned their names in the ceiling, mementos in case they never came back, and it's a moving experience to read them today. But the pub is most famous as the local of Francis Crick and James Watson. When they discovered DNA in 1953, Crick burst in on diners to announce that they had 'discovered the secret of life'.

THE ELM TREE [3]

16a Orchard St, Cambridge CB1 1JT

www.theelmtreecambridge.co.uk

The Cambridge drinker clearly has a lot of affection for Belgian beers. Rob Wain of The Elm Tree discovered Belgian Trappist ales in the early noughties on a trip to Bruges, and now stocks more than 50 Belgian bottled beers in his pub, divided between the main menu and the 'red menu' of special sharing bottles. This is just one quirk of a pub that stands out proudly in many wonderful ways against the city's chain-owned hostelries.

THE FAT CAT

49 West End Street, Norwich NR2 4NA

www.fatcatpub.co.uk

The name and the devotion to cask ale were originally borrowed from Dave Wickett's legendary Sheffield pub, with his blessing, and The Fat Cat, opened in 1991 down a quiet Norwich backstreet, is now regarded by many as the best cask ale pub in Norfolk. The quiet reverence of beer here encourages you not just to drink, but to saviour and appreciate, with no hint of high-handed beer nerdiness.

THE KITCHENER ARMS

Brockford Station, Wetheringsett, near Stowmarket, Suffolk IP14 5PW

A pedant could argue that The Kitchener Arms is not technically a pub: it's a railway carriage on a siding in a disused train line-cum-railway museum that serves beer, and only opens on 'certain days during the season'. But to the true pub enthusiast, the randomness of the set-up is at the heart of its appeal. Great pubs can spring up absolutely anywhere and this one simply does what it wants, when it feels like it.

THE LIVE AND LET LIVE

40 Mawson Road, Cambridge CB1 2EA

Hidden down an eerily quiet backstreet, the 'Live and Let' is a symphony of varnished and careworn wood, tatty books and magazines, posters and press clippings. It's the kind of place where local newspaper front pages cause evening-long debates around the bar. Fairy lights strung along the heavy roof beams are the only clue of any progression from the mid-20th century. This is a truly wonderful bolthole in which to hide away temporarily from the world.

THE LORD NELSON INN [4]

East Street, Southwold, Suffolk IP18 6EJ

www.thelordnelsonsouthwold.co.uk

Southwold brewer Adnams owns a lot of fine pubs in this genteel seaside town. All of them are worth shouting about and several of them could well claim to be the best in Southwold. But the special atmosphere of 'the Nellie', its mementos from the Battle of Trafalgar, its perfectly kept ales and its relaxed seaside-induced atmosphere combine to make it the universal favourite among locals, day trippers and second-homers alike.

THE QUEEN'S HEAD 🍴! 🍺🍴

Fowlmere Rd, Newton, Cambridgeshire CB22 7PG

Soup.

When you're considering the attributes and attractions of a pub, it's not a word most of us would ever put near the top of the list. But every great pub has its own unique quirks. And if an infinite number of monkeys with typewriters will one day eventually reproduce the works of Shakespeare, then with tens of thousands of pubs, eventually there might just be a pub that is famous for its soup.

No, it still doesn't sound any better, does it? OK, let's deal with the other stuff first.

Soup is probably not the main attraction for the locals who drink in here every night, in a network of rooms that provides intimate nooks while still allowing a benign buzz to circulate. Soup is certainly not as important to CAMRA as the pub's antiquity or its superbly kept range of local real ales served direct from the cask behind the bar.

The Queen's Head is one of only five pubs to have featured in every single edition of CAMRA's *Good Beer Guide*, now well into its third decade, and it has every single edition here, in tattered and faded stacks, to prove it.

There are many ways to fall in love with this pub: if the hop plants growing wild in the car park don't get you, the pensive-looking stag's head garlanded with hops in the lounge bar might. If you turn right instead of left as you enter, the antique but still-used skittles table might be the first thing to pique your interest. Or maybe it'll be the neat display of Terry's Chocolate Oranges and boxes of Maltesers lined up enticingly behind the bar.

But when you enter, the smell that assails you, that charges out from behind the bar to hug you, is one of sliced and diced and sautéed and boiled and caramelized vegetables and, possibly, other things. It's maddeningly soothing, exotically mundane, an olfactory comfort blanket that does for this pub what

the aromas of freshly baked bread and freshly ground coffee supposedly do for hopeful house sellers and supermarket owners.

You may ask what flavour the soup is. This is a very good question. The flavour of the Queen's Head soup is not like the flavour of other foods. The stockpot that contains it evolves, layer upon layer. The pub's menu contains a separate laminated sheet with a colour chart. 'To find out what the soup of the day is, match the colour of the soup with the colour on the chart. ("Other colours may occur"), it explains.

The spectrum runs through shades of brown to 'yellowish brown', with the garish outlier 'greenish' lurking at the bottom, like a pea-shooting business ball.

On the day of my visit, the closest match is 'reddish brown'. The tasting notes for this particular delicacy read, 'A close relative of dark brown, this sumptuous soup invades your taste buds with all its redder exotic attributes.' I'm able to identify bits of tomato, possibly some mushroom, definitely carrot. From my extensive experience of soup, I'd say that it most closely corresponds to oxtail in the real world, but it's earthier and more urgent. It's also so addictive that, I'm wondering if a mystery ingredient, or whatever they put in Pringles, might also be part of the recipe.

My soup is served in a mug, and when I finish it, I feel a sense of loss. I wonder if anyone ever buys rounds of it, like beer, and which colour is best to session on, or if anyone ever has more than they can handle. Or maybe there's a quota imposed, a personal ration to ensure everyone gets their share.

More pubs should do this – it's a natural extension of the welcome offered by the perfect pub. We could then have a *Good Soup Guide* to match the *Good Beer Guide*. I'm baggsying chief taster when that happens.

OPPOSITE TOP: The Queen's Head, Newton, hiding its soupy secrets.

OPPOSITE BOTTOM LEFT: Now there's a queen who needs a nourishing bowl of soup.

OPPOSITE BOTTOM RIGHT: Is this the best pub menu in the whole of Britain? Yes hands down it is.

THE QUEEN'S HEAD, NEWTON
SOUP OF THE DAY CHART

TO FIND OUT WHAT THE SOUP OF THE DAY IS, MATCH THE
COLOUR OF THE SOUP WITH THE COLOUR ON THE CHART. (OTHER
COLOURS MAY OCCUR). IF UNSURE PLEASE ENQUIRE AT THE BAR

DARK BROWN>> STILL THE HEAVYWEIGHT OF ALL Q.H SOUPS
ITS DARK, RICH AND COMPLEX FLAVOURS MAKES THIS
THE MOST POPULAR POTAGE.

REDDISH BROWN>> A CLOSE RELATIVE OF DARK BROWN THIS
SUMPTOUS SOUP INVADES YOUR TASTEBUDS WITH ALL
ITS REDDER EXOTIC ATTRIBUTES.

MEDIUM BROWN>> MOVING TO THE OTHER END OF THE
SPECTRUM, THIS SOUP IS LIGHTER THAN THE DARKER
VARIETYS YET STILL OFFERS AN AMAZING WELL ROUNDED
FLAVOUR.

LIGHT BROWN>> ALSO KNOWN AS 'FAWN' OR MORE
TRADITIONALLY AS 'KHAKI' THIS SOUP IS ANOTHER Q.H
HEAVY WEIGHT YET AT THE OTHER END OF THE SCALE.

YELLOWISH BROWN>> SIMILAR TO THE LIGHT BROWN ABOVE.
YELLOWISH-BROWN TENDS TO HAVE A LITTLE EXTRA IN
THE WAY OF EXOTIC INGREDIENTS AND INTRIGUING
SEASONING.

GREENISH>>
LIGHT GREEN TO DARK GREEN, THIS SOUP MAY
CONTAIN PEAS!

ALL INGREDIENTS HAVE BEEN SLICED, DICED, BOILED AND
CARAMELISED WITH TENDER LOVING CARE

... NOT SUITABLE FOR VEGETARIANS

THE NUTSHELL

The Traverse, Bury St Edmunds, Suffolk IP33 1BJ

www.thenutshellpub.co.uk

Widely acclaimed to be the UK's smallest pub, although if the measurements are correct, it's been beaten to that title by another pub in this section. Whatever, it's certainly small, looking from the outside like a limpet stuck to the neighbouring building. Inside, you have no option but to make friends with anyone else who has managed to squeeze in. It can get very intimate in here.

PINT SHOP [2]

10 Peas Hill, Cambridge CB2 3PN

www.pintshop.co.uk

Inspired by the history of beer houses in the 1830s, two successful entrepreneurs from the food and drink industry discovered a disused office building that was once an 1830s ale house and saw its potential. Pint Shop combines wonderful food and great craft beer in a way that avoids cliché, introducing new trends to a mainstream audience and proving the new beer revolution is no fad.

QUEEN'S HEAD [1]

7 Cross St, Eye, Suffolk IP23 7AB

www.queensheadeye.co.uk

The Queen of the title is Boudicca, who reigned around these parts until her rebellion against Roman rule. This medieval building honours her with a pub sign based on a stained glass impression of her copied from a nearby church. The walls of the pub are covered in framed pictures, while in the nicely designed 'ego room', mirrors line the walls. Meanwhile, you'll find cask ale in the main bar.

THE RED LION [3]

32 High St, Hinxton, Cambridge CB10 1QY

www.redlionhinxton.co.uk

Hidden down a narrow lane off the main road, the village of Hinxton feels cut off from the world. Its pub is a true destination though. Festooned with awards for its restaurant, it manages to avoid the common gastropub trap of forgetting it's also a pub. The low, 16th-century ceilings create an intimate atmosphere, and the beer is dazzlingly fresh.

THE ROSE

235 Queens Rd, Norwich, Norfolk NR1 3EA

www.rosenorwich.co.uk

With one of the best and broadest selections of beer in the city, The Rose under former landlady Dawn Hopkins, was instrumental in putting Norwich on the beer map with its annual City of Ale celebration. The new owners are carrying on the tradition for beer, great quizzes, and providing a focal point for home football supporters on busy match days at Norwich City.

THE ROSE AND CROWN [4]

Old Church Road, Snettisham, Norfolk PE31 7LX

www.roseandcrownsnettisham.co.uk

This perfect country pub overlooks the village green and is home to the local cricket team. Its roots are deep, going back six or seven centuries, when it was reputedly opened to cater for the labourers building the astonishing village church. The current landlords, in place for 20 years, and winners of many pub awards, know they are simply the caretakers for a pub that will be here for centuries to come.

THE RED LION 👥❗🍺

27 High St, Histon, Cambridgeshire CB24 9JD
www.theredlionhiston.co.uk

The village of Histon is unusual in that, for a place so small, it still has six pubs operating in close proximity to one other. At first glance, The Red Lion doesn't look like the most inviting of them – it seems a bit ordinary. But look a little closer, and it's anything but.

What appears to be the main door turns out to be a painted panel on the wall. The signs, which you know will be saying things like 'a range of fine ales', because they always do, also advertise features such as 'EU Compliant Light Bulbs', 'Mains Water Supply', 'Non-Toxic Carpets' and 'Illuminated Fire Exit Signs'.

Like many aspects of a pub, these signs telegraph the personality of the publican. Online reviews of The Red Lion refer to its gaffer in a range of terms stretching from 'eccentric' to 'nut job'. None of these descriptions is entirely without foundation.

Mark Donnachy claims that when he took over at The Red Lion in 1994, he had business in the town pretty much his own way. Recently, however, the other pubs have upped their game, and he's had to respond. One nearby pub launched a Happy Hour, slashing prices in the early evenings. So Mark responded by advertising a Miserable Hour, during which he added 10p to the price of a pint.

Business boomed.

Unsure whether or not this was another of Donnachy's jokes, people flocked to the pub. They found that he was being entirely serious. The 10p premium on drinks was to be donated to charity. People voted with their humour and decency, and the nearby happy hour of the competition was soon dropped.

One year, Donnachy didn't feel like putting up Christmas decorations. On Twelfth Night, he relented and decorated the pub, then proceeded to leave the decorations up for the whole year thereafter.

There's method to the Red Lion's madness. The best pubs, and the best publicans, take their vocation seriously, themselves less so. Obstinacy, wilful contrarianism and often downright bloody-mindedness can be powerful tools to guarantee a pub's success.

Take beer festivals. More and more pubs are staging their own, getting in a bit of racking, perhaps even a marquee and maybe a barbecue or hog roast, and selling a dozen or so local cask ales over the period of a weekend.

My visit to The Red Lion coincides with the first night of its beer festival. There is a huge marquee in the garden selling 60 different cask ales from across the country. There are more in reserve, so the pub can guarantee 60 beers ever night of the week. The climax will be the German night on Saturday, featuring bierkeller bands, German food and traditional Bavarian dress. Tickets are £40 ($58), which seems a bit steep for a beer festival. They went on sale at 7pm this evening, when the beer festival opened. An hour later, three quarters of the tickets have been sold.

Other pubs might put on a local covers band as part of their festival. Here, The Psychobombs play a set of heavy mod, psychedelia and R&B that's so tight, so loud and so driven, I feel like I'm seeing the 1960s unfold for the very first time.

There's a man standing in front of me, watching me write this in my notebook, with a look of absolute horror and disgust on his face. He couldn't seem more appalled if I had spat in his pint. It may only be a Monday evening, but the vibe has hit. The joint is jumping. Somewhere, it's always the Friday night of your dreams. Here, it's whatever night of the week, and whatever month of the year, Mark Donnachy says it is. It's Mark's world. The rest of us just live in it, by invitation only.

GLUTEN FREE TOILETS

DIVERSITY COMPLIANT MENUS

LACONS YARMOUTH BEERS

THE RED LION
FREE HOUSE
A WIDE SELECTION OF
CASK CONDITIONED ALES
GARDEN AND CAR PARK AT REAR

THE RED LION

WARM HOSPITALITY
EVER PRESENT
"It's not easy..!"

E.U. COMPLIANT
LIGHT BULBS

[1] [2]

[3]

[3]

BLACKSHORE
STOUT

4. REDWELL
WHITE IPA

7. REDWELL
STEAM LAGER

ASPALL
SUFFOLK CYDER

5. ASPALL
HARRY SPARROW

CIDER

8. MEANTIME
LONDON LAGER

EDWELL
WEST COAST
PACE

6. REDWELL
HELLES

9. FREEDOM
FOUR LAGER

[4]

[4]

THE SIGNAL BOX INN [1]

Lakeside Station, Kings Road, Cleethorpes,
Lincolnshire DN35 0AG

www.ccir.co.uk/signalboxinn

At 3.8sq m (40sq ft) smaller than
Bury's Nutshell, the Signal Box Inn
has stolen the tiny crown of Smallest
Pub in the World. It's a genuine
Victorian signal box that was bought
by the Cleethorpes Light Railway –
a narrow gauge tourist delight – and
can comfortably fit six people at a
time while serving a good selection of
cask ales, spirit and cider. It certainly
looks cosy in there.

THE STATION HOTEL [2]

Station Rd, Framlingham, Suffolk IP13 9EE

www.thestationframlingham.com

The cask ale is the star on the bar in
this pub that's owned by the Earl Soham
Brewery, which reopened it in 1997
after a long period of closure. But
the place is, if anything, even more
celebrated for its food. With both a
wood-fired pizza oven and a hog roast
kit backing up the main kitchen, all
options spanning traditional to modern
pub food are covered. Ed Sheeran has
also been known to pop in for a pint or
two, as it's his local pub.

THE STRUGGLER'S INN

83 Westgate, Lincoln LN1 3BG

www.strugglers-lincoln.co.uk

No, that's not a misprint – the
'strugglers' were people condemned
to hang in nearby Lincoln Castle, as
depicted on the pub's sign. The morbid
theme carries on with stories of the
pub being haunted by a ghost – not of
one of the hangman's victims, but of a
hanged man's dog who last set eyes on
his master here. Lincoln's best real ale
pub takes the haunting in its stride,
bursting at the seams with great cask
ales and those who enjoy them.

THE TICKELL ARMS [3]

North Road, Whittlesford, Cambrideshire
CB22 4NZ

www.cambscuisine.com

With an exterior painted a pretty pale
sky blue and windows that look like
they're from a fairy-tale house, the
front of this pub certainly grabs your
attention. Inside, most of the space is
given over to restaurant seating, but
the pub area has a neat practicality.
'Feel free to play the board games
badly or the piano well,' implores a
blackboard in the living-room-style
Marlborough Room. Meanwhile, the
dining area has a relaxed atmosphere.

THE TOBIE NORRIS

12 St Paul's St, Stamford, Lincolnshire PE9 2BE

www.kneadpubs.co.uk

The core of this rambling, wonky
building dates back to 1280, but it
hasn't always been a pub. The name
comes from a 16th-century bell-maker
who bought the premises and turned
it into a foundry. For much of the 20th
century it was an RAF Association
Club and it's only been operating as a
pub in its current guise since 2008,
since when it has quickly become a
firm local favourite.

THE VICTORIA

Earl Soham, Suffolk IP13 7RL

www.earlsohamvictoria.co.uk

An old-fashioned, unfussy pub that
provides a showcase for the beers
of the local Earl Soham Brewery.
It's stripped back, with the air of a
well-scrubbed farmhouse kitchen
serving simple but satisfying food.
It comes complete with a set of
outside toilets for the gents. The
brewery used to be out back, but has
now expanded and relocated. It may
be spartan, but it contains all the
elements you need for a proper pub.

THE WHITE HORSE [4]

The Street, Neatishead, Norwich NR12 8AD

www.thewhitehorseinnneatishead.com

Without doubt, this is the best beer
pub you'll find on the Norfolk Broads.
Moor at Gaye's Staithe off the River
Ant on the North Broads and stroll ten
minutes up the road to the village, and
you'll find this perfect blend of cosy,
traditional pub atmosphere and craft
beer-led modernity. The in-house
brewery complements a perfectly
chosen list from the most exciting
breweries in the UK as well as
established local favourites.

Also Try...

THE ANGEL

High St, Grantham, Lincolnshire NG31 6PN

www.angelandroyal.co.uk

THE OLD ENGLISH GENTLEMAN

11 Gold St, Saffron Walden, Essex CB10 1EJ

www.oldenglishgentleman.com

THE OLD FERRYBOAT

Holywell, St Ives, Huntingdon, Cambridgeshire
PE27 4TG

www.oldenglishinns.co.uk

THE THREE HORSESHOES 🍽❗🍺🍴

The Street, Warham, Norfolk NR23 1NL
www.warhamhorseshoes.co.uk

When you enter the tiny village of Warham, it's like stepping back into the 1950s. The exterior of The Three Horseshoes is red brick with patches of pebbly flint, an attractive feature of the local architecture. Two massive briars of roses rear out from the walls, the red of their petals so vivid you can almost hear it.

Inside, The Three Horseshoes is the kind of pub you hope still exists, but secretly fear might have been swept away. The bar itself is a delight: a whole room-sized area that's bigger than the public bar, complete with an old stone sink and shelves full of tiny compartments stocking useful things. The local ales stand on stillage down one side. A few products with garish 21st-century branding look out of place, and seem almost apologetic.

The menu, ranged over three crowded blackboards that can hardly contain their enthusiasm, boasts a staggering array of home-cooked food made from local ingredients, with a particular preponderance of pies – lamb and garlic, Warham sausage, and fennel and butter bean turn up to support the usual suspects. Two old men on one of the red leather settles have just finished their meal and they urge us to go for the rabbit with bacon and onion. 'Whatever you have, it'll be very good,' says one.

Having ordered a pair of pies (and a homemade pickled egg because it was there), we wander through the rest of the pub, trying to decide where we want to sit.

The next room past the public bar resembles a Victorian sitting room. A big portrait of Her Imperial Majesty, flanked by another local hero, Lord Nelson (born just a few miles from here in Burnham Thorpe), hangs above a burnished piano and makes us instinctively stand up straighter.

The next room is more of a scullery. A rug covers cracked and chipped red tiles. The walls are the colour of mint ice cream, which should really hurt, but somehow it works as a background for ancient posters advertising mustard powder, tea, Oxo, soap and bile beans – apparently an effective cure for constipation.

When our pies arrive, their crusts have risen so far from the dish that they resemble brains ready for dissection. The contents are hotter than the sun, but with a depth and richness of flavour that suggest a lifetime's devotion to the art of pie making. The accompanying vegetables look like they're from the 1950s, and have been on the boil since then.

Once service has finished and the pub is ten minutes away from closing for the afternoon, there's absolute silence throughout. The only noise we can hear is the chattering of the swifts, nesting in the eaves outside. You can almost hear the building breathe.

Later, I check the website. I find that the landlord, who has been here for over 25 years has 'filled [the pub] with vintage charm with its gas lighting and fascinating bits of breweriana and quirky bygone touches'.

For a moment, this saddens me. What had seemed like an effortless accumulation of decades of detritus has in fact been carefully designed. The pub probably didn't look much like this 30 years ago.

But then I decide it's fine, because it's so well done, it works. It might not be 'authentic', whatever that means, but it feels like it is. Nostalgia is often for times and places we don't remember and have never visited, and possibly never existed in the first place, so who are we to say how authentic an old-fashioned space is? You could be harsh and call the Three Horseshoes a theme pub. I'm sure the landlord doesn't think of it that way. And he's made such a good job of the theme, the distinction between real and artificial has dissolved into the pie gravy.

THE MIDLANDS

The huge industrial conurbation in the Midlands holds lovingly preserved pubs that reflect the gritty character of factory workers who relied on beer for hydration. Outside the cities lie some of the UK's most beautiful country pubs.

1. **The Barrels** *(page 176)*, 69 St Owen St, Hereford HR1 2JQ
2. **The Bartons Arms** *(page 176)*, 144 High St, Aston, Birmingham B6 4UP
3. **The Borehole** *(page 176)*, Unit 2, Mount Rd Industrial Estate, Stone, Staffordshire ST15 8LL
4. **Burton Bridge Inn** *(page 177)*, 24 Bridge St, Burton-on-Trent, Staffordshire DE14 1SY
5. **The Brunswick** *(page 177)*, 1 Railway Terrace, Derby DE1 2RU
6. **The Castle Inn** *(page 177)*, Edge Hill (nr Ratley), Banbury, Warwickshire OX15 6DJ
7. **The Cider House** *(page 181)*, Woodmancote, Defford, Worcestershire WR8 9BW
8. **The Coopers Tavern** *(page 174)*, 43 Cross St, Burton-on-Trent, Staffordshire DE14 1EG
9. **The Craven Arms** *(page 181)*, 47 Upper Gough St, City Centre, Birmingham B1 1JL
10. **The Crown Inn** *(page 178)*, Woolhope, Hereford HR1 4QP
11. **The Crown Inn** *(page 181)*, Church Street, Beeston, Nottingham NG9 1FY
12. **The Fleece Inn** *(page 181)*, The Cross, Bretforton, Worcestershire WR11 7JE
13. **The Galton Arms** *(page 181)*, Harrow Lane, Himbleton, Worcestershire WR9 7LQ
14. **The Merchant's Inn** *(page 181)*, 5 Little Church St, Rugby CV21 3AW
15. **The Nag's Head** *(page 182)*, 19–21 Bank St, Malvern, Worcestershire WR14 2JG
16. **Ye Olde Trip to Jerusalem** *(page 181)*, Brewhouse Yard, Nottingham NG1 6AD
17. **The Olive Branch** *(page 181)*, Main St, Clipsham, Oakham, Rutland LE15 7SH
18. **The Plough** *(page 181)*, 23 Fish Street, Worcester WR1 2HN
19. **The Post Office Vaults** *(page 184)*, 84 New St, Birmingham B2 4BA
20. **Purecraft Bar** *(page 184)*, 30 Waterloo St, Birmingham B2 5TJ
21. **The Royal Exchange** *(page 184)*, Radford St, Stone, Staffordshire ST15 8DA
22. **The Royal Oak** *(page 184)*, 25 High Street, Eccleshall, Staffordshire ST21 6BW
23. **The Star Inn** *(page 184)*, Manor Road, Sulgrave, Northamptonshire OX17 2SA
24. **The Three Kings Inn** *(page 184)*, Hanley Castle, Worcester, Worcestershire WR8 0BL
25. **The Victoria** *(page 185)*, 85 Dovecote Lane, Beeston, Nottingham NG9 1JG
26. **The Vine Inn** *(page 186)*, 10 Delph Rd, Brierley Hill, West Midlands DY5 2TN
27. **The Wellington** *(page 185)*, 37 Bennett's Hill, Birmingham B2 5SN
28. **The Yew Tree** *(page 185)*, 3 Church Lane, Cauldon, Staffordshire ST10 3EJ

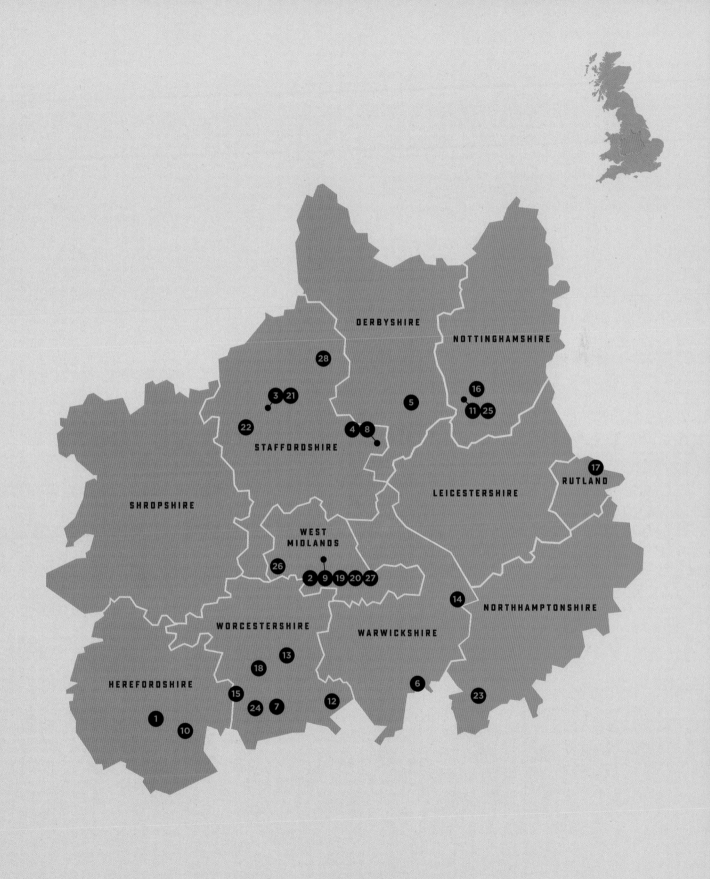

DERBYSHIRE

NOTTINGHAMSHIRE

28

3 21

22

STAFFORDSHIRE

4 8

5

16

11 25

SHROPSHIRE

LEICESTERSHIRE

17

RUTLAND

WEST
MIDLANDS

26

2 9 19 20 27

14

NORTHHAMPTONSHIRE

WORCESTERSHIRE

WARWICKSHIRE

13

18

6

23

HEREFORDSHIRE

15

24 7

12

1

10

THE COOPERS TAVERN

43 Cross St, Burton-on-Trent, Staffordshire DE14 1EG
www.cooperstavern.co.uk

Some pubs are taverns, and some pubs are inns. Some are gastropubs or craft beer bars or, hideously, a 'bar and kitchen' or 'tap and eating rooms'. But some of the very best pubs are 'public houses' in every sense of the term.

The Coopers sits in a back street, and you won't find it unless you go looking for it. It's not that it tries to hide itself – the big sign painted on the front of the building with the pub's name on it is about as loud an advert as you can get – but the building itself is like a nice double-fronted house rather than a pub and still manages to blend in, fading into its surroundings.

Inside, the first room you encounter feels like a parlour, with cracked, shiny floor tiles, modest furnishings and lots of etched glass and pictures reminding you of Burton-on-Trent's brewing heritage, celebrating the unlikely story of the town that was for a while the unlikely brewing capital of the world. To your left is a lounge with an artificial fire and the formal, working-class air of a room that's only 'used for best'.

There's no bar visible, which is odd, but there seems to be something happening at the far end of the room. So you go through the parlour, which is always quiet, to the far end, where there is always chatter, and into one of the strangest rooms you'll ever encounter in a pub.

The main bar in the Coopers doesn't feel so much like a room, more a collection of walls, angles and crannies that have got together to try to make a room, found that it's not as easy as they thought, and given up halfway through.

To your left there's a crowded bookshelf. To your right is a space that seems to be made entirely of corners, with an indistinguishable number of benches along bits of wall, and hogsheads serving as tables. In front of you is a raised area that reminds you of the pews at the front of old churches that were reserved for the local gentry. Here – you just *know* – that bench is reserved for the master brewers of old Burton, a town shaped and still dominated by the breweries within it.

But we still haven't got to the bar.

The mechanics of the bar are all present and correct. Beer taps are lined up along it, and on the back bar there are spirits, snacks, bottled beers and barrels on stillage. There's just one usual feature about it: it faces onto a brick wall. It's been built down a seemingly random dead-end corridor flung off the main room. There's just enough space for one customer to stand at the corner, by the hatch where staff go behind the bar, to get served. Handily, the ever-changing selection of cask ales is detailed on small slates hung above the brewers' pew.

This room feels like the heart of the pub, the way a kitchen does in the best kind of home. But there is no kitchen in the Coopers. This doesn't stop Mary, the publican, devising different ways to try to offer food. A few years ago there was the 'English Tapas bowl', comprising handfuls of different bar snacks, a bit of pork pie and some cheese and crackers. At the time of writing, this has been replaced by a brilliantly original take on the idea of a cheeseboard. If you're in the Coopers when Mary gets back from taking her dogs out, or from going out for a meal with her husband Bob, it can feel like you're sitting in her living room as she takes a seat among the regulars and holds court. You'd feel as though you were intruding if it wasn't for every single aspect of the pub making you feel welcome, as if you've been drinking here your whole life. Orwell may have thought his Moon Under Water didn't exist. I wish with all my heart that I could have bought him a pint here.

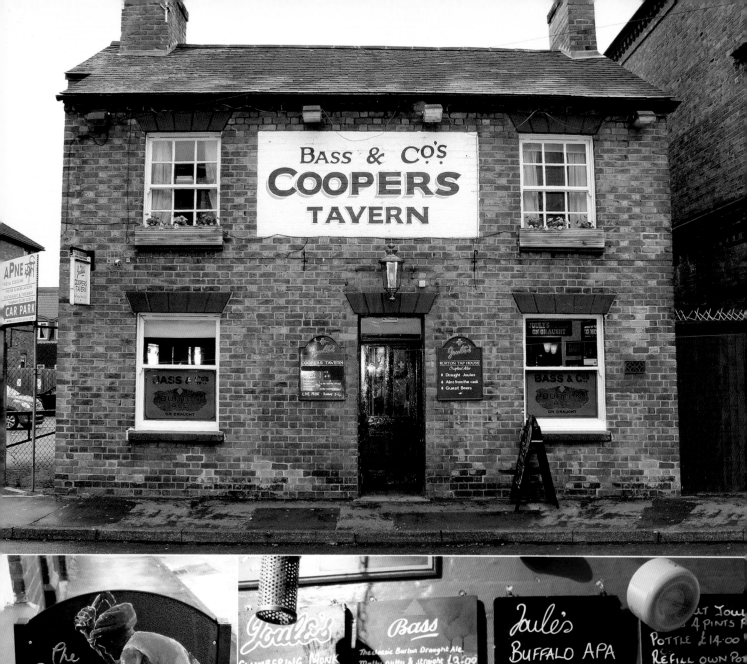

BASS & CO'S
COOPERS
TAVERN

The Coopers Tavern

EST 1777

Joule's
SLUMBERING MONK
.5%   £2.90

Bass
The classic Burton Draught Ale.
Malty, nutty & straight £3.09
from the Barrel!   4.4%

Joule's
BUFFALO APA
5.2%   CRAFT KEG   £3.50

T JOU
4 PINTS P
POTTLE £14.00
REFILL OWN POT
CASK ALES
ONLY   £11.00

Joule's
Pale Ale
.1%   £2.90

GUEST BEER
OAKHAM ALES
CITRA
4.1%   £3.10

Joule's
BLONDE
%   £2.90

GUEST BEER
FROTH BLOWERS
BREWING CO
GOLLOP WITH ZEST
4.5% £3.10

GUEST BEER
FAT CAT BREWERY
STOUT CAT
4.6% £3.10   HANDPULL

GUEST BEE
WOODS B
SHROPSHIRE
4.5% £3.10

From the

THE BARRELS [1]

69 St. Owen St, Hereford HR1 2JQ

www.wyevalleybrewery.co.uk

Once the home of the Wye Valley
Brewery, until it far outgrew these
premises, The Barrels is so steeped in
beer it still feels like a brewery as much
as a pub. It pulls off the brilliant trick of
appearing to carry on its way, oblivious
to modern trends, and yet at the same
time offer successive generations of
Hereford pubgoers exactly what they're
looking for. Worth visiting for the Wye
Valley HPA alone. It keeps true to its
soul as a community pub, so expect no
meals or gimmicks but plenty of good
conversation and conviviality.

THE BARTONS ARMS

144 High St, Aston, Birmingham B6 4UP

www.thebartonsarms.com

The stunning tiles, stained glass and
snob screens of this outrageously
elegant pub have survived neglect, fire,
violent rioting and even Laurel and
Hardy serving pints behind the bar
(I'm not joking.) A Grade II listing in
1976 saved it from an even greater
danger – indifferent neglect and the
attention of developers –since this
1901 building has a nationally
important historic pub interior. It
was thankfully rescued in 2002 by
Oakham Ales, which now keeps the
vast cellars full of excellent beer.

THE BOREHOLE [2]

Unit 2, Mount Road Industrial Estate, Stone,
Staffordshire ST15 8LL

This micropub is the brewery tap for
the Lymestone Brewery, so it's fitting
that it was converted from an office on
an industrial state that was originally
the site of the long gone Bent's Brewery.
With its small, cosy rooms, log burner
and neat shelves behind the bar
containing jars of nuts and pickled
eggs, it still has the welcome air of a
workers cafe, while serving fantastic
Lymestone Brewery beers. Nice
touches include quirky retro decor
such as a Wi-Fi router that is, in fact,
part of an old telephone exchange.

BURTON BRIDGE INN [3]

24 Bridge St, Burton-on-Trent, Staffordshire
DE14 1SY

www.burtonbridgeinn.co.uk

The brewery tap of the Burton Bridge Brewery, which is in the yard at the back, is one of the few remaining signs that Burton-on-Trent was once the foremost brewing town on the planet. This pub dates from the 17th century. Today it feels like a dignified and trim old man wearing his best suit, approachable but demanding respect, as do the oak beams and the brewery memorabilia from a different era. The house beers are, of course, excellent, and include a special gold medal ale.

THE BRUNSWICK [4]

1 Railway Terrace, Derby DE1 2RU

www.brunswickderby.co.uk

This lovely pub is just a stone's throw from the train station, which is handy for the real ale fans who make trips to Derby specifically to drink here. It is one of Britain's oldest railwaymen's pubs. There's an in-house brewery and up to 16 beers on tap, plus a collection of brewing memorabilia featuring old train photographs and prints, as well as visual evidence of the history and restoration of the pub. This, plus the wonky shape of the building and its unchanging rooms, make the Brunswick a delightful place to explore.

THE CASTLE INN [5]

Edge Hill, Banbury, Warwickshire OX15 6DJ

www.castleatedgehill.co.uk

There are lots of pubs with the word 'Castle' in their name, but this is the only pub I know that actually *is* a castle. It overlooks the site of the first battle of the English Civil War, and sits on the spot where Charles I gathered his commanders to prepare the attack. Its carefully refurbished interior and overall style definitely remain more Cavalier than Roundhead. Constructed as a gothic folly in 1742, it now contains a bar and four dining areas, as well as lots of authentic period details such as stone fireplaces and arched doorways.

THE CROWN INN 👥 🪓 🌳 🍺 🍴

Woolhope, Hereford HR1 4QP
www.crowninnwoolhope.co.uk

The countryside around Ledbury in Herefordshire is dotted with beautiful small villages amid hundreds of acres of orchards and farmland. This is cider country, with many of the world's greatest cider makers not much more than an apple's throw from each other. There's just one problem if you want to enjoy their produce: outside the main towns, there are hardly any pubs, and hardly any shops.

In areas like this, village pubs are closing. When custom during the week dries up thanks to people commuting or buying up nearby houses as seldom-used holiday homes, it's simply not viable to stay open. Successful pubs here are few and far between. So how do you make a pub succeed here?

There are two possible strategies. Firstly, you could set out to become indispensable to the small local population. Or, secondly, you could turn yourself into a destination pub that attracts people from further afield, making sure they are prepared to drive here over some distance to experience a special offering you can't get elsewhere. The Crown at Woolhope succeeds in both.

On May Day weekend, the pub is crammed full of diners like it is every weekend throughout the year. This is a place that's famous for its food, and the car park often spills over down into the narrow winding lane up to the pub.

Today there's no room in the car park at all. A large marquee sits at one end, with a dozen local ciders and perries, including one of each made here, on the premises. As is traditional, the bungs were popped only this morning, after the barrels have been left to ferment since late October all through the winter. There are a few local ales too, extending the modest but perfectly chosen range to be found on the main bar indoors.

Each beer and cider was chosen personally by publican, chef and in-house cider maker Matt Slocombe, who personally knows each of the people he buys from.

Live bands play in the corner of the marquee by the bar, and there's a large audience gathered to watch them. Here then, we have enough beer, cider and drinkers to fill two pubs, all packed into the one space.

In the beer garden at the back, steadily falling blossom from the apple trees creates a slow, mesmeric narrative, miles away from the frenetic energy out front. There's a bouncy castle, a whole hog roast set up inside a small wooden outside bar, and another wooden shelter with a table football game inside.

None of this – with the possible exception of the bouncy castle – feels like it's a stretch from the norm for this pub. It's all an extension of Matt's personality. Today, he's taken control of the cider bar in the marquee, because that's what he loves, and he wants to show off his new cider. I head back round the front to get another glass of it, and we agree that, being so young and raw, it's still a bit sharp, and needs to calm down a little, but that it's on the way to being very good indeed. (When I return five months later, it's phenomenal.)

You can always tell when a country pub is regarded as being a little bit special by the people who know it. With a pub like this, people don't refer to it as the Crown *in* Woolhope, like you might tell someone there's a WH Smith in Woolhope or a Wetherspoon's in Woolhope (there isn't, by the way). Instead, they refer to the Crown *at* Woolhope. It's a subtle code that suggests the pub isn't merely part of the village: it's the reason to go to the village in the first place. I live 166 miles (267km) away from this village. It's frankly weird how often I seem to end up drinking here.

OPPOSITE TOP: Publican Matt Slocombe wears his cheeky red blazer whenever he's in his happy place, which is most of the time.

OPPOSITE BOTTOM: The Crown is at Woolhope, not in Woolhope. This distinction is an important one in understanding pubs.

[1]

[2]

[3]

THE CIDER HOUSE [1]

Woodmancote, Defford, Worcestershire WR8 9BW

Cider – and only cider – is served from across the top half of a stable-style farmhouse door into the parlour. Standards have improved recently – if you don't want to sit outside, there's now a single light bulb illuminating the shed where a few benches are provided. It's known locally as the 'Monkey House', after a customer who arrived home in a dishevelled state from drinking here, and blamed his condition on monkeys attacking him from the trees.

THE CRAVEN ARMS [2]

47 Upper Gough St, City Centre, Birmingham B1 1JL

www.blackcountryales.co.uk

Many fans of this pub enjoy pointing out the contrast between the nearby Mailbox – a shopping centre full of premium brands – and the graceful charm of this little pub. The Victorian majolica tiles covering the outside are more beautiful than anything in a designer store. Inside, the service is personal and knowledgeable, the beers excellent and the bar snacks are, of course, homemade. A true premium experience in a pub that's run by Black Country Ales.

THE CROWN INN

Church Street, Beeston, Nottingham NG9 1FY

www.everards.co.uk

The Crown was an early success story in the Project William scheme run by Everards Brewery that revives failed pubs in conjuction with small brewers, in this case local brewers Browns. It's both stately and welcoming, modern and traditional, a world away from the knackered boozer it was before this brilliant initiative saved it.

THE FLEECE INN [3]

The Cross, Evesham, Worcestershire WR11 7JE

www.hefleeceinn.co.uk

This country pub was built in the early 15th century and stayed in the same family until Lola Taplin, a formidable guv'nor and direct descendent of the man who built it, passed away in front of the fire after living her whole 77 years here. There have been so few changes over the centuries that there are still circles around the fireplaces – to prevent witches from entering the pub via the chimneys.

THE GALTON ARMS

Harrow Lane, Himbleton, Worcestershire WR9 7LQ

This Grade II-listed country pub dating from the 17th century wasn't quite open when Guy Fawkes and the other gunpowder plotters met in Himbleton. Had it been, the excellent Bathams bitter and old-fashioned burgers might have dissuaded them from their task. Ancient beams split the room into the 'top bar' and the 'bottom bar', even though they are level. There's an ongoing rivalry between drinkers from the 'two' bars that extends to them even having played cricket against each other.

THE MERCHANT'S INN

5 Little Church St, Rugby CV21 3AW

www.merchantsinn.co.uk

Revered for the quality and range of its ales, the beer festivals here are truly special. Each year there's a theme, and the whole of the outside of the building is painted to resemble a selection of beach huts, a zebra or a cow. They're also fanatical about a certain game that was invented just down the road, which I can't for the life of me even remember the name of now.

YE OLDE TRIP TO JERUSALEM

Brewhouse Yard, Nottingham NG1 6AD

www.triptojerusalem.com

Dismissed by many ardent pub lovers as a tourist trap, its claim to be the oldest inn in Britain is debatable. Even the company that's running the place has another inn a few minutes' walk away that claims to be the oldest in Nottingham. Nevertheless, there's a genuine charm to the maze of rooms hewn from the rock beneath Nottingham Castle, and a real sense of timelessness and warmth in this ancient place.

THE OLIVE BRANCH

Main St, Clipsham, Oakham, Rutland LE15 7SH

www.theolivebranchpub.com

When a landowner demolished the locals' favourite pub, the outcry was so loud that he knocked three cottages into one to create a replacement, hence the name of this pub that opened in 1890. It's widely celebrated for food that goes heavy on local provenance and means you need to reserve a table days in advance, but it still looks and feels like an old country pub that's perfect for losing a rainy afternoon in.

THE PLOUGH

23 Fish Street, Worcester WR1 2HN

www.theplough-worcester.com

As you walk into this corner building, the bar is directly in front of you, and you must walk up a few steps to approach it, like an altar. Once you've got your beer (or selected a dram from an astonishingly large and eclectic range of malt whiskies) you have a choice of a comfy, cluttered lounge to the left, or a utilitarian public bar to the right, where old boys sit solemnly holding court along the bench on the back wall.

THE NAG'S HEAD 🐾❗🍺🍴

19–21 Bank St, Malvern, Worcestershire WR14 2JG
www.nagsheadmalvern.co.uk

Opponents of the British pub often have one great misunderstanding about its nature: they see it as a shop that sells alcohol, and see the consumption of alcohol as a functional way of becoming intoxicated and nothing more.

It's a bleak view of life that reflects nothing of the true appeal of drinking, or pubs. Leaving aside for the moment the many other benefits of drinking alcoholic drinks apart from intoxication, there are many reasons we do so in the pub. Given that we usually go to the pub with friends, why do we meet them there rather than buying alcohol more cheaply in supermarkets and drinking it at home?

Pubgoers know the answer to that question, even if it's something they feel instinctively and struggle to put into words. But for anyone who's stumped by it, I'd suggest a visit to The Nag's Head as soon as possible.

The vertiginous slopes of Great Malvern are insane, and the Nag's Head clings to the mountainside like a Hitchcock heroine. With its wooden façade and low roof, it looks more like a Swiss chalet than an English pub.

At 7pm on a Friday night in June, the garden is buzzing with people. An old-fashioned red telephone box sits by a hedge, its branches winding through its body and waving from where the windows used to be.

When you get to the door, you're greeted by a sign, warning you that you'll be in serious trouble if you swear.

Once inside, you're at the corner of a bar that stretches away from you at right angles. The bar itself is crowded with beer tap handles, so dense they look like a hastily erected barricade. In the tiny space behind, six bar staff somehow manage to weave around each other, constantly pulling pints and firing them out from behind the stockade, like a benign version of the besieged British troops at Rorke's Drift. A church hymn board has beer names slotted into it instead of numbers, each a small black tile with the beer's logo carefully reproduced in coloured chalks.

More signs tell us that as well as swearing, blaspheming is also outlawed to ensure our welfare. The landlord is absent tonight, but he's watching us from the walls, imposing his presence on this busy maze.

The place seems to generate random rooms spontaneously, making itself up as it goes along. Three steps down here there's an alcove, round a corner there, behind a half-wall yonder, there's always another small room. And we've been sitting for 20 minutes before we realize there's a second mountainside of a beer garden at the back. Halfway up one wall, about head height, there's a small arched wooden doorway. I'm half-convinced it leads to some kind of magic kingdom – and that's before the excellent Batham's Bitter kicks in.

After a while, I notice a small area cordoned off by wrought-iron ropes. It's protecting a glass floor. Looking down, it reveals a human skeleton splayed over barrels in the beer cellar, which can only be taken as a warning about any swearing and blaspheming transgressions.

There's no music, but the bar is filled with the loud buzz of people talking at volume – not shouting, but amplified by their excitement at being here on a sunny Friday night, in a special space that seems random and can no doubt occasionally be scary too.

It doesn't have to make sense. It's an adult version of an adventure playground, and that's why we come here, and why we go to all the other pubs where the publican expresses some kind of individual vision that no corporation could ever copy, even if they wanted to, which I doubt they would: they'd have to understand its appeal first.

OPPOSITE TOP: The Nag's Head prepares to welcome the hordes – at least, those members of the hordes who are able to climb up really steep hills.

OPPOSITE BOTTOM LEFT: You've been told. Behave.

OPPOSITE BOTTOM RIGHT: The most normal-looking room in a very eccentric pub.

Welcome to our Pub! In order to look after you all we have a NO SWEARING RULE which we will enforce. Thankyou...

[1]   [2]

THE POST OFFICE VAULTS

84 New Street, Birmingham B2 4BA

www.postofficevaults.co.uk

You'll probably have to be shown where this subterranean bar is by a regular – even when you know where to look, it's difficult to spot. Inside is a wonderful combination of old world beer appreciation and new generation craft – the beer list of bottled beers available (the 'Beer Bible') merits the name, and the easy-going vibe attracts everyone from grimy T-shirted real ale geeks to smart office workers seeking a quick *kriek* at lunchtime.

PURECRAFT BAR [1]

30 Waterloo St, Birmingham B2 5TJ

www.purecraftbars.com

Very much a new-generation craft beer bar, the minimalist industrial decor may scream hip and trendy, but the business is relentlessly dedicated to welcoming everyone to great beer. The New World craft selection is expertly chosen. The cask ales are kept in phenomenal condition, and the bar snacks – including Indian spiced sausage rolls – are without equal.

THE ROYAL EXCHANGE [2]

Radford Street, Stone, Staffordshire ST15 8DA

www.titanicbrewery.co.uk

A multi-award winning community hub that's always pleasantly lively, this place creates its own customs and traditions and immediately initiates you into them, not least its own blends of Titanic ales, which drinkers have taken and adapted to create into their own beers: half a Plum Porter mixed with half a Steerage? That'll be a pint of Plumage, thank you.

THE ROYAL OAK

25 High Street, Eccleshall, Staffordshire ST21 6BW

www.royaloakeccleshall.co.uk

Once run-down and set to be closed, this pub has now been restored to, or even surpassed, its former glory. Renovated with original or reclaimed materials, with lead-lined, stained-glass windows, The Royal Oak offers free sausage rolls every Friday at 5pm, which always vanish by eight minutes past. The pub's even better now than when England football legend Geoff Hurst owned it, and it feels like it's been here, just like this, for ever.

THE STAR INN

Manor Rd, Sulgrave, Northamptonshire OX17 2SA

www.thestarinnsulgrave.com

This beautiful, centuries-old pub is a firm favourite with both locals and tourists, one of whom was John Wayne, enjoying what is purported to be his only ever visit to a British pub. With its low beams, worn flagstones and Aunt Sally team (this is a traditional pub game, a bit like skittles but based on creatively murdering a chicken), the Duke no doubt encountered a perfect example of what the countryside pub is all about.

THE THREE KINGS INN [3]

Hanley Castle, Worcester, Worcestershire WR8 0BL

This gloriously scruffy pub is a wonderful antidote to the plastic theme-park sanitization of other pubs its age. The 1970s meet the 1670s in the Grade II-listed interior. Landlord Sue Roberts, the third generation of the family that took over in 1911, is a hero to a band of ale-loving regulars who would probably fight to the death anyone who wanted to change the pub.

THE VICTORIA [4]

85 Dovecote Lane, Beeston, Nottingham NG9 1JG

www.victoriabeeston.co.uk

Originally built as a refreshment stop for railway passengers, the high-ceilinged interior of this elegant pub has been restored to its original grandeur, with diamond-cut glass panels, classic parquet flooring and original back bar fittings. The 16 rotating cask ales also probably have something to do with its popularity.

THE WELLINGTON

37 Bennett's Hill, Birmingham B2 5SN

www.thewellingtonrealale.co.uk

There can't be many pubs these days where you struggle to find a seat in the middle of a weekday afternoon – especially when that pub is as generously proportioned as The Wellington. But this 'specialist real ale pub' is crowded from 10am till midnight, seven days a week. Screens around the pub – and broadcast on the website – give thoroughly modern, up-to-the-minute information on the 16 cask ales on the bar, their price, strength and style.

THE YEW TREE

3 Church Lane, Cauldon, Staffordshire ST10 3EJ

www.yewtreeinncauldon.com

On the edge of the Peak District, this place feels like it takes forever to get to, but once there you won't want to leave. The interior is a great example of the pub as junk shop – or perhaps a treasure-trove would be more accurate. *The Good Pub Guide* awards a star to pubs it thinks are truly special. This is the only pub in the annual *Guide* that has been given two stars.

Also Try...

THE DRUM AND MONKEY

Newbridge Green, Upton upon Severn, Worcester WR8 0QP

www.the-drum-and-monkey.co.uk

THE MAJOR'S ARMS

Jacob's Cottage, Bishop's Frome, Worcester WR6 5AX

www.themajorsarms.co.uk

THE OLD NAG'S HEAD

Edale, Hope Valley, Derbyshire S33 7ZD

www.the-old-nags-head.co.uk

THE PRINCE OF WALES

Church Lane, Ledbury, Herefordshire HR8 1DL

www.powledbury.co.uk

THE VINE INN 👥 🍺

10 Delph Rd, Brierley Hill, West Midlands DY5 2TN
www.bathams.com

When I started writing about beer, it wasn't long before friends who had grown up in the Black Country felt they urgently needed to make me aware of a local legend.

If I got into a conversation about beer with anyone from Birmingham or the West Midlands, They'd nod patiently, ask a few questions, sizing me up, and wait for an opening to ask 'Tell me, have you have had Batham's Bitter?' When I replied that I hadn't, they could rarely hide their disappointment. I had failed some kind of test.

I had to find out more.

There are legends around Batham's and, like all legends, they're a mix of truth and fantasy.

They say there are only a handful of pubs that are allowed to have it. They say demand exceeds supply to such an extent that some pubs obtain bootleg Batham's, and are then banned from ever selling the real stuff if they're found out. They say you can buy bottles, but if you do, you must take the empties back or you'll never get any more. The truth – probably – is that Batham's is brewed by a small brewery attached to a pub and it can only produce enough beer to satisfy a modest, local market. I decide that to try Batham's for myself, I need to go to the source.

The Bull and Bladder – known officially as The Vine Hotel – is the Batham's brewery tap. It sits on a street that seems perpetually shiny with rain, in an unlovely part of an old industrial town now swallowed by Birmingham's sprawl. It's a hulk of a building – one of those Victorian pubs that seem to have been designed to withstand a full frontal assault by its drinkers – further bulked out by the addition of the brewery on the side.

The pub is a local legend in its own right. It seems unchanged since the 1930s, one of those places that has resisted every single trend, technological development and interior design fad of the last 30 years. It has carpets. And separate rooms. Aged banquettes create a barrier between groups but still allow those groups to eye each other up. It has an inbuilt hierarchy so clear that as you walk in for the first time, you immediately know which rooms are open to you as a stranger, and which are not. A random collection of brilliant and nonsensical stuff on the walls could keep you gawking for hours.

The Bull and Bladder serves both types of beer: Batham's Bitter *and* Mild. Nothing else is necessary. And the only food you need is pork scratchings – another local delicacy – so sit down and stop asking questions.

I take a first sip and decide that Batham's is a typical session beer, nothing out of the ordinary. It's a little sweet for my taste, and could do with a bit more hop. I go back for a second sip to confirm my first impression and realize that I've already drained the pint glass. That was odd.

I try again. Again, the beer seems to lift the glass to my mouth and pour itself down my throat of its own volition. My conscious brain is still trying to decide whether I like the beer or not, but some deeper, more primal part of my brain made that decision long ago.

It goes to my head straight away. A group of ladies sit in the next booth, dressed up for a big Friday night out in the way women south of here just don't do. In my mind's eye, the next morning they are joined by old women in headscarves drinking halves of mild, men in flat caps and waistcoats, a procession of drinkers going back over the last century.

The beer is only 4.3% ABV, but clearly has some other power that is not just alcohol, that works together with the pub to weave its magic. 'Bostin.' As they say around here.

GREAT PUBS IN THE
NORTH & NORTH WEST

Lake District pubs have an obvious charm. But the best pubs of cities like Liverpool and Manchester tell you much more about their fierce identities than any tourist brochure is able to do.

1: **The 23 Club** *(page 194)*, 23 Hope St, Liverpool L1 9BY

2: **The Albion Inn** *(page 194)*, Park St, Chester, Cheshire CH1 1RN

3: **The Baltic Fleet** *(page 194)*, 33A Wapping, Liverpool L1 8DQ

4: **The Baum** *(page 194)*, 33–37 Toad Lane, Rochdale, Greater Manchester OL12 0NU

5: **The Belvedere** *(page 194)*, 5 Sugnall St, Liverpool L7 7EB

6: **The Black Bull** *(page 194)*, 1 Yewdale Rd, Coniston, Cumbria LA21 8DU

7: **The Black Horse** *(page 190)*, 166 Friargate, Preston, Lancashire PR1 2EJ

8: **The Bridge Bier Huis** *(page 84)*, 2 Bank Parade, Burnley, Lancashire BB11 1UH

9: **The Briton's Protection** *(page 192)*, 50 Great Bridgewater St, Manchester M1 5LE

10: **The Cartford Inn** *(page 196)*, Cartford Lane, Little Eccleston, Preston, Lancashire PR3 0YP

11: **The Church Inn & Saddleworth Brewery** *(page 195)*, Running Hill Gate, Oldham, Lancashire OL3 6LW

12: **The Dispensary** *(page 195)*, 87 Renshaw St, Liverpool L1 2SP

13: **The Drunken Duck** *(page 195)*, Barngates, Ambleside, Cumbria LA22 0NG

14: **The Golden Rule** *(page 195)*, Smithy Brow, Ambleside, Cumbria LA22 9AS

15: **Hawskhead Brewery & Beer Hall** *(page 195)*, Staveley Mill Yard, Back Lane, Kendal, Cumbria LA8 9LR

16: **Hole in T' Wall** *(page 195)*, Robinson Place, Bowness-on-Windermere, Cumbria LA23 3DH

17: **The Kirkstile Inn** *(page 198)*, Loweswater, Cumbria CA13 0RU

18: **The Marble Arch Inn** *(page 198)*, 73 Rochdale Rd, Manchester M4 4HY

19: **Ye Olde Man & Scythe** *(page 198)*, 6–8 Churchgate, Bolton, Lancashire BL1 1HL

20: **Peveril of the Peak** *(page 198)*, 127 Great Bridgewater St, Manchester M1 5JQ

21: **The Philharmonic Dining Rooms** *(page 50)*, 36 Hope St, Liverpool L1 9BX

22: **The Taps** *(page 200)*, 12 Henry St, Lytham St Annes, Lancashire FY8 5LE

23: **The Wasdale Head Inn** *(page 198)*, Wasdale Head, Gosforth, Cumbria CA20 1EX

24: **The White Cross** *(page 198)*, Quarry Rd, Lancaster LA1 4XT

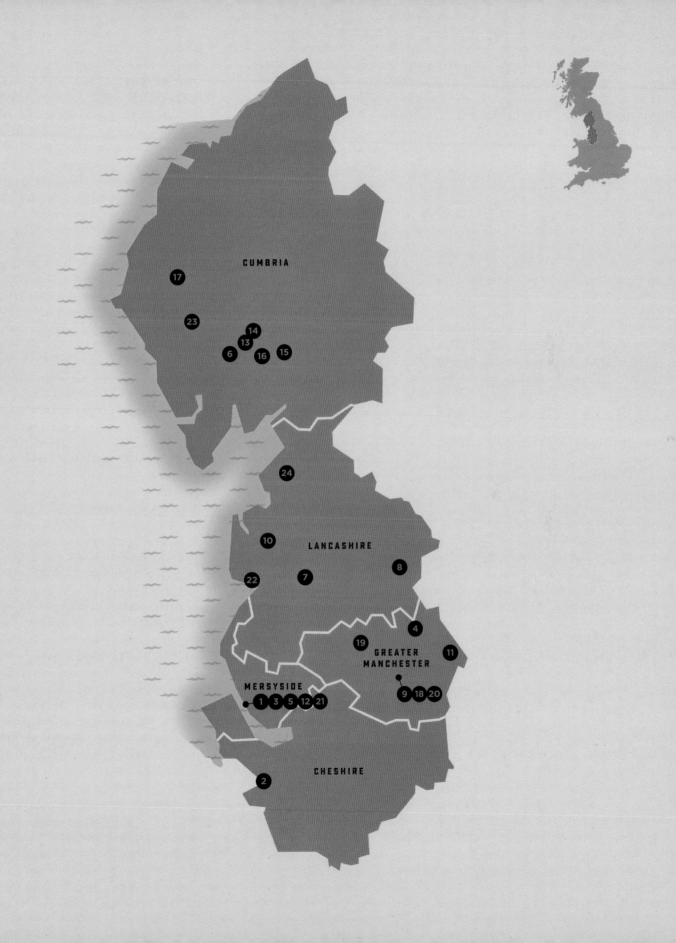

CUMBRIA

17

23

14
13
6   16   15

24

10   LANCASHIRE

22   7

8

4

19   GREATER
MANCHESTER

11

MERSYSIDE

1   3   5   12   21

9   18   20

CHESHIRE

2

THE BLACK HORSE

166 Friargate, Preston, Lancashire PR1 2EJ
www.blackhorse.robinsonsbrewery.com

There's something unusual in the make-up of breweries and pubs in the north west of England: in industry terms, the region is about half a century out of date.

Until the 1950s, Britain was a patchwork of regional and local breweries, hardly any of which had a national reach. Each brewery owned, or 'tied', the pubs that sold its beer, so as you travelled the country you'd drink Bass beer in Bass pubs in Burton, Banks's beers in Banks's pubs in Wolverhampton, Tetley's beers in Tetley's pubs in Leeds, and so on.

But in the 1950s and 1960s, rapid consolidation saw the emergence of the 'Big Six' national brewers. Bigger conglomerates bought smaller companies for their pubs, often closing the breweries themselves. After 1989's Beer Orders and the emergence of the non-brewery-tied pub companies (pubcos) we now have a beer market dominated by global brewing corporations. Many pubs are owned by the pubcos or by large regional brewing concerns such as Greene King or Marston's (who now brew Banks's and, under contract, also brew Bass and Tetley's for the global giants that in turn own them).

This is true everywhere except the north west where, somehow, traditional family-run brewers such as Robinson's, Hydes, Holt's, J W Lees, Moorhouse's and Thwaites largely escaped the mergers. They're all still going strong today, most of them still with modest estates of tied pubs.

These traditional family brewers can be criticized for being too conservative in a rapidly changing beer world. But it means that they're more careful with their heritage than are faceless corporations with no historical ties.

The Black Horse, owned by Robinson's, is a case in point. The interior is Grade II listed, but it doesn't feel preserved so much as simply *unchanged* – an important difference. There have actually been significant structural changes, but you'd never know unless you remembered what it was like before.

The pub boasts of having 'the highest bar in Lancashire', but that's almost missing the point when it comes to describing this opulent interior. The Black Horse was rebuilt as a hotel in 1898, and this goes a long way to explaining why the surroundings are so special.

The bar is indeed high – over 1.2m (4ft) tall. It's semi-circular in shape and curves inwards towards the floor, tiled regally in brown and yellow. The floor itself is not to be outdone – a wide expanse of delicate mosaic covers the whole of the main bar area.

Three drinking rooms open off the main bar, each of them ornately pretty. Stained and frosted glass, much of it featuring the Robinson's unicorn, lets the light in, but keeps the world out.

The wonderful thing about this space is that, while it is undeniably grand, it doesn't humble the drinker. You still feel like you're sitting in a traditional town-centre backstreet pub, with a garrulous landlord and the sport on the TV.

The north is famous for its understatement. I was once sitting in another Robinson's pub, when a visitor who hadn't seen it since its refurbishment arrived. 'Hey, you could bring the wife in 'ere,' he said. I soon realized he had no intention to bring the wife at all: he was simply saying it was nice enough that you could, which meant that she would like it, which meant he thought it was smart and beautiful, but this was not something he could ever say directly.

Some punters have brought their wives to The Black Horse. Others sit there silently, conscious of their surroundings but not being obvious about it. I almost say aloud, 'Hey, you could bring the Queen in 'ere,' but I don't want to disturb the ambience. And anyway, there's a match on.

OPPOSITE: The Black Horse originally doubled as a small hotel, hence the highly appointed drinking areas arranged as small smoke rooms either side of a mosaic-floored corridor. The *pièce de résistance*, though, is the breathtaking semi-circular ceramic counter, offering one of the finest displays of pub ceramics in England.

THE BRITON'S PROTECTION

50 Great Bridgewater St, Manchester M1 5LE
www.britonsprotection.com

Some pubs in northern cities wear their scars with pride. They were built to serve people who toiled in mines and mills, factories and furnaces, and when the industries they powered disappeared, whole districts were flattened. Here and there, they stand like battered prizefighters, the buildings they once neighboured now long gone. Traffic thunders constantly, speeding people through places that are often no longer places at all, just nothings separating more desirable, thriving districts.

I approach the Briton's Protection from under the arches of a railway viaduct haunted by incessant drips wearing grooves into the stone. Across a precarious matrix of crossings and lights, the pub waits, forbidding. It's not exactly hostile, but its brooding bulk and sober name make it feel reserved, keeping itself to itself.

This misconception is shattered as soon as I push open the door. The warmth of the welcome is as big a contrast with the desolate exterior, as is the fire's glow with the drizzly night.

The long, narrow front bar gives the mistaken impression of a pub that's much smaller than it looks from outside. The deep mahogany bar is divided into three arched sections that invite you to creep down and see what's lurking in the next one. Behind the bar, shelves shine gold with the 300-odd whiskies the pub boasts.

As you stand to get served, you realize there are more rooms through the bar on the other side. I take my pint (a chalkboard above the bar lists the real ales and the distances they have travelled from their respective breweries) and head round to explore.

Small, post-work groups chat softly beside fireplaces at every turn. One quiet room glows red, thanks to coloured light bulbs glowing onto matching seats, like a benign boudoir. The place feels like it could offer even the most faithful regular an undiscovered nook if they looked hard enough.

A tiled mural in the corridor connecting the front bar to these rooms depicts scenes from the Peterloo Massacre, the 1819 tragedy when peaceful protestors demanding the vote were slaughtered by a sabre-wielding cavalry charge. Fifteen people were killed, and as many as 700 injured. The Briton's Protection was just a few hundred metres from the scene, and the 15th Hussars, Manchester and Cheshire Yeomanry rode past its doors on their way into 'battle'. The Yeomanry were part-time soldiers recruited from local businessmen, mainly publicans. But it's unlikely the landlord of The Briton's Protection was among them: the pub is famous for having sheltered civilians from the carnage.

I take a seat at a small round table in the front room. Both seating and table are unusually low, making me feel tiny in front of the bar's wide arches. The crackled caramel wall tiles and beaten copper tabletops add to a soothing warmth as we hunker down. I watch the door, and when people come through they sometimes seem to sag with relief, as if falling into a partner's arms for a much-needed hug at the end of another gruelling day.

St Peter's Street, site of the massacre, is now a glass and aluminium-fronted corridor of hotels, lawyers' offices and hip bars. As I watch the barman, a distinguished man in his late fifties, with crisp white shirtsleeves rolled to the elbows and a shiny black waistcoat, chatting gently to one such tired customer, the thought forms that The Briton's Protection feels like a remnant from a bygone age. Immediately, the pub seems to answer back. 'Bygone age?' it asks. 'How can it be gone if I'm still here? If I'm still needed like I was on that terrible day?'

'Fair point,' I whisper back to the tiles.

OPPOSITE TOP: The Briton's Protection stands battered but still resolute, an old survivor amid many new high-rise city buildings.

OPPOSITE BOTTOM: Inside is a haven to the people of Manchester today, just as it's always been.

[1]

[2]

THE 23 CLUB

23 Hope St, Liverpool L1 9BY
www.theclovehitch.com/the-23-club
This cosy basement craft beer bar
seemingly couldn't help also becoming
a great pub with a dedicated cadre of
locals and established traditions within
a couple of years of opening. The nook
where 'the Unstable Table' used to be
is now a brilliant bottle shop. Regulars
have their tabs chalked on boards
around the bar, and sometimes
succeed in rubbing them out while
waiting to be served.

THE ALBION INN

Park St, Chester, Cheshire CH1 1RN
www.albioninnchester.co.uk
It would be easy for a pub themed as a
middle-class house from 1914 to feel
tacky and contrived, but here it works
beautifully. The food helps – excellent
and hearty dishes such as shepherd's
pie and corn beef hash – as does the
idiosyncratic approach to both drink
and drinkers. One of many forthright
chalkboards and signs around the
place announces that the guest lager
is 'I Can't Believe It's Not Piss'.

THE BALTIC FLEET [1]

33A Wapping, Liverpool L1 8DQ
www.balticfleetpubliverpool.com
Down by the redeveloped docks, this
wedge-shaped bulwark is home to the
excellent Wapping Brewery. On the
night we go, one of its light, airy rooms
has been colonized by pirates, who
seem to have scared off the pub's four
resident ghosts. Everyone here seems
to know each other, but you soon
realize it's just that Liverpool makes
it impossible to remain a stranger for
more than five minutes.

THE BAUM [2]

33–37 Toad Lane, Rochdale OL12 0NU
www.thebaum.co.uk
The Baum demonstrates the
timelessness of what makes pubs
great without being stuck in the past.
It's only been a pub for 30 years,
having previously been a hardware
store. But its insistence on great beer
and the careful, subtle nurturing of a
proper pub atmosphere have seen it
twice named British Pub of the Year
by CAMRA, as well as becoming a
fierce favourite among locals.

THE BELVEDERE

5 Sugnall St, Liverpool L7 7EB
www.belvedereliverpool.com
This tiny pub has been wonderfully
preserved and partially restored, with
a light, bright atmosphere and a main
room so small you can't help but make
friends. A great survivor since 1836, it
now looks forward to a bright future in
a regenerated district. If the clientele
seem a little formally dressed, don't
worry – it's just the orchestra from the
nearby Philharmonic Hall, nipping out
for a quick pint during the interval.

THE BLACK BULL

1 Yewdale Rd, Coniston, Cumbria LA21 8DU
www.blackbullconiston.co.uk
Sitting in the forbidding shadow of
Coniston Old Man, this 400-year-old
coaching inn still offers refuge to
travellers. The cosy, unpretentious bar
also offers some remarkably good beers.
The in-house brewery's Bluebird
Bitter won Champion Beer of Britain
in 1998, and in 2012 the potent,
Madeira-like No. 9 Barley Wine
repeated the feat. They even brew
a very good lager.

THE CHURCH INN
& SADDLEWORTH BREWERY

Running Hill Gate, Oldham OL3 6LW

www.churchinnsaddleworth.co.uk

Straddling the border between
Lancashire and Yorkshire, the Inn
and nearby church look out across a
beautiful green valley sloping down
from the Peak District at its back.
The Taylor family revived a ruined,
century-old brewhouse in 1997, and
now produces an attractive range of
real ales for the pub.

THE DISPENSARY

87 Renshaw St, Liverpool L1 2SP

Ask any Liverpudlian about great
pubs, and they'll insist you visit The
Dispensary. You'll love it, they say.
Just make sure that you don't ask for
a glass of water. Don't leave your coat
on a chair (coat hooks are provided).
Don't try to use a plug socket. Don't
ask for tasters of the many real ales.
This is Dave's pub, and if you follow
Dave's rules – whatever they might
be today – you'll have a great time.
It sounds intimidating, but on my
visit I have a great time.

THE DRUNKEN DUCK

Barngates, Ambleside, Cumbria LA22 0NG

www.drunkenduckinn.co.uk

A sleepy boozer that's been turned
into a gastropub with the full Farrow
& Ball subtle colour treatment, this
place's saving grace is that it's also
home to Barngates brewery. Shortly
after the hop harvest, the fresh
garlands hanging from the ceiling are
so bounteous it's like eating in a hop
garden. The food is excellent, and fun
to pair with the wide range of beers
brewed on site.

THE GOLDEN RULE

Smithy Brow, Ambleside, Cumbria LA22 9AS

www.goldenrule-ambleside.co.uk

This gloriously unfussy, stripped-
down pub offers no more and no less
than any pub on this site will have
offered at any point in the last century.
The atmosphere is that special mix
you get only when a pub genuinely
caters for everyone. Tucked away
down a side street in a town full of
lowest common denominator tourist
traps, this is where those in search
of a proper pub find home.

HAWSKHEAD BREWERY
& BEER HALL [3]

Staveley Mill Yard, Back Lane, Kendal, Cumbria
LA8 9LR

www.hawksheadbrewery.co.uk/the-beer-hall

There's a growing trend for popular
craft breweries to throw open their
doors on Saturdays and accommodate
weekend drinkers. Hawkshead has
gone a stage further and built a bar
that would work on its own, even if
large stainless steel fermenters
weren't flanking the tables. A great
range of beers – and a huge car park
– mean the place is always busy.

HOLE IN T' WALL [4]

Robinson Place, Bowness-on-Windermere,
Cumbria LA23 3DH

www.newhallinn.robinsonsbrewery.com

The New Hall Inn, as it is officially
known, dates back to 1612. The pub
grudgingly admits to having installed
electricity and central heating since
then, but little else has changed. The
ancient stoves and fireplaces look like
they've always been here. It's hard to
find – between two narrow lanes off a
junction – but well worth the effort.

THE CARTFORD INN 🍴

Cartford Lane, Little Eccleston, Preston, Lancashire PR3 0YP
www.thecartfordinn.co.uk

The Cartford Inn comes highly recommended. But have you ever been in that situation where a friend recommends a place, a book or a film and says, 'You'll absolutely LOVE it. It's right up your street,' and you follow their recommendation and end up thinking, 'Does this person even *know* me?'

To get to The Cartford Inn you have to drive through a recently built village of large, well-to-do houses that feel a little cold and imposing. The steady stream of Range Rovers and Audis coming the other way makes me feel uneasy. I start to imagine a pub full of footballers' wives and lost reality TV show finalists.

Such fears, as usual, are unfounded. The pub was originally built as a 17th-century coaching inn, and today looks a little careworn from the outside, sitting at a crossing over the tidal River Wyre on low, flat marshland. Inside, what seems at first glance to be a typically antiseptic gastropub template, all design-hotel restaurant-chic complete with award-winning rosettes and certificates, soon reveals itself to be something cleverer and more complex.

The decor evokes its landscape, with lots of reclaimed wood and a sense of flotsam and jetsam. The wallpaper features a stunning design of white elderflower on a pink background. Around it, surfaces are littered with angels – lots of angels, sitting pensively on fireplaces or holding candles – and mushrooms. Mushrooms are clearly a passion here. Carved wooden mushrooms stand on every surface. There are heavy glass mushroom paperweights, mushrooms painted onto worn, re-covered tables, and expertly photographed mushrooms hanging in the hallway.

There's also a curious line in locally produced art, with pictures leaning against the walls, all for sale. These include sad, scary clowns, cows that look as though they're on LSD, and, of course, mushrooms. Maybe that explains the state the cows seem to be in.

The whole arrangement echoes the quirky outsider art of the traditional, characterful pub but, like everything else here, it's done with a modern twist and design eye. The use of random everyday objects, arranged to create something different, given roles for which they weren't intended, is exactly the same in principle as if the walls were full of horse brasses or miner's lamps. It's just that here it's mushrooms and angels instead. This stylish environment makes you realize how quickly the standard Farrow & Ball treatment of the typical gastropub is dating.

The subliminal cues work. From a menu that's crammed with locally sourced ingredients and full of stories about how they were obtained, I choose a field mushroom salad for lunch. It's extremely good: warm mushrooms, orzo pasta and red onion, all tossed in fresh baby leaves. It's one of those healthy meals that doesn't make you feel like you're missing out. And the local ales are great.

Despite the huge car park and the big houses nearby, the rosettes out front and the clear design eye, the whole place feels very relaxed. The fire is lit, the staff are genuinely friendly, neither servile nor aloof. Once the dinner plates have been cleared, it would be easy to settle in for the afternoon.

I really hadn't expected to like this place as much as I do, but there's such an authenticity and integrity to it. The Fylde peninsula is one of those flat, spacey areas that feels like it's between the sea and the land, even though we're some miles from the coast here. The stylish yet ever so slightly trippy vibe of The Cartford Inn feels just right in this environment, unique to this place, rooted wonderfully within it.

OPPOSITE TOP: Patched up and partially rebuilt over the years, the Cartford wears its age with pride.

OPPOSITE BOTTOM LEFT: Today's main course, remembered in oils, decorates the wall.

OPPOSITE BOTTOM RIGHT: The search for the nation's best pubs constantly brings you snatched moments of unanticipated beauty.

THE KIRKSTILE INN [1]

Loweswater, Cumbria CA13 0RU

www.kirkstile.com

Outside, especially in the beer garden where you can picnic on rare sunny days, the view gives you the urge to charge up mountains and the belief that you're capable of doing so. Inside, the gentle glow, the food that has people booking tables days in advance, and the in-house, award-winning beers make you think better of physical exercise, and hunker down for as long as you can.

THE MARBLE ARCH INN

73 Rochdale Rd, Manchester M4 4HY

www.marblebeers.com/marble-arch

It would be so easy for the owners of, without doubt, the most beautiful pub in Manchester, to simply polish the gorgeous mosaic floor and the lacquered tiles that cover the walls, and count the money. Happily, this is the flagship of the Marble Brewery, and thrives thanks to a loving touch. The beer range is astonishing, and the menu includes a range of 22 different cheeses, each with detailed tasting notes. Also home to the Laurel and Hardy Preservation Society.

YE OLDE MAN & SCYTHE

6–8 Churchgate, Bolton, Lancashire BL1 1HL

www.facebook.com/man.nscythe

Mentioned by name in a charter from 1251, this pub has a pretty good claim to being one of the oldest in England (it was rebuilt in 1636). The timber-framed, gabled building is beautifully preserved and one of the most popular pubs in town, partly because of the excellent cider, and partly because of the English Civil War ghost that has allegedly been captured on CCTV.

PEVERIL OF THE PEAK [2]

127 Great Bridgewater St, Manchester M1 5JQ

www.facebook.com/peverilmanchester

On a rainy night in January, the golden tiles that cover the outside of the 'Pev' seem to shine in the lamp light, immediately diverting your steps so you're through the door before you know it. Inside, photos of Morrissey and Oasis are Blu-tacked to the walls like a student's bedroom, hinting at the pub's esteemed place within the city's music culture. It's gloriously ramshackle and utterly beautiful at the same time.

THE WASDALE HEAD INN [3]

Wasdale Head, Gosforth, Cumbria CA20 1EX

www.wasdale.com

At the fringes of the Lake District, around pretty Windermere, the pubs present themselves for car-bound sightseers. The deeper you go into the hills, the more rugged the pubs become. By the time you hit Wasdale, they're catering out and out for walkers, climbers and shepherds. Here, the slate-floored bar is perfect for soggy waterproofs and muddy dogs, slightly austere yet also wonderfully welcoming.

THE WHITE CROSS

Quarry Rd, Lancaster, Lancashire LA1 4XT

www.thewhitecross.co.uk

This canal-side pub was converted from an old cotton mill, and has rugged charm if not conventional beauty. The current landlord took over in 2004 and by switching the focus to real ale, he's increased the turnover tenfold. The pub now boasts 14 ales, most of them on regular rotation, appealing to an older generation of ale drinkers as well as the town's student population.

Also Try...

THE BELLS OF PEOVER

The Cobbles, Near Knutsford, Cheshire WA16 9PZ

www.thebellsofpeover.com

THE BRITANNIA INN

Elterwater, Ambleside, Cumbria LA22 9HP

www.thebritanniainn.com

THE CIRCUS TAVERN

86 Portland St, Manchester M1 4GX

THE NURSERY INN

258 Green Lane, Stockport, Heaton Norris, Cheshire SK4 2NA

www.nurseryinn.co.uk

THOMAS RIGBYS

23-25 Dale St, Liverpool, Merseyside L2 2EZ

THE WHITE LION

35 Warmingham Rd, Coppenhall, Crewe, Cheshire CW1 4PS

www.thewhitelion.biz

WILSONS
PEVERIL OF
THE PEAK

BAR FOOD

BAR GAMES

Wines &

INN

THE TAPS 👥 🍺

12 Henry St, Lytham St Annes, Lancashire FY8 5LE
www.thetaps.net

The Taps has had a facelift.

It happens. Nothing – not even pubs – can stay the same forever. If a pub is an expression of the landlord's personality, when the landlord leaves, what does it do?

For 20 years, Ian Rigg made The Taps his own place. During that time, he acquired a national reputation for being the publican's publican, a consummate professional who was able to sell mind-boggling amounts of beer for such a relatively quiet place, who often frustrated his bosses at Greene King HQ with his determination to do things his own way, but he never failed to delight his regulars.

Royal Lytham St Anne's golf course is on the doorstep. When the Open Golf Championship was held here, Riggy would have the entire pub turfed. Other times, sand would be dumped throughout to give beach parties the final touch they needed. On Sundays, trays full of roast potatoes would be handed out free around the pub. People came here especially for them, and Riggy would always make sure no one hogged them and that everyone got their fair share.

More than anything (except his regulars), Riggy loved his beer. There was a glass wall so punters could see into the cellar, a work of art in its own right. It was an honour to be allowed to set foot in there – whether you were a drinker or a member of staff.

When Riggy took a well-deserved retirement in 2012, aged 63, it was time for a change.

On my first visit to The Taps since Riggy's retirement, I'm not sure what to expect. A couple of early signs are not good. As I walk around the corner, the comforting redbrick building, which looks like two houses that have been knocked through, is just as it was – apart from the new Greene King corporate branding. (The special appeal of pubs is that they're all

different from one another. Why would a company want to make them all look the same?) Inside, the cellar has gone, moved behind the scenes to make room for more seating. There's been some extensive redevelopment, and there are hints of posh – The Taps always used to seem a little bit scruffy, but in the best possible way.

But that's where my misgivings end. The long line of hand pumps is still in place on the bar, a mix of old favourites and beers I've never seen before. The welcome is disarmingly friendly, which is not always the case in pubs where the regulars are as close-knit as this. And the beer is phenomenal. A 4% ABV golden ale can often seem uninteresting in the midst of a craft beer revolution that's constantly pushing into new territories. But when it's kept this well, this fresh, it is able to surprise and delight even the most jaded beer palate. The key to cask ale is that the final part of the brewing process happens in the cellar of the pub when the beer is tapped and vented, then nurtured carefully through its brief shelf life. If the pub has lost anything with Riggy's departure, it has most certainly retained his obsession with, and skill for, keeping and serving a truly perfect pint of ale.

The pub has also retained its humour and mood. Everyone drinking here comports themselves like they're at home, totally comfortable, completely relaxed. I feel like I would only have to stay until the end of the day to become one of them. But it's time to go. As I leave the pub, people are pouring into it like a crowd going to a football match or concert, already laughing and joking. I quickly scan posters to see if I've missed some kind of event. But no, it's just an ordinary Saturday afternoon in an extraordinary pub.

OPPOSITE TOP: The Taps. For once, the blurb painted on the pub exterior is absolutely true.

OPPOSITE BOTTOM LEFT: Small preserving jars of beer in front of the bar help people identify the different colours and kinds of beer that are on offer.

OPPOSITE BOTTOM RIGHT: An enticing and moveable feast of ale on the ever-changing blackboard.

THE TAPS

purveyors of the finest cask ales

GREEN... drink 3.5...
An easy-drink... & quite...
moreish session
ale

MOORHOUSES   MORLAND
PENDLE WITCHES BREN   OLD SPECKLED HEN
Light amber, fruity 5.1%   A PREMIUM AMBER ALE 4.5%
AND INTENSELY SWEET   MALTY AND FRUITY

ALLGATES   MOORHOUSES
BUGLE HORN   BLACK CAT
A light, hoppy 4.3%   An award-winning 3.4%
pale ale   Dark Mild. chocolatey!

DUKERIES BLONDE   COTLEIGH
WELL BALANCED,   BARN OWL
LIGHT, HOPPY 3.8%   A light brown ale 4.5%
                                       malty & smooth.

GREENE KING   BELHAVEN
ABBOT RESERVE   GRAND SLAM
DARK, MALTY   AMBER, SWEET MALT 4.0%
FRUITY 6.5%   AROMA, SWEET BITTER FINISH

LILLEYS LEMON &   WESTONS
GINGER CIDER
Sweet, smooth ginger

GREAT PUBS IN THE
NORTH EAST

Yorkshire has always been proud of its beer and pubs. While the rest of the North East shares with God's Own County a glamour I wish I could resist calling 'gritty', the whole region is a testament to the fierce pride of its people in doing pubs well.

1: **The Bath Hotel** *(page 206)*, 66-68 Victoria St, Sheffield, South Yorkshire S3 7QL

2: **The Bingley Arms** *(page 206)*, Church Lane, Leeds, West Yorkshire LS17 9DR

3: **The Birch Hall Inn** *(page 206)*, Beck Hole Rd, Whitby, North Yorkshire YO22 5LE

4: **The Blue Bell** *(page 206)*, 53 Fossgate, York, North Yorkshire YO1 9TF

5: **The Bridge Tavern** *(page 206)*, 7 Akenside Hill, Newcastle upon Tyne NE1 3UF

6: **The Cumberland Arms** *(page 216)*, James Place St, Newcastle Upon Tyne NE6 1LD

7: **The Devonshire Cat** *(page 206)*, 49 Wellington St, Sheffield S1 4HG

8: **The Fat Cat** *(page 204)*, 23 Alma St, Sheffield, South Yorkshire S3 8SA

9: **The Feathers** *(page 207)*, Hedley on the Hill, Stocksfield, Northumberland NE43 7SW

10: **The Free Trade Inn** *(page 207)*, St Lawrence Rd, Newcastle upon Tyne, NE6 1AP

11: **Friends of Ham** *(page 207)*, 4–8 New Station St, Leeds LS1 5DL

12: **The Garden Gate** *(page 207)*, 3 Whitfield Place, Hunslet, Leeds LS10 2QB

13: **The Grapes Inn** *(page 207)*, Railway St, Slingsby, North Yorkshire YO62 4AL

14: **The Grove Inn** *(page 207)*, 2 Spring Grove St, Huddersfield HD1 4BP

15: **The Grove Inn** *(page 210)*, Back Row, Leeds LS11 5PL

16: **The Hallamshire House** *(page 210)*, 49–51 Commonside, Sheffield S10 1GF

17: **The Hop** *(page 210)*, 19 Bank St, Wakefield, West Yorkshire WF1 1EH

18: **The Kelham Island Tavern** *(page 210)*, 62 Russell St, Sheffield S3 8RW

19: **The Kings Arms** *(page 210)*, Heath, Sharlston Common, Wakefield WF1 5SL

20: **The Lion Inn** *(page 210)*, Blakey Ridge, Kirkbymoorside, North Yorkshire YO62 7LQ

21: **The Old Hill Inn** *(page 215)*, Chapel-le-Dale, Ingleton, North Yorkshire LA6 3AR

22: **The Old No 7** *(page 215)*, 7 Market Hill, Barnsley, South Yorkshire S70 2PX

23: **The Rat Inn** *(page 215)*, Anick, Hexham, Northumberland NE46 4LN

24: **The Rat and Ratchet** *(page 215)*, 40 Chapel Hill, Huddersfield HD1 3EB

25: **The Rutland Arms** *(page 208)*, 86 Brown St, Sheffield S1 2BS

26: **The Sheffield Tap** *(page 72)*, Platform 1B, Sheffield Station, Sheaf St, Sheffield S1 2BP

27: **The Strines Inn** *(page 212)*, Bradfield Dale, Bradfield, Sheffield, South Yorkshire S6 6JE

28: **The Talbot Inn** *(page 54)*, Towngate, Barnsley, South Yorkshire S75 6AS

29: **The Tan Hill Inn** *(page 64)*, Reeth Richmond, Swaledale, North Yorkshire DL11 6ED

30: **The York Tap** *(page 215)*, York Railway Station, Station Rd, York YO24 1AB

31: **The Whalebone** *(page 215)*, 165 Wincolmlee, Hull HU2 0PA

32: **Whitelocks** *(page 215)*, 4 Turk's Head Yard, Leeds LS1 6HB

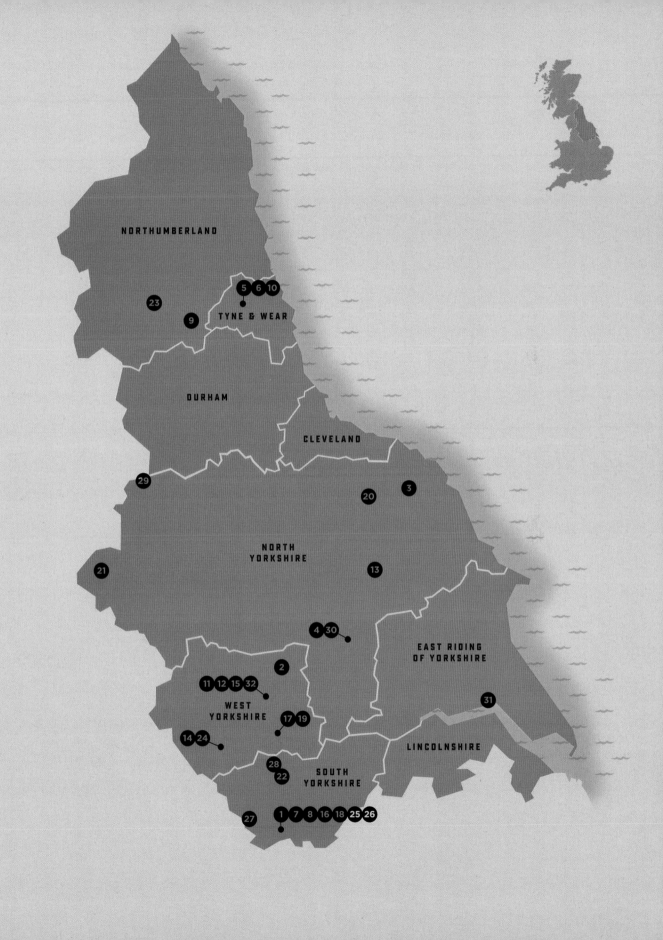

NORTHUMBERLAND

TYNE & WEAR

DURHAM

CLEVELAND

NORTH
YORKSHIRE

EAST RIDING
OF YORKSHIRE

WEST
YORKSHIRE

SOUTH
YORKSHIRE

LINCOLNSHIRE

THE FAT CAT 🍺

23 Alma St, Sheffield S3 8SA
www.thefatcat.co.uk

Walking into The Fat Cat reminds you that pubs are – to give them their full title – Public Houses. The front door opens into a tiled parlour and you're immediately confronted by the smells of home cooking; no-nonsense meat-and-two veg-aromas that evoke Sunday afternoons with grandparents, tea cosies and sticky roasting tins left to soak.

It's an aroma that makes me want to stand up straight and make sure my hair is tidy, worrying briefly that someone might appear with a spit-moistened handkerchief to dab stains from my chin. But this worry is almost immediately exploded by the pub's architectural informality. There are doors to your right and left, and then a second door on the right that gives access behind the bar, and doubles up as a serving hatch when the bottom half is closed. A few people stand here in the corridor chatting, pints in hand, beneath the press cuttings and award certificates that crowd the walls, and the chalkboard detailing the long list of the real ales on offer.

If you want to have a look at these beers before ordering one, you need to go through the first door on the right and into the main bar room. This homely space, shaped like an angular question mark around the bar itself, has the careworn but judiciously scrubbed air of a generations-old family home awaiting guests. Effortlessly welcoming.

The actual bar is a work of art, an ornately carved wooden installation rescued from an old butcher's shop, and it is lined now with more real ale hand pulls than you thought possible, crowding every inch of bar top, dense like porcupine quills.

The frosted windows bring the day to a standstill. Time passes slowly inside The Fat Cat, for sure.

A smattering of middle-aged men consults sheaves of notes and arcane-looking guidebooks. These are the tickers, collectors of draught beer who regularly travel up to 100 miles (160 km) and more to visit this pub and check it for real ales they've not yet sampled.

The Fat Cat has been a beacon to them for almost 40 years. When Dave Wickett opened Sheffield's first devoted real ale pub in 1980, in an industrial area that was being devastated by the collapse of the steel industry, people told him he was mad. On the opening night, the queues stretched around the block.

The Fat Cat has a close relative in Rochester, New York. The Old Toad is a real ale pub run entirely by business students on their gap years from Sheffield Hallam University, thanks to a scheme Wickett set up to give them practical experience.

Dave Wickett died too young in 2012, but his spirit lives on here and in the Kelham Island Brewery, another first for Sheffield when he founded it, and a forerunner in the current boom in British microbreweries. If Sheffield gets more than its fair share of pubs in this book, it's because it is arguably the best city for good beer in the UK, and that's down in large part to the vision of Dave Wickett – a man who possessed a rare combination of a genuine passion for beer and shrewd business acumen. Not every brewer he hired got on with him. But many who left his employ were sufficiently inspired by what they'd learned there that they went and opened a brewery of their own just down the road. That's why Sheffield now has far more breweries than it should.

Dave Wickett's influence continues to define what was once Steel City, and is now very much Beer City. He was a very different kind of fat cat, and his adoptive city will certainly not forget him.

OPPOSITE TOP: The main bar in The Fat Cat, looking far better now than when it was in a butcher's shop.

OPPOSITE BOTTOM LEFT: The pub sign declares that it has been ferociously independent from 1980 to the present day.

OPPOSITE BOTTOM RIGHT: The first beacon of regeneration in what was once an abandoned district, and is now at the heart of Sheffield's peerless beer scene.

[1]

[3]

THE BATH HOTEL

66–68 Victoria St, Sheffield S3 7QL

www.beerinthebath.co.uk

The pub equivalent of winning the lottery is when you buy a dilapidated old boozer, commit to spending an awful lot of money on refurbishing it, then tear out the tatty detritus to find a perfectly preserved Victorian interior beneath. The whole identity of this pub flows from the beautiful rediscovered tiled floor, which helps to create a homely hybrid of craft beer bar and Victorian pub.

THE BINGLEY ARMS

Church Lane, Leeds LS17 9DR

www.bingleyarms.co.uk

One of at least two pubs in this book that claims *Guinness World Records* lists it as the oldest pub in England. (In fact, *Guinness* doesn't list any pub as definitively the oldest in England.) No matter, it's obviously very old, with an interior full of odd nooks and crannies to draw you in, great beer and licensees who clearly love what they do.

THE BIRCH HALL INN

Beck Hole Rd, Whitby, North Yorkshire YO22 5LE

www.beckhole.info/bhi

This delightful pub, which sits by a bridge over the Eller Beck, holds an awful lot of charm within its restricted space. The Big Bar (hint: it's not very big at all) is the main and oldest part of the pub, with an open fire at one end and a serving hatch at the other. On your way through to the Little Bar, you pass a tiny, in-house sweetshop. And why not?

THE BLUE BELL [1]

53 Fossgate, York YO1 9TF

Widely attacked for maintaining a 'selective' door policy, this pub can be 'closed for a private party' on busy nights, to deter stag and hen parties from colonizing the place. But accusations of discrimination against tourists and non-regulars are nonsense. There's a warm and courteous welcome, great beer and amazing pork pies in this excellent pub, the interior of which hasn't been refurbished since 1903.

THE BRIDGE TAVERN [2]

7 Akenside Hill, Newcastle upon Tyne NE1 3UF

www.thebridgetavern.com

Built between the legs of the Tyne Bridge, the highlight is the terrace at the back where, in the words of the owner, the bridge is your ceiling. This makes you feel a sense of wonder, like you're in some hybrid of Newcastle and New York. An in-house microbrewery helps, creating one-off beers that are pumped straight to the taps.

THE DEVONSHIRE CAT

49 Wellington St, Sheffield S1 4HG

www.devonshirecat.co.uk

As a rule, a pub shoehorned into the ground floor of a 21st-century-built student hall of residence should be resolutely of the lowest common denominator. The Devonshire Cat begs to differ. While it may look like a carpet showroom, with its big windows and cheap business-hotel-style decor, its 12 perfectly kept cask ales and a bottle cellar to rival any Brussels beer bar soon tempt students away from their Rekorderlig cider.

THE FEATHERS [3]

Hedley on the Hill, Stocksfield,
Northumberland NE43 7SW

www.thefeathers.net

On Easter Monday, the locals here
hold a race up the steep slopes to the
hilltop pub, carrying empty beer
barrels. Inside, they find a place that
combines 'gastro' and 'pub' quite
beautifully, with award-winning food
made from local and often foraged
ingredients, served in an assertively
old-school pub atmosphere, unfussy
and unpretentious.

THE FREE TRADE INN

St Lawrence Rd, Newcastle upon Tyne NE6 1AP

Standing alone on a corner above the
Ouseburn Valley, this gloriously
ramshackle pub has the best views
of Newcastle, especially at sunset.
It seems to have effortlessly made a
transition from old boozer to craft
beer venue without losing the twinkle
in its eye. One can rarely say this, but
the graffiti in the men's toilets is an
essential (if unrepeatable) read. It
alone makes the pub worth a visit.

FRIENDS OF HAM [4]

4–8 New Station St, Leeds LS1 5DL

www.friendsofham.com

Some ideas are so simple you ask,
'Hang on, where's the catch?' Some are
so brilliant that there is none. Friends
of Ham is a Spanish-inspired tapas-
style bar specializing in really great
meat and cheese, because these items
are produced in the north of England
as well as in Spain. It complements
these with an amazing range of northern
craft beers. Simply wonderful.

THE GARDEN GATE

3 Whitfield Place, Hunslet, Leeds LS10 2QB

www.gardengatesleeds.co.uk

It's distressing to think that anyone
with a soul could seriously think of
destroying this, one of the most
beautiful pubs in the country. But in
an area that's been redeveloped into
housing estates and big-box shopping,
locals had to fight hard to preserve it,
until it was saved by Leeds Brewery
and a Grade II listing. If this pub
interior were in Venice, it would be a
globally celebrated tourist attraction.

THE GRAPES INN

Railway St, Slingsby, North Yorkshire YO62 4AL

www.thegrapesinn-slingsby.co.uk

A great example of a tired, neglected
pub that so inspired one young couple
coming to the village for a visit, they
decided to take it on, with no previous
experience of running a pub. The
Grapes is a stately Georgian building,
and the various rooms inside take you
from a country walker's pub to an
elegant sitting room. Full of lovely old
stuff and furniture, deployed with a
keen, modern designer's eye.

THE GROVE INN

2 Spring Grove St, Huddersfield HD1 4BP

www.thegrove.pub

Described by other publicans in the
town of Huddersfield as the place that
sets the trend, the beer selection here
at the Grove rivals any in the country.
It provides a ridiculous number of
cask and keg taps and over 200 bottled
beers. And yet it's still defiantly a
proper northern pub, right down to its
tiled floors and wooden benches - a
nice, suburban corner boozer.

THE RUTLAND ARMS ❗🍺🍴

86 Brown St, Sheffield S1 2BS
www.therutlandarmssheffield.co.uk

Not so long ago, one of the key facets of any great pub would be that it had a cracking jukebox.

There it stood against a back wall, tempting people to humiliation. You stood in plain sight of the rest of the pub, and paid good money in order to say to them, 'Look, this is my taste in music, and I'm going to make you listen to it now.' In doing so, you risked anything from a dirty look to the ultimate sanction: the bar staff quietly skipping your choice and going on to the next song.

Of course, the staff controlled the discs that were on there in the first place, so when a jukebox consisted of seven-inch singles, you couldn't go too far wrong. Then we got CD jukeboxes that had hundreds of songs, and the control started to shift behind the bar. Nowadays, pub music is increasingly sourced from Spotify or iTunes. The selection is practically infinite, but it seems pubgoers can no longer be trusted to choose it. The staff tend to decide what we're listening to, in another example of the infantilization of modern life.

So this is the first reason I love The Rutland Arms. It still has a jukebox packed full of CDs. Even better, it has a sign above it reading 'Play Music Box Thing', and a blackboard beside that listing the music choices that are currently forbidden. These tell you a lot about the staff, the drinkers and how they interact: on the day of this particular visit, the banned list includes The Lightning Seeds, The Bluetones, and 'Paul Weller (solo and Style Council)'. The careful exclusion of The Jam from this list is a beautiful touch.

The Rutland expresses itself via its blackboards. One features a list of 'Danger Booze', which includes beers that are strong, expensive, weird or, indeed, all three. Another is titled, 'This week we are drinking...' The text below completes the sentence with, 'the tears of our enemies'.

The danger booze complements a smartly chosen range of drinks that's heavy on local craft beer and cask ale. It also complements what I would call the 'danger food'. The menu at the Rutland is singular, unbound by convention. There's a strong Indian influence, mixed in with traditional pub fare, a hint of modern European, and something unique. Slow-cooked lamb shoulder and tandoori sea bass hold up the respectable end, but the menu gradually loses its mind as you read down and across, until it ends up at a section titled 'Chip Hilarity/Butty fun', which starts with a straightforward chip butty 'because you're worth it', then runs through the 'Rutty Butty' and its damaged cousin, the 'Slutty Rutty Butty', to the *pièce de résistance*, the 'Bhaji Butty', which is every bit as repulsive and utterly irresistible as it sounds. Depending on your mood, you can choose between the most disgustingly unhealthy pub food I've ever attempted to force into my body, and some dazzlingly healthy and tasty veggie options that are superior to anything I've seen in other pubs.

Combining the best bits of a traditional northern, real ale pub, student wackiness that never gets out of hand, the contemporary craft beer movement and the indefinable something every great pub possesses, the Rutland speaks to you in its own singular voice. It's not the voice of the landlord or the staff, or the punters, but a composite voice of the pub itself. It's a very appealing, friendly, likeable voice, and it tells you to come back again soon, when hopefully the music of The Bluetones will be out of the sin bin and replaced by indie band Placebo. One day, I'll pluck up the courage to ask exactly why that is.

OPPOSITE TOP: The Rutland Arms is another architectural survivor in an area where many streets have disappeared.

OPPOSITE BOTTOM LEFT: Sheffield has an astonishing number of talented street artists, and the walls around the Rutland offer them a blank canvas.

OPPOSITE BOTTOM RIGHT: The Rutland's drinks selection is a truly impressive one.

[2]

[3]

THE GROVE INN

Back Row, Leeds LS11 5PL

www.thegroveinn.com

So old and careworn you might feel it shouldn't still be here, the Grove is, in fact, in rude health. As well as being a superb real ale pub that's hardly changed in decades, this is the perfect place to hide on rainy weekday afternoons. It's also a famous folk venue with live gigs four nights a week in the back room. Look out for the homemade Scotch eggs too.

THE HALLAMSHIRE HOUSE [1]

49–51 Commonside, Sheffield S10 1GF

www.myhallamshire.co.uk

Having been bought and rescued by the Thornbridge Brewery, the Hallamshire takes the concept of the Victorian gin palace and redefines it beautifully for the modern era. It's a city community boozer yet it also feels like a countryside stately home. Sheffield's only full-size snooker room and table is the focal point at which the world of the pub and the manor house find a perfectly easy and comfortable fusion.

THE HOP

19 Bank St, Wakefield WF1 1EH

www.thehopwakefield.com

The line between pub and playground is a thin one. The Wakefield Hop gleefully smashes it, making the most of a vast space by turning it into an adult's adventure playground. One bar is a VW camper van. Upstairs there's a 1960s sitting room. If you're over 30 and still have a soul, it's the kind of place that makes you ask, 'Why didn't we have anything like this when we were twenty?'

THE KELHAM ISLAND TAVERN [2]

62 Russell St, Sheffield S3 8RW

www.kelhamtavern.co.uk

The only pub to be named CAMRA's National Pub of the Year two years running, this place feels like it's been here for ever, so it's astonishing to discover it only (re)opened in its current form in 2002. Revered for the range and quality of its beer, it should also be celebrated for its cellophane-wrapped rolls, pork pies, garden full of palm trees, pub quiz, folk nights and pub cat.

THE KINGS ARMS

Heath, Sharlston Common, Wakefield WF1 5SL

www.thekingsarmsheath.co.uk

Somehow, the tiny village of Heath has escaped any new building since the 19th century, and most of it is much older. The Kings Arms is the heart of the place, an old coaching inn that's still gas-lit. It so enfolds you in its maze of corridors and rooms, you quickly forget when and where you are. This place is magical.

THE LION INN [3]

Blakey Ridge, Kirkbymoorside, North Yorkshire YO62 7LQ

www.lionblakey.co.uk

You know you've found somewhere special when it feels like you're in the middle of nowhere as you approach it, high in desolate hills with no sign of life. Then, when you finally enter, you're delighted to see it full of people. The Lion has the usual blueprint of northern country pub: stone and wood, cask ale, immense portions of homely food. It just somehow manages to executes the formula better than most.

THE STRINES INN 🏰🌳

Bradfield Dale, Bradfield, Sheffield S6 6JE
www.thestrinesinn.webs.com

I first realized the power of pubs as a way of bringing people together about six years before I ever tasted beer.

My family home was rarely a happy one – it was a case of four people living more or less independently under the same roof rather than a family unit. But every now and then, there was something that would genuinely bring us together, something that made everyone equally happy, for the same reasons. On long summer Sunday evenings, any one of us might say, 'Do you fancy a run out to the Strines?' We'd pile into the car, and dad would drive us out into the stark beauty of the Peak District, along a tiny road running above the Ladybower reservoir (which is famous for being the place where the Dambusters practised their bombing runs during World War Two) to this grey, rambling 13th-century inn. Fizzy pop and crisps never tasted better as we sat outside, soaking up the silence of the hills, sharing chips with the noisy peacocks that roamed the grounds.

Thirty years later, The Strines is pretty much unchanged. Families like mine speak seldom as they search for a connection over pie and aggressively boiled veg. A young couple sit across from each other, looking around anxiously and tentatively wondering if their first date is going OK. Moorland walkers and leather-clad bikers remind us that the Strines isn't really on the way to anywhere, that getting here is partly the point of its existence.

It was first built as a manor house, and bits of it just seem to keep settling on the place as the years go by. It's been an inn since 1771, and still offers bed and breakfast accommodation. 'Try a romantic night or two away from the rat race,' say the posters. 'This is the ideal place.'

The Strines gains new things as and when it needs them and gets rid of stuff that is no longer useful whenever it feels like it. An antiquated pay-phone sits on the wall, still occasionally necessary in a place mercifully free from mobile signals. A yellowed poster informs us that the pub holds the Roy Castle Good Air Award for providing a smoke-free area, almost a decade after smoking in pubs was outlawed. A stuffed hawk in a case sits below an antique meat grinder, next to brass engine plates from the Ark Royal. Stuffed squirrels and sheep's heads nestle up to cooking pots, all surrounded by more horse brasses than I've ever seen. There is no sense of anyone trying to create 'a look' here, unless 'coaching inn/naval history/taxidermy is a new concept in design circles: the pub just customizes itself organically. You could almost believe that some of this stuff simply appears on the walls by its own volition, filling spaces that need to be filled.

Almost every option on the menu seems to include a pie or a giant Yorkshire pudding. You can have the latter with sausages or as a vegetarian option. You can have it on its own as a starter. It hides, almost apologetically, at the bottom of the descriptions of the homemade butter-bean stew and the homemade chilli. After spending a few minutes with the menu, it seems outrageous that you can't have a steak and ale pie inside a giant Yorkshire pudding, like they've missed the obvious.

'Ooh, mixed grill. I do fancy a big plate of meat,' says a lady at the next table.

When Yorkshire people come to the Strines, they subconsciously smooth some of the edges from their accents, rounding out vowel sounds and completing 'the' where there's usually just a glottal stop.

Like the mixed grill, everything about the Strines is a treat: not exotic – that would never do – but just a little bit special.

OPPOSITE TOP: The Strines Inn, gateway to the Peak District. Well, detour on the way to the Peak District. OK, total distraction that makes you forget about going to the Peak District.

OPPOSITE BOTTOM LEFT AND RIGHT: Inside, the Strines feels like the original template for what has become standard pub decoration everywhere.

[1]

[2]

[3]

[4]

THE OLD HILL INN

Chapel-le-Dale, Ingleton, North Yorkshire LA6 3AR

www.oldhillinn.co.uk

Nestled among Yorkshire's Three Peaks, this former drover's inn is pretty much exactly how you'd imagine a Yorkshire Dales country pub to be. Inside, it's all bare stone walls, wooden cartwheels, fireplaces and good old-fashioned Yorkshire bitter on the bar. The hidden secret is that it's run by a family of chefs, so the food stands out.

THE OLD NO 7

7 Market Hill, Barnsley S70 2PX

www.oldno7barnsley.co.uk

Superb local brewery Acorn rescued this Barnsley town centre institution after former owners Enterprise Inns closed it and sold it at auction. They've managed not only to breathe new life into it, but with their own beers on cask and a brilliantly chosen range of Belgian ales, British ciders and international craft beers, they've made it one of Yorkshire's best beer and cider pubs.

THE RAT INN [1]

Anick, Hexham, Northumberland NE46 4LN

www.theratinn.com

One of those country inns that has it all: in the summer, it commands stunning views across the Tyne Valley. In winter, it's the perfect place for huddling down by the open fires with a glass of something warming. The collection of chamber pots on the ceiling helps keep the vibe decidedly pubby, despite the award-winning food being the main attraction.

THE RAT AND RATCHET [2]

40 Chapel Hill, Huddersfield HD1 3EB

www.ossett-brewery.co.uk

There are lots of pubs with in-house breweries now. But few, if any, can claim to sell their beers nationwide and also win the national title of Cask Ale Pub of the Year. The brewery is in the cellar. The pub is open and expansive, elegant yet plain. Meanwhile, a jukebox and a vintage pinball machine round off the ambience of a pub that could prosper on its beer alone, but manages to offer so much more as well.

THE YORK TAP

York Railway Station, Station Rd, York YO24 1AB

www.yorktap.com

The York Tap, another beautiful railway pub restoration job from the team that created The Sheffield Tap, is sited directly on the station concourse. There's a circular bar in the middle and a light, airy space all around. It still feels as prim and proper as a typical York tearoom, only now it sells a massive range of well-chosen craft beers to thirsty travellers.

THE WHALEBONE

165 Wincolmlee, Hull HU2 0PA

If you're looking for pubs that define a specific area and a community in Hull, people unfailingly point you to The Whalebone. It's been a dockers' pub for two centuries, and despite many changes of ownership and direction, it's maintained its core identity. There is now a handy brewery in the cottage next door, and Hull's full range of up-and-coming craft breweries also feature on the bar.

WHITELOCKS

4 Turk's Head Yard, Leeds LS1 6HB

www.whitelocksleeds.com

The oldest pub in Leeds is long and thin, with low ceilings and an accumulated mass of folksy decoration. The cramped space forces people up against each other, creating new friendships. The 8in- (20cm-) step up behind the bar means the staff look down on you across the copper bar tops. Gazing up to choose from the beer fonts, you feel like a child in a magical, alcohol-fuelled sweet shop.

Also Try...

BIG SIX

10 Horsfall St, Halifax HX1 3HG

www.thebig6inn.co.uk

THE BRIDGE INN

Grinton, Richmond, North Yorkshire DL11 6HH

www.bridgeinn-grinton.co.uk

THE CENTRAL

Half Moon Lane, Gateshead, Tyne & Wear NE8 2AN

www.theheadofsteam.co.uk

THE CLUNY

36 Lime St, Newcastle upon Tyne NE1 2PQ

www.thecluny.com

NORTH BAR [3]

24 New Briggate, Leeds LS1 6NU

www.northbar.com

THE SCARBROUGH HOTEL

Bishopsgate St, Leeds LS1 5DY

www.nicholsonspubs.co.uk/restaurants

THE THREE PIGEONS [4]

1 Sun Fold, Halifax HX1 2LX

www.ossett-brewery.co.uk

THE CUMBERLAND ARMS ♜ 👥 🎤 ! 🍺

James Place St, Newcastle upon Tyne NE6 1LD
www.thecumberlandarms.co.uk

If you're looking for the kind of pub where you walk in and see a wide range of beers on the bar, and you're working out what you haven't had before and which are from local breweries and a man in his 60s standing next to you says, 'Go on, be adventurous,' and then engages you in conversation for an hour, making you laugh so much you forget to take any notes until you're too tipsy to write properly, this is your place.

The Cumberland Arms sits on a hillside looking down on central Newcastle. It was originally built as part of a cramped Victorian terrace and is the only survivor. After the slums were demolished, they were replaced by post-war tower blocks. Now, those too have gone and the Cumberland is still here, a redbrick suburban building in a post-industrial area, where the countryside is reasserting itself, surrounded on all sides by the city.

Inside, the pub is careworn, the wood chipped and shined by use. The walls are a mix of bare brick and varnished wood, with simple planks making up the floor. In one corner there's a bookcase full of *Good Beer Guides* and more books, together with a tatty pile of old board games. The walls surrounding it are heavy with awards for the beers, which doesn't come as a surprise, and for folk dancing, which does. There's a beer, cider and music festival here in April, and a square outside the pub that's used for dancing, so that might explain it.

Right now, there's a folk session happening next door, in the smaller back bar. I enter to find someone playing the piano, and other musicians brush past, carrying instruments. One table in the corner has a chalkboard on it reading 'Reserved for musicians from 8.30pm.' I can't help feeling the musicians would like this sign to apply to the whole room, so I head back next door. The piano music wafts through via the bar area that serves both rooms, and I get the best of each.

My new friend, who really, definitely had to be going before I bought him a pint, has now forgotten I exist and doesn't acknowledge me when I return to the bar. He's now talking to a young student of Asian origin, repeating the patter he gave me 20 minutes ago to his new companion, almost word for word.

The professional pub loafer is an endangered species. He (it's always he) is part of the folklore of the archetypal pub, but if you don't visit the right kind of pub, you might not encounter him for years.

There's a touch of the conman to his approach, but at his best, like this bloke, he's too clever to offend anyone. He never actually asks for a drink. He simply waits until you're about to buy another one, and then announces that he really must be off home to his long-suffering wife, who'll kill him if he's late again. In doing so, he taps into the programming that guides any serious pubgoer: if you're about to order another drink and someone says they're leaving, you offer to buy them a pint without thinking. It's the code.

All this happens under the watchful eye of the bar staff. It always takes place at the bar, because it's neutral territory, and the staff will intervene if there's any sense of the visitor being harassed.

I'm sure there really is a wife at home. Well, almost sure. But if he'd rather stay in The Cumberland Arms for another pint, I can see why. I wonder if he ever brings the wife in with him, and if she enjoys the pub as much as he does. Because as the loafer, the couples in the corner, the student and the musicians all demonstrate, this is a pub that has something for everyone. Even if some of the people would rather be in a separate room.

OPPOSITE TOP: A comforting mix of careworn wooden furniture and walls is both welcoming and informal.

OPPOSITE BOTTOM LEFT: The Cumberland Arms has survived waves of turmoil and emerged as a space that looks and feels fresh and contemporary by virtue of never having changed much.

OPPOSITE BOTTOM RIGHT: Musicians and dancers perform regularly in this lively suburban Newcastle pub.

NORTHERN IRELAND

When you visit Northern Ireland, it's easy to see how 'The Troubles' that blighted it for a generation impacted every aspect of life. A decade after the ceasefire, beer and pubs are re-emerging optimistically, helping to heal wounds and build bonds.

1: **The Anchor Bar** *(page 222)*, 9–11 Bryansford Rd, Newcastle, County Down BT33 0HJ

2: **Blakes of the Hollow** *(page 222)*, 6 Church St, Enniskillen, County Fermanagh BT74 7EJ

3: **The Cross Keys Inn** *(page 222)*, 40 Grange Rd, Toomebridge, County Antrim BT41 3QB

4: **The Crown Liquor Saloon** *(page 224)*, 46 Great Victoria St, Belfast, County Antrim BT2 7BA

5: **Groucho's** *(page 220)*, 1 The Square, Richhill, County Armagh BT61 9PP

6: **The Harbour Bar** *(page 222)*, The Harbour, Portrush, County Antrim BT56 8DF

7: **The Harp Bar** *(page228)*, 35 Hill St, Belfast, County Antrim BT1 2LB

8: **The John Hewitt** *(page 227)*, 51 Donegall St, Belfast, County Antrim BT1 2FH

9: **Peadar O'Donnell's** *(page 227)*, 59–63 Waterloo St, Londonderry BT48 6HD

10: **The Sunflower** *(page 227)*, Union St, Belfast, County Antrim BT1 2JG

11: **The White Horse Inn** *(page 227)*, 49–53 Main St, Saintfield, Ballynahinch, County Down BT24 7AB

GROUCHO'S 🏰 ! 🍴 🍎 🍺

1 The Square, Richhill, County Armagh BT61 9PP
www.grouchosonthesquare.com

I love trying to decode a characterful pub when I walk into it for the first time.

A good pub expresses a personality, telling you something about the building, the area, the time it was built, the people who run it. Sometimes its story is obvious. In mediocre pubs there's no story at all. And sometimes, you have to sit and absorb the place, and try to work out what it's saying.

I encounter Groucho's on Halloween weekend, which is also the weekend of the Richhill Apple Harvest Fayre. The square on which Groucho's stands is full of stalls selling local produce, and there's a marquee in which chefs – including Groucho's own – are giving cookery demonstrations.

Groucho's beer garden has been turned into an exhibition space for the burgeoning local cider scene. Armagh has long been an important apple-growing region, and the Armagh Bramley was awarded Protected Geographical Indication (PGI) status in 2012. Over the past few years, many local orchards have set up cider-making businesses, creating high quality, full-juice ciders that combine full flavour and moreish drinkability.

Inside, the main bar of Groucho's resembles an old barn, with a massive gabled ceiling forming a tall atrium that takes you by surprise because it's not immediately apparent from the street. The heavy beams supporting the ceiling form a kind of narrow mezzanine around the main bar space which is crammed with clutter on a grand scale, including a full-size metal ploughshare, a row of rusty bayonets and a pile of old suitcases.

An incredible amount of effort has gone into the Halloween decorations. An 8ft- (2.4m-) tall ghost dominates one corner. Coffin lids have been nailed over the high windows, and a life-size mummy guards the bar.

So I'm not quite sure what to make of the place. A converted barn with a Halloween fetish? A serious food pub? Some of the tourist websites refer to it as a cafe-bar and music lounge, others an olde worlde pub.

When I find owner Peter Lyness, tall and magnificently bearded as he is, he's able to shed some light.

'We designed this place never to be sold,' he says softly. 'The plough up there belonged to my great-great-great-grandfather. Those bayonets on the beam were found up in the loft, after being stashed there when people weren't allowed weapons.'

And so the history of the place reveals itself. What is now Groucho's was originally built as a coaching inn around four centuries ago. It's linked by tunnel to Richhill Castle, Ulster's first non-fortified manor house, and shares a close history with the place. The square was a stop on the coaching routes from Armagh to Belfast and Dublin, and the inn catered for travellers who would alight at the bottom of the hill and walk up the steep slope to refresh themselves at the inn. It was an inconvenience, but not as bad as bumping up the hill in a carriage with no suspension.

Groucho's website nails it when it says the place has been continuously evolving for the last four hundred years. It's an old coaching inn, a gastropub, a traditional Ulster boozer, a European-style coffee bar – whatever you want it to be, really. Like almost all pubs in Northern Ireland, it's celebrated for its live music. Like the best pubs anywhere in Britain, the standard of its food is high, and it keeps a close eye on a developing range of whiskies, beers and ciders. It evolves to be what people want it to be, and says what you want to hear. Who knows what its customers will be calling it another hundred years from now?

OPPOSITE TOP: Look up, and this pub is a museum to its own history, part of a plan to ensure it is never sold.

OPPOSITE BOTTOM: Great beer, great cider, great food, great coffee, sport on the TV for those who want it – Groucho's certainly offers something for everyone in its community.

THE ANCHOR BAR [3]

9–11 Bryansford Rd, Newcastle, County Down
BT33 0HJ

A blackboard boasts 28 gins, 39 whiskies, 11 vodkas, 19 rums and 14 bourbons. The beer selection is pretty good too. At the bar, we talk to two men who travel 35 miles (56km) to sample new Irish craft ales here. A huge room at the back has pool tables, dartboard, games machines, stage and big screen, keeping noisy attractions away from the great drinks.

BLAKES OF THE HOLLOW [1]

6 Church St, Enniskillen, County Fermanagh
BT74 7EJ

blakesofthehollow.com

The writer John McGahern said it all about this unspoilt Victorian bar when he wrote, 'The patterned tilework of the floor is identical to that in the Catholic church 100 metres or so above the Hollow, which was built more than a decade before, but the tiles in Blakes are more cracked and worn than the church tiles.'

THE CROSS KEYS INN [2]

40 Grange Rd, Toomebridge, County Antrim
BT41 3QB

This former coaching inn was built in the 17th century and is a must for anyone who wants to experience pubs how they once were. It still has a thatched roof above the whitewashed walls. That can sound a little flat in print, but it fills you with pleasure when you see it with your own eyes, a delightful escape from modernity.

THE HARBOUR BAR

The Harbour, Portrush, County Antrim BT56 8DF

www.ramorerestaurant.com/harbourbar

Showing there's more to Northern Ireland than quaint tradition (wonderful though that is), this bar, in a successful harbourside hotel, combines the peaceful, idyllic setting of a coastal village with cosmopolitan sophistication, premium spirits and cool cocktails, as well as a genuinely warm welcome that keeps visitors coming back year after year.

THE CROWN LIQUOR SALOON 🍽 🏛 🍺

46 Great Victoria St, Belfast, County Antrim BT2 7BA
www.nicholsonspubs.co.uk

The special nature of the pub is all to do with the meaning of space. There are permeable barriers between public and private, and in today's large, one-room pubs, those walls are invisible. People can chat to and flirt with you at the bar, but when you go and sit at a table with your friends, you create a private space that others have to be invited to join.

This distinction was once physical in many pubs, and remains so at the Crown. All around the walls are 5ft- (1.5m-) high partitions that create private booths. Inside each booth is a table with a banquette seat around it. Screens block out the view, but the open space between the top of the screen and the ceiling allows sound to travel freely, so you still get the sense of being in a pub with other people.

The former Railway Hotel was nothing special when father and son Michael and Patrick Flanagan took it over in 1880. Patrick was fascinated by architecture, and had toured Italy and Spain, admiring their churches and palaces. So when the Catholic Church embarked on a major building programme in Belfast, Patrick lured some of the Italian architects who had been brought in for the project to drink in the pub after hours, and persuaded them to do a little moonlighting.

They covered the outside with polychromatic tiles that shone in the lamplight. They laid an intricate mosaic of a crown in the entrance hall, and designed the entire floor in patterns made from small tiles. They painted beautiful birds and flowers on the glass of the snug screens, and designed the pillars to look as though they were flowing black scales, each individual scale edged in gold. They carved the mahogany snug walls, appointing lions and griffins to guard the narrow doors, and built the bar altar-style, with a red granite top and embossed tiles curving down to a brass foot rail that was heated.

During the Troubles, the Crown had its windows blown out by bombs, and scraped by in a city where no one went out after dark. The National Trust acquired it in 1978, and restored the tiles, windows, mosaics, even the gas lamps. The Crown was the most stunning pub of its day, and now it is again.

And it still has a heated foot rail at the bar.

Refurbishments have continued steadily ever since. After the smoking ban came into force, the National Trust cleaned the ceiling and discovered it wasn't black. Apparently, it's a deep red, but on an autumn Saturday evening it looks like rippling chocolate.

In the days of gin palaces, pubs like the Crown were criticized by right-wing politicians because they felt such places were giving working-class people ideas above their station – they simply didn't deserve places like this and wouldn't know how to appreciate them. And they were attacked by liberal and left-wing politicians for luring honest working people to their alcoholic doom with bright lights and gaudy glamour.

(Did I mention yet that they even installed a heated foot rail at the bar?)

No one discussed a third point of view: that surroundings like this simply elevate the soul. Now, 130 years after the Crown opened, a crowd of mainly local people talk in the high pitch you get when your throat tightens slightly, because you're feeling excitement, or love, or both.

There's a heated foot rail at the bar. And if you had holes in your cardboard-soled shoes when you came in from the rainy streets after a gruelling day's work, even if you couldn't afford one of the fancy booths, it must have felt like the pub was wrapping a blanket around you and kissing you on the forehead.

OPPOSITE TOP: The Italian-influenced magnificence of the main space in the Crown Liquor Saloon.

OPPOSITE BOTTOM LEFT: Small snugs provide private drinking spaces where the ambience of the pub still bleeds through.

OPPOSITE BOTTOM RIGHT: The main entrance to the Crown: let no surface go needlessly unadorned.

THE JOHN HEWITT

51 Donegall St, Belfast, County Antrim BT1 2FH

www.thejohnhewitt.com

When the Belfast Unemployed Resource Centre struggled for funding, they decided to set up a pub in the building next door as a revenue stream for projects helping the unemployed and disadvantaged. The former newspaper building is now a wonderfully warm venue full of Irish craft beer, live music and deliriously tasty food. Beware the champ – a traditional Irish potato dish – it's seriously addictive.

PEADAR O'DONNELL'S

59–63 Waterloo St, Londonderry BT48 6HD

www.peadars.com

There's live music every night at this tourist magnet, where world flags cover the ceiling. But it manages to attract international visitors without losing the ramshackle charm of a proper Irish pub, and the tunes and the quality of the Guinness mean it's still popular with locals too.

THE SUNFLOWER

Union St, Belfast, County Antrim BT1 2JG

There's a security cage around the door, to prevent unwanted entry and allow searches. This was a common sight back in the Troubles, and it survives today as a memento. A slogan on the wall next to it reads, 'No topless bathing. Ulster has suffered enough.' Humour is a popular response to the Troubles, and The Sunflower is big on tolerance, openness, peace – and damn fine pizza.

THE WHITE HORSE INN

49–53 Main St, Saintfield, Ballynahinch, County Down BT24 7AB

www.whitehorsesaintfield.com

The brewery tap of Whitewater – Northern Ireland's largest craft brewery – is a modern craft beer bar, but it's also an inn that dates back over 200 years, and a sense of history survives. Real ale in Ireland is growing but still rare, and this pub is an important marker for its development.

Also Try...

BREW BOT

451 Ormeau Rd, Belfast, County Antrim BT7 3GQ

www.brewbotbelfast.com

THE BREWER'S HOUSE

73 Castlecaulfield Rd, Dungannon, County Tyrone BT70 3HB

www.thebrewershouse.com

THE DUKE OF YORK [2]

7–11 Commercial Court, Belfast, County Antrim BT1 2NB

www.dukeofyorkbelfast.com

MCCOLLAMS

23 Mill Street, Cushendall, Ballymena, County Antrim BT44 0RR

www.mccollamsbar.com

THE PLOUGH

3 The Square, Hillsborough, County Down BT26 6AG

www.ploughgroup.com/ploughinn

THE HARP BAR 🎙️ ! 🖼️

35 Hill St, Belfast, County Antrim BT1 2LB
www.harpbarbelfast.com

As a fan of Scottish single malts, I'm surprised to learn that not too long ago, Irish whisky (we'll come back to that spelling in a moment) was the world's most popular. Its biggest export market was the US, and there was a healthy trade across Britain. But in the 1920s, the effects of Prohibition in the States and the Irish War of Independence back home struck twin hammer blows. Within a decade the industry was all but dead.

'This place used to be a bonded whisky warehouse before prohibition,' says Willie Jack. 'We're near the docks here. All this was bonded warehouses. They all went.'

The local press always refer to Willie Jack simply as Willie Jack – they never feel the need to preface this with 'local businessman' or 'popular bar owner' or any other note of explanation – they just assume everyone already knows who he is. When people talk to him in person, they always call him Willie Jack – never just 'Willie', and certainly not 'Mr Jack'.He's Willie Jack, the guy who owns that brilliant pub the Duke of York, the Dark Horse on the other side of the narrow lane from it, and now The Harp Bar across the road from the end of the lane.

Willie Jack opened The Harp Bar in 2013, claiming he'd been waiting 20 years for the perfect spot. Since its days as a bonded warehouse, that perfect spot has been a succession of bar and restaurant concepts. You'd never guess that now. The Harp looks like it's been a Northern Irish institution even longer than Van Morrison has. (Van played here on New Year's Eve 2013, by the way, just after the place opened.)

'People come here straight from the airport,' says Willie Jack. 'They get off the plane and ask the taxi driver to take them to the best bar in Belfast, and they bring them straight here with their suitcases.'

The dimensions of The Harp, its location and the notices outside about queuing etiquette all hint at a lowest common denominator superpub. But the detail reveals something quite different. Willie Jack is proud of a stocking policy that includes no alcopops or cheap, gaudy shots and slammers. The seats are covered with plush velvet. And behind the bar, much of it in locked cases, is one of the finest troves of Irish whisk(e)y anywhere in the world.

Willie Jack is a collector. Many bar operators try to create the feel of a traditional English or Irish pub by buying junkshop tat by the skip-load and scattering it on the walls in a random approximation of age and tradition. But Willie Jack tirelessly scours junk shops and antique shops with a very specific focus.

Branded trays from distillers such as Bushmills, Dunville's, Hewitt's and Comber crowd the walls, and reveal that in its prime, Irish whisky was spelled without the 'e'. As Scotch whisky took advantage of the gap created by Ireland's difficulties, Irish producers came together and agreed that their product should be called whiskey, a superior drink. On old etched mirrors and painted trays – and even on some of the ancient, priceless bottles behind the bar – you find both spellings.

Like so much else in Northern Ireland, the peace process has reawakened the whiskey industry. At the time of writing, there are 26 new distilleries at various stages of development. Willie Jack has created their perfect showcase – not some stuffy, exclusive bar for crusty old men, but an opulent, ebullient pub where the walls drip with riches, the Guinness is smooth and clean, and the live music every night of the week means the *craic* is always good.

OPPOSITE TOP: A small part of one of the greatest pub whisk(e)y collections in the world.

OPPOSITE BOTTOM LEFT AND RIGHT: Willie Jack has turned this corner of Belfast's former docks into the heart of nightlife, in a city that was until recently crippled by damaging sectarian violence.

SCOTLAND

The Scottish pub is often overlooked as a separate type of pub in its own right. It's not just the increased focus on whisky; there's a utilitarian grandeur that sets Scotland apart – a different country indeed.

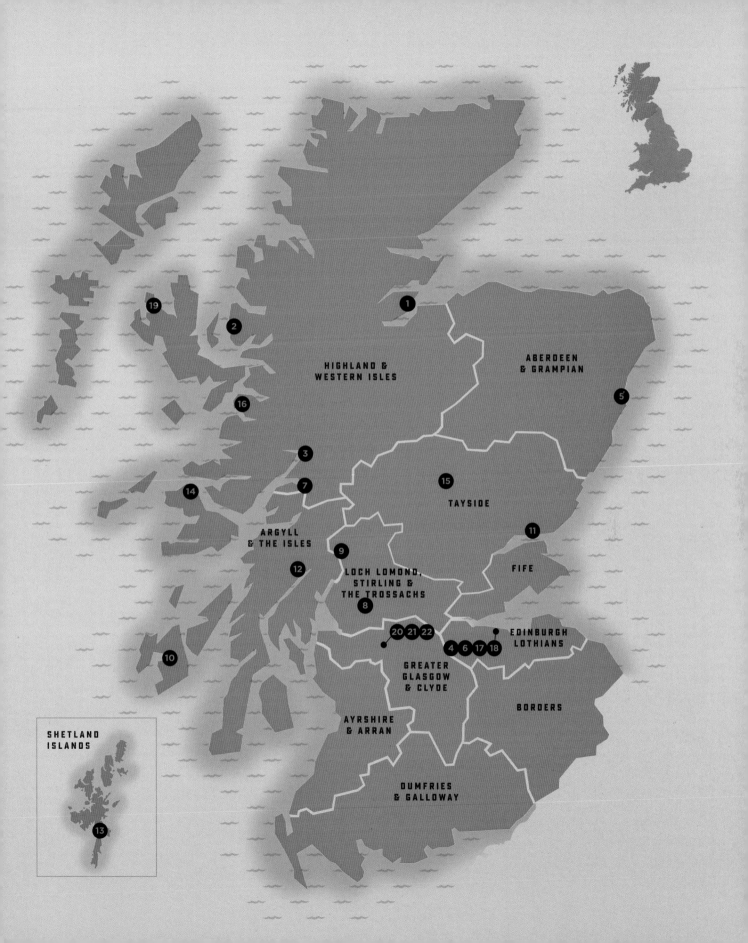

SHETLAND
ISLANDS

HIGHLAND &
WESTERN ISLES

ABERDEEN
& GRAMPIAN

TAYSIDE

ARGYLL
& THE ISLES

FIFE

LOCH LOMOND,
STIRLING &
THE TROSSACHS

EDINBURGH
LOTHIANS

GREATER
GLASGOW
& CLYDE

BORDERS

AYRSHIRE
& ARRAN

DUMFRIES
& GALLOWAY

THE ANDERSON [1]

Union St, Fortrose by Inverness,
Ross-Shire, Highlands IV10 8TD

www.theanderson.co.uk

If I said The Anderson had one of the
best drinks lists in eastern Scotland,
as many reviewers do, I might be
unwittingly implying that it's good for
this part of the country, but wouldn't
be as special somewhere else. So for
the record: the Anderson has one of
the best drinks lists anywhere in the
UK. And it's a wonderfully warm,
welcoming pub too.

APPLECROSS INN [2]

Shore St, Strathcarron, Wester Ross IV54 8LR

www.applecross.uk.com/inn

Slap-bang on the harbourside of a tiny
coastal village with views across to the
Isle of Skye, it's as beautiful here as it
is remote. Although it takes a real
effort of will and a great deal of time to
get here, it's worth putting the effort
in, if only to be rewarded by the
welcome you receive. The menu is
bursting with locally caught seafood,
and the staff are renowned for being
extremely friendly.

THE BEN NEVIS INN [3]

Claggan, Achintee, Fort William PH33 6TE

www.ben-nevis-inn.co.uk

'The wee inn at the foot of the Ben' is
as stripped back and hunkered down
as you'd expect out here, resolutely
practical and unfussy. But this restored
200-year-old barn has been fitted out
with long benches that give it a festive,
beer-hall feel, which encourages the
sharing of hiking war stories between
courageous groups of robust walkers
and the local mountain rescue team
over foaming pints of restorative ale.

BENNETS BAR

8 Leven St, Edinburgh EH3 9LG

www.bennetsbaredinburgh.co.uk

Edinburgh pubs are often long, narrow spaces, the bar down one side and a row of banquettes and tables down the other. Here, the illuminated back bar's wooden arches frame an extensive collection of single malts, and the tables are overlooked by tall arched mirrors framed by scenes from Greek mythology. It's a perfect combination of practical drinking space and unlooked-for elegance.

THE CLACHAIG INN [4]

Glencoe, Argyll PH49 4HX

www.clachaig.com

Three different bars sprawl around this homely food, drink and accommodation site in the heart of Glencoe, offering something for everyone, whether it's a welcome respite from the mountains for walkers, or a decent meal followed by a range of fine single malts for those touring the highlands and staying at the best places they can find along the route.

THE CLACHAN INN [5]

Drymen Square, Drymen, Glasgow G63 0BL

www.clachaninndrymen.co.uk

The oldest registered licensed pub in Scotland leaves you in no doubt where you are with its fiercely tartan carpets. Catering to walkers on the West Highland Way, tourists visiting Loch Lomond or the Trossachs National Park, and locals from nearby Drymen, this inn doesn't pretend to be anything other than what it is – a traditional, typical Scottish pub – and it succeeds just because of that.

BREWDOG

17 Gallowgate, Aberdeen AB25 1EB
www.brewdog.com/bars/uk/aberdeen

What's the difference between a pub and a bar?

The precise distinction is open to debate, but there are clues in those names. The bar is the space where drink is served, while 'pub' is short for 'public house'. A little simplistic, perhaps, but when we go to a bar we expect to drink in cool, stylish surroundings. When we go to a pub, we expect more – a warm welcome, a place to hang out rather than simply drink, almost a sense of shared ownership.

With its stripped back decor, uncompromising range of craft beers and punky vibe, the original outlet in BrewDog's rapidly expanding empire certainly looks like a bar. It was designed to create a statement, a break from the complacent norm. But, cleverly, the experience of drinking here still manages to retain the most important aspects of the traditional pub.

One of the most inaccurate adjectives that has been attached to the craft beer revolution is 'snobbish'. Craft beer 'snobs' are often accused of wilfully choosing a beer that's different, often bizarre, then telling you they're superior to you because you don't know about it – and if you did, you probably wouldn't appreciate it anyway.

BrewDog are widely regarded as the original driving force in the British craft beer revolution. They have a confrontational attitude to the mainstream beer industry. Therefore, the argument goes, they must be dreadful craft beer snobs themselves.

But they aren't. In fact, they are the complete opposite, if anything.

I know BrewDog's beers well. But when I approach the bar, with all the beers listed above it in cinema-style marquee lettering, I always check for specials or limited editions. As I increasingly resemble a craft beer drinker's dad rather than the drinker himself, my hesitation can be mistaken for uncertainty.

'Hi there, would you like to try anything?'

'Have you had any of our beers before?'

'Shall I talk you through our range?'

'Try this, it's a limited edition and it's my favourite and I'm trying to get them to brew it again.'

'No, don't listen to her, try this one instead. It's far better.'

BrewDog has completely shattered the myth in the pub industry that it's a waste of time training young bar staff members who don't see this as a real job and will move on in a few months. Their staff-training scheme is the best there is, and the brand is so strong that potential employees arrive already passionate about the beers and the places that serve them.

And this is the result: every time you go to a BrewDog bar, you get a warm, genuinely friendly welcome, and a crash course – should you want it – in their beer range and the craft beer movement in general.

In that respect, BrewDog bars are way more like the ideal pub than many other pubs are. As I take my pint of Punk IPA to a vacant table in BrewDog Aberdeen, plug in my laptop, scan the walls for the free Wi-Fi password ('welovebeer') and take a look at the latest beer list and free magazine on my table, I reflect that this is very much a place in which to settle down and hang out rather than simply drink beer. A few of the tables are taken by some kind of local business that's holding either a team-bonding day or a new product launch over beers and a selection of sandwiches. An old couple sit in one corner, chatting away over their hop-bomb IPAs.

We may still cling to the idea, as Orwell did, that a proper pub needs to be, or at least feel, Victorian or older. But break down the elements of what makes a great pub as opposed to a bar, and they're all here at BrewDog. The aggressive bark of their PR is far worse than their bite.

OPPOSITE TOP: Many pubs hide their price list. BrewDog turns theirs into the main attraction.

OPPOSITE MIDDLE LEFT: A BrewDog. He wants so much to tell you about his favourite beer.

OPPOSITE BOTTOM LEFT AND RIGHT: BrewDog Aberdeen was the prototype for a concept that has now rolled out around the world.

* BREWDOG DRAFT *			* GUEST DRAFT *		
NANNY STATE	0.5%	£3.95	...STONE...		
DEAD PONY CLUB	3.8%	£3.95	POINTS UNKNOWN IPA	9.5%	£4.0 ⅓
THIS IS LAGER.	4.7%	£4.10	...EVIL TWIN...		
FIVE AM RED ALE	5.0%	£4.25	MOLOTOV LITE	8.5%	£ ½
HOP FICTION	5.2%	£4.25	...OSKAR BLUES...		
PUNK IPA	5.4%	£4.25	G'KNIGHT	8.7%	£
BLACK ALE	7.2%	£4.20 ⅔	TEN FIDY 2012	10.5%	£
SUMMER	7.2%	£4.30 ⅔	...TO OL...		
MASHTAG 2015	10.0%	£4.00	NELSON SURVIN	9.0%	£3.40 ⅓
	.% £.		SPILDT MAELK	13.0%	£3.60 ⅓
HARDCORE IPA	9.2%	£3.80 ½			
IN THE HOPCANNONWITH...					
GRAPEFRUIT & CHILLI	9.2%	£3.80 ⅓			

BREWDOG ABERDEEN

BREW DOG

[1]

[1]

[2]

[3]

[4]

[5]

THE DROVERS INN [1]

Inverarnan, North Loch Lomond G83 7DX

www.thedroversinn.co.uk

This stone hulk has stood at the foot of the mountains by Loch Lomond since 1705, and now looks so old and weathered it seems to be merging into the rock behind. Inside, you'll find claymores, shields and a worryingly large collection of taxidermy wildlife capped off by a frankly terrifying man-sized bear, followed by a great selection of whiskies to calm any frazzled nerves you may have.

THE FISHERMAN'S TAVERN

12–16 Fort St, Dundee, Angus DD5 2AD

www.fishermanstavern-broughtyferry.co.uk

Housed within a row of three 17th-century listed cottages, this is one of those pubs that goes on further than you think and is timeless. The only Scottish pub to feature in every edition of the *Good Beer Guide*, it doesn't stray too far from the basics, but does them extremely well.

THE GEORGE HOTEL [2]

Main St E, Inveraray PA32 8TT

www.thegeorgehotel.co.uk

The formula for a successful rural Scottish pub may look deceptively simple, but it has to be perfectly executed. It includes roaring fires, and there are four wood- and peat-burning fireplaces here that instantly help create a welcome that you will find hard to leave. With Loch Fyne just outside the front door, this is a perfect place to discover how well whisky matches with seafood.

THE LOUNGE BAR

4 Mounthooly St, Lerwick, Shetland, Shetland Islands ZE1 0BJ

If you're one of the most remote pubs in the British Isles, you either become insular and weird or outrageously garrulous and friendly. If you want to see which way The Lounge Bar went without getting on a plane to Shetland, simply watch the clips of live music sessions on their Facebook page. And then get on a plane to Shetland.

THE MISHNISH

Main St, Tobermory, Isle of Mull PA75 6NT

www.themishnish.co.uk

Decorated with the flotsam and jetsam of shipwrecks, with furniture seemingly cobbled together from driftwood, this place feels like a cross between a 17th-century pirates' haunt and a traditional Scottish pub. Right on the harbour front, it offers fantastic views across the bay, and the Tobermory distillery is only a couple of hundred yards away. What more do you need?

MOULIN INN

Kirkmichael Rd, Moulin, Pitlochry, Perthshire PH16 5EW

www.moulinhotel.co.uk/inn/pub

Built as an inn in 1695, the various buildings that make up the Moulin Inn, pub and brewery still sit prettily around a U-shaped courtyard. The brewery opened on the pub's 300th anniversary, in what used to be the coach house. Now, aged locals tell tall stories to tourists visiting the 'gateway to the Highlands', earning pints of the in-house beer for their efforts.

THE OLD FORGE [3]

Knoydart, Mallaig, Inverness-Shire PH41 4PL

www.theoldforge.co.uk

Claiming to be Britain's remotest mainland pub, this place certainly has a good case. There are no roads worthy of the name in or out of the hamlet of Knoydart, and most people and supplies arrive by ferry from Mallaig. But once you get here, it seems like the entire world has arrived to party amid what is also some of the country's most stunning scenery.

THE OXFORD BAR [4]

8 Young St, Edinburgh EH2 4JB

www.oxfordbar.co.uk

The pub made famous by Ian Rankin in his Rebus novels would still be noteworthy even if the fictional detective had never set foot in here. Rankin is merely the latest in a long succession of literary figures who have taken their liquid inspiration in 'The Ox', and it's easy to see why. Austere and yet beautiful, it's both a refuge and a place from which stories pour forth.

THE PORT O' LEITH

58 Constitution St, Edinburgh EH6 6RS

Beware of making assumptions about pubs when you first walk in, and beware too of stereotyping people whose backgrounds you don't share. Those who miss the point of pubs like this would call it 'rough'. The tabletops may be sticky and the music can be deafeningly loud, but the service is disarmingly friendly and the playlist is superb. The shipping flags covering the ceiling point to an international crowd of devoted regulars.

THE STEIN INN [5]

Macleods Terrace, Isle of Skye, Highland IV55 8GA

www.steininn.co.uk

Right on the waterside, the location of this wonderful 18th-century inn is heartbreakingly beautiful. Settings like this inspire Scottish pubs to offer a warm welcome and a quiet retreat – it would be difficult indeed to do something mundane in these surroundings. Skye's oldest pub lives up to its billing, all stone and wood, malt and seafood, served up with pride and warmth.

THE CANNY MAN'S 🏰 ❗ 🖼

237 Morningside Rd, Edinburgh EH10 4QU
www.cannymans.co.uk

Some of the best pubs in the world possess a quality that is so hard to pin down, not everyone gets it. Sometimes it's about a simplicity that's so austere, the appeal is almost invisible – the pub is so plain, there's seemingly nothing to get excited about.

At the other end of the spectrum there is the Canny Man's.

This grotto of opulent eccentricity warns passing trade with a heavy sign – literally carved in stone – by the door, reading:

NO SMOKING
NO CREDIT CARDS
NO MOBILE PHONES
NO CAMERAS
NO BACKPACKERS

These statutes help preserve an air inside that could be described as stepping back in time. But that phrase falls short, because you can't really be sure what era you're stepping into.

At first glance you're in a Victorian sitting room. But then the place quickly evokes a childhood memory in me (which may or may not be real) of watching a Connery-era James Bond movie in my great aunt's house in 1975. The crimson walls have a whiff of the Raj about them. The small, copper-topped round tables and Venetian red upholstered stools lure you to a time that could be anywhere between the 1930s and 1970s.

The music, too, shuffles along the pub's timeline, juke-box style, from classical orchestra to 1940s crooning. It emanates from unseen speakers – possibly hidden behind the huge moose head hung on the wall, or maybe above the Chinese parasol suspended from the ceiling.

Built in 1871 and run by the same family ever since, the pub's detritus is not forcibly quirky – it's simply that it belongs to a family that never throws away anything that is either useful or interesting to look at. Beer labels on some of the walls are now fading into the wood under layers of heavily weathered varnish.

Until 2011, the real star of The Canny Man's was its proprietor, Watson Kerr, great-grandson of the founder, James Kerr. Watson was described in a guide to the pub written in 2004 and still available on The Canny Man's website as 'the fat guy, somewhere between 60 and death, holding Cuba in his mouth and drinking wine. Although he is what could be termed as a functional alcoholic, he is still very capable of working and running a tight ship.'

That Kerr himself approved this description, and the family who survive him and run the pub along the lines laid down by him still publish it, says a great deal about a character who was, perhaps understandably, much misunderstood by the long line of people he barred from the pub simply because he didn't like the look of them. As online reviews illustrate, it's still possible to be ejected from The Canny Man's in the most severe manner. The pub is almost as likely to receive a one-star as a five-star review – though it rarely gets anything in between.

Some mistake the attitude as straight-forward snobbery, but I've never detected any, and real snobs sniff me out in an instant. It's not the warmest welcome you'll ever receive in a pub, but it does feel like you've managed to get into an exclusive club under sufferance.

Kerr's supporters insist he just wanted to keep the place perfect for the regulars who kept him in business. 'Loved by those who know it and hated by those who do not understand it,' concludes Tom, the regular who was employed to write the pub's history/guide/rule book.

The Canny Man's is still Watson Kerr's pub – his wife and sons make sure of that. It has changed little and long may it remain the same.

OPPOSITE TOP: Rumours that the musical instruments hanging from the ceiling of The Canny Man's belong to buskers who came in during the Edinburgh festival and never came out again have not been fully substantiated.

OPPOSITE BOTTOM LEFT TO RIGHT: The old school charm of The Canny Man's plays by its own rules, and you either get it or you don't. For your own good, you should really try to get it.

DUFFIES BAR AT THE LOCHSIDE HOTEL ⚓ 🍴 🖼

20 Shore St, Bowmore, Isle of Islay PA43 7LB
www.lochsidehotel.co.uk

Wherever you go, pubs perform the same basic function of offering hospitality and refreshment. But the nature, or flavour, of this function varies depending on exactly where you are.

In Scotland, as in more weather-beaten parts of England and Wales, pubs hunker down, shielding you from the elements. Up here, pubs can look craggier and more rugged. From the outside, thick, stone walls and small windows are fortress-like against the elements. But get inside, and they *glow*.

In the height of summer, overlooking rolling green hills, few things are better than sitting at a beer garden table with a pint of something light and fresh, soaking up the view. But the winter pub offers a magic that's deeper. Making it to the pub in the first place can feel like an achievement. And once inside, a blazing fire and a warming glass of something dark will laugh in the face of the rain that batters the windows like handfuls of flung gravel. The pub envelops you and warms you, as if to reassure you that you're safe.

The Lochside Hotel is right on the water in the small town of Bowmore, the main centre of civilization on the isle of Islay. It's built to withstand wind, rain and crashing waves, and when they're absent, it offers stunning sea views and amazing sunsets.

But while the views are great, for me this is a place to visit after dark, when Duffies Bar, the beating heart of the hotel, warms the whole place with its spirit.

Islay is famous for its single malt whiskies. To some, their intense peatiness is medicinal, an eye-watering assault on the palate. For others, they represent the highest expression of both the whisky maker's art, and the role of *terroir* in drinks. Any whisky maker will tell you that, for the most part, whisky gets its character not from the distilled liquid itself,

but from the long ageing process in the barrel. Whisk(e)y aged in fresh oak will have a completely different character to whisky aged in sherry barrels, for instance. But when peat is used to dry the malted barley that is then brewed to create the wash – the base beverage for whisky – the peat character carries through the distillation process and dominates the finished product. It's fiery and intense, tying the whisky to the land of its birth, and providing the perfect warming comfort to anyone who has been lashed by Islay's weather.

Duffies Bar stocks between 250 and 300 whiskies, most of them from Islay. Even if you don't fancy a dram yourself, the bar is fascinating as a museum, an exhibition of Scotland's national drink. There are bottles here from distilleries that closed decades ago, and bottles of incredibly rare expressions such as Black Bowmore, distilled in 1964 in the distillery just across the road, matured for years in dark cellars with the crashing sea audible against the other side of the wall, and now retailing for around £8,000 ($11,400) a bottle.

Your immediate environment has a huge impact on your perception of flavour, and Duffies is tailor-made to heighten your whisky-drinking experience. The range of bottles, some of them protected in locked glass cases, conveys a sure sense of privilege and excitement. But, at the same time, the plain wood and simple bar stools say that this is a democratic place, open to anyone. Even a dram of something you can buy in your local supermarket is going to taste better here than it does at home.

Malt whisky warms you from the throat and stomach out. And Duffies, recognized as one of the best whisky bars in the world, warms you from the outside in. The elements outside, mighty as they are, are powerless here.

TENNENTS

191 Byres Rd, Glasgow G12 8TN

www.thetennentsbarglasgow.co.uk

This large Victorian corner pub may look a little frayed at the edges, but as one regular told me, 'You can't move in here on match day, and yet you'll always get served straight away.' A rank of up to a dozen cask ale pumps certainly back up the claim that this is 'Glasgow's finest ale house'.

THE UBIQUITOUS CHIP

12 Ashton Ln, Glasgow G12 8SJ

www.ubiquitouschip.co.uk

This former dairy and stable retains whitewashed walls and vaulted ceilings of black wooden beams. It's a curious space – a restaurant in the middle linking at least two separate pubs with bridges and mezzanines. The Upper Bar is several times bigger than the 'wee pub' downstairs. It doesn't look much like a pub, but certainly feels like one – a pub in a different language.

WEST [1]

Templeton Building, Glasgow Green, Glasgow G40 1AW

www.westbeer.com

Petra Wetzel founded the WEST brewery after moving to Glasgow from Germany. She loved everything about her adoptive home, apart from the beer, so founded one of the best lager breweries in the UK with a philosophy of 'Glaswegian heart, German head'.

The bar, in an old carpet factory built to resemble a Venetian palace, sees this through – a German bierkeller suffused with Glasgow chic.

Also Try…

THE BOW BAR

80 West Bow, Edinburgh EH1 2HH

www.thebowbar.co.uk

THE SHIP INN

The Toft, Elie, Fife KY9 1DT

www.shipinn.scot

STATION BAR

Wemyss Bay Rd, Wemyss Bay, Renfrewshire PA18 6AA

WALES

Easy to overlook and often mocked, Wales has found its mojo over the last twenty years and is fast becoming the UK's best-kept food and drink secret. Some of the country's best food, beer, cider, hospitality and countryside are waiting for you here.

1: **The Bell** *(page 245)*, Bulmore Rd, Caerleon, Glamorgan NP18 1QQ

2: **The Black Lion** *(page 245)*, Glan Mor Terrace, New Quay, Ceredigion SA45 9PT

3: **The Blue Bell Inn** *(page 244)*, Rhosesmor Rd, Halkyn, Flintshire CH8 8DL

4: **The Bridge End Inn** *(page 245)*, Bridge St, Ruabon, Wrexham LL14 6DA

5: **Bunch of Grapes** *(page 250)*, Ynysyngharad Rd, Pontypridd, Glamorgan CF37 4DA

6: **The City Arms** *(page 245)*, 10–12 Quay St, Cardiff CF10 1EA

7: **The Clytha Arms** *(page 246)*, Abergavenny, Monmouthshire NP7 9BW

8: **Nantyffin Cider Mill** *(page 249)*, Brecon Rd, Crickhowell, Powys NP8 1SG

9: **The Shoemakers Arms** *(page 249)*, Pentre-bach, Brecon, Powys LD3 8UB

10: **The Sportsman** *(page 249)*, 17 Severn St, Newtown, Powys SY16 2AQ

11: **Tafarn Sinc** *(page 249)*, Rosebush, Pembrokeshire SA66 7QU

12: **The Ty Coch Inn** *(page 68)*, Porthdinllaen, Pwllheli, Gwynedd LL53 6DB

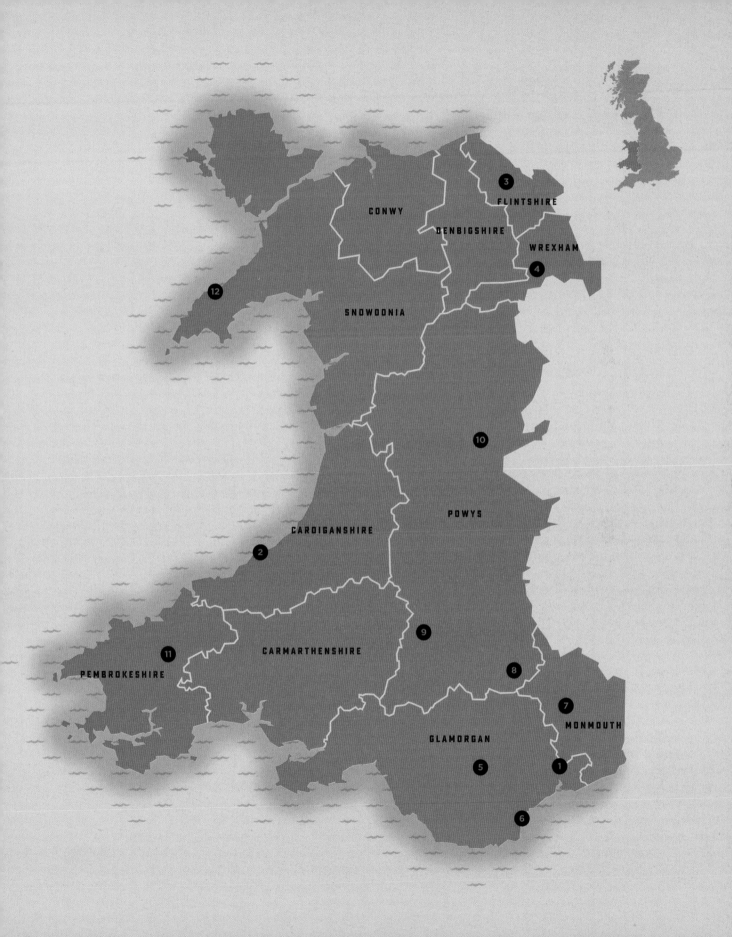

CONWY

FLINTSHIRE

DENBIGSHIRE

WREXHAM

SNOWDONIA

POWYS

CARDIGANSHIRE

CARMARTHENSHIRE

PEMBROKESHIRE

GLAMORGAN

MONMOUTH

THE BLUE BELL INN

Rhosesmor Rd, Halkyn, Flintshire CH8 8DL
www.bluebell.uk.eu.org

Philosophically, there are two opposing views on human nature. One says that we're innately competitive and selfish, that it's still all about the survival of the fittest, that we take what we can get and we're only nice to each other because we benefit from people being nice back to us.

The other view is that we're innately social creatures, and that by working together we all benefit from the overall greater good.

Unwittingly, The Blue Bell Inn at Halkyn has created an experiment to see which of these theories is true – for its regulars at least, if not the whole of humanity.

Since it voluntarily closed its restaurant in order to accommodate the local Post Office in the space instead, the Blue Bell doesn't really offer food, although it can be arranged for functions. But every few months, Saturday night at the Blue Bell is Cheese and Pickled night. Guests are invited to bring along a piece of cheese – as much as you like, of whatever type, though there's a gentle encouragement to be adventurous. The pub provides bread, crackers and plates. Each person hands over their cheese on arrival, and it's taken into the back room where it's assembled onto large serving plates, with little flags indicating the name of each variety. Anyone in the pub can then help themselves to as much cheese as they like. There is no admission charge, ticket, or fee for a plate.

Now, if the atavistic view of human nature were correct, the pub would run out of cheese pretty quickly. People would bring the bare minimum and take more than they brought. There's nothing to stop anyone turning up when the evening is in full flow and helping themselves without having brought anything. It would be natural and obvious to take advantage of other people's naïve generosity.

But instead, there's always far more cheese than anyone can eat, with piles left over at the end of the evening.

Most people bring more than they take. Not only that, people have started baking cakes and biscuits and bringing them along to add to the table. And so the regulars at the Blue Bell prove themselves to be innately generous and social.

It would be interesting to see if other pubs would see the same result. The atmosphere in any pub is shaped largely by the people who own and run it, and landlord Steve Marquis and his wife Ness create a sense of welcome and generosity that is irresistible.

The Blue Bell Inn is a free house, and Steve selects every beer, cider and whisky that goes on the bar. He personally writes tasting notes for every single one and publishes them on the pub's website, which is kept meticulously up to date regarding what's currently on the pumps. The back bar is lined with small shot glasses ready to offer tasters, and it's difficult to buy a pint of beer or cider without being offered at least two or three others to try before you make your decision.

The stunning care taken over the excellent range of drinks makes the Blue Bell worth climbing a small mountain for – which is just as well, because it's on top of one. Halkyn Mountain rears up unexpectedly, offering stunning views over the Dee estuary, with Liverpool clearly visible in the distance. The mountain is still common land that has never been enclosed, and around 200 households in this tiny community have the right to graze sheep on the land. Many still do.

So maybe the community spirit and fellowship of the Blue Bell is in the soil of the place. Or maybe it's all down to one very special publican. Or it could simply be that great pubs bring out the very best in people.

THE BELL

Bulmore Rd, Caerleon, Glamorgan NP18 1QQ

www.thebellatcaerleon.co.uk

This 400-year-old coaching inn just outside Newport has everything: beautiful old rooms, a well-respected restaurant, a great wine list and a superb range of beers and ciders. Locally sourced beer and food are used extensively in the menu, and it's worth a visit for the cider-infused Scotch egg alone.

THE BLACK LION

Glan Mor Terrace, New Quay, Ceredigion SA45 9PT

www.blacklionnewquay.co.uk

Back in the days when Dylan Thomas lived in New Quay, The Black Lion was apparently a hangout for skint, creative types. Today, pub and town are quiet, lacking the poet's hell-raising behaviour. In photos he gazes down for the wall, watching as people lose themselves in the stunning sea view over Cardigan Bay, and drift.

THE BRIDGE END INN

Bridge St, Ruabon, Wrexham LL14 6DA

www.mcgivernales.co.uk

With its low-beamed ceilings, smouldering wood fire and piles of board games, old magazines and books, this pub has the air of a decadent front room of some benign eccentric rather than a traditional pub. Excellent ales and ciders are complemented by simple rolls and pork pies from the local butcher, and the delicious aroma of wood smoke.

Owned by McGivern ales, the pub effortlessly wins regular awards.

THE CITY ARMS [1]

10–12 Quay St, Cardiff CF10 1EA

www.thecityarmscardiff.com

The nice thing about this Brains-owned pub is that it doesn't have to be as good as it is. It's a great old building in a perfect location near the Millennium Stadium, and it could make a mint simply pushing out the usual Brains range with minimal care or effort. That it has one of the best beer selections in the city, served in comforting surroundings, and attracts passionate staff who are committed to keeping them well and making this a flagship pub for the city, is a great credit to Wales' largest brewer.

THE CLYTHA ARMS 🌳🍺🍴🍎

Abergavenny, Monmouthshire NP7 9BW
www.clytha-arms.com

The green hills around Abergavenny are blessed with great food pubs – just don't call them gastropubs. While one or two have had the Farrow & Ball and celebrity chef treatment rested on them, most serve good food simply because that's what you do around here. These are places where the landlord can tell you the name of the farm that the beef on your plate came from – and the name of the farmer, if not the cow – not in response to a growing interest in local provenance or anything like that, but simply because they've always done things that way.

At the Clytha, it's not just the food that's locally sourced. The wide range of cask ales comes mainly from local brewers, as do the bag-in-box ciders stacked at one end of the bar. 'I have to keep them up there,' says landlord Andrew Canning, 'If I keep them in the cellar they turn the ales cloudy.'

Canning has run the Clytha for a quarter of a century. In that time, he's embedded the pub in its landscape and worked with it, making the pub a true expression of the local area. 'Cider has always been made locally around Monmouthshire,' he says. 'We're only a dozen miles south of the estate of Lord Scudamore, who revolutionized cider making in the 17th century. When cider became less popular, the local farmers never grubbed up all their orchards, so now there's plenty of fruit if you know where to look.'

Cider-making in Wales is undergoing a revival. It is very much part of the identity of the area, so it's important to Canning that it's part of the pub's make-up too.

There are lots of indigenous apple and pear trees around here, not just in working orchards but on roadsides, in forgotten corners of fields and in back gardens. Some of them grow fruit varieties not seen anywhere else. There's one big, ancient tree in the grounds of the Clytha that usually produces a bounteous crop of culinary pears. There are five old Welsh perry varietals in an orchard two miles (three km) north, and Andrew gets a good crop from there, combines them with his and makes his own perry – three or four barrels a year – which is served exclusively at the Clytha. It's so tannic, he ages it for two years to mellow and soften before serving.

The Clytha is a beautifully welcoming old pub, with open wood fires that make you want to settle in for days. You might have to step over one of the pub dogs to enter, and once inside they'll probably come and check you out. The smell of woodsmoke hangs in the air, and the pub feels old and cranky without being shabby or dilapidated.

It's only when you look at the menu that you realise this might be a seriously good food destination too. The menu announces its intent with just enough careful description of the dishes to let you know this isn't just standard pub food, but never gets too florid. The bacon, laverbread and cockles are nothing short of addictive, and the stuffed ham cooked with cider is a perennial favourite. When your meals arrive, the dogs look soulfully into your eyes. However good the food, you always feel like you're eating in a pub rather than a wannabe restaurant.

Every May, The Clytha Arms puts on a cider festival, with camping available in the grounds of the pub. It has a reputation for being quite a party. And this is what makes the Clytha so special as a country pub: it caters for everyone. It's quite hard to imagine many other places being lauded equally by muddy festivalgoers and *Country Living* magazine, but this place pulls it off in a self-effacing, modest, typically Welsh fashion.

OPPOSITE TOP: The Clytha Arms puts on its best face for those passing on the busy road out front.

OPPOSITE BOTTOM: An authentic, accessible pub housed in a deceptively beautiful building.

[2]

NANTYFFIN CIDER MILL

Brecon Rd, Crickhowell, Powys NP8 1SG

www.cidermill.co.uk

Originally a 16th-century cattle-drovers' inn, this place first became famous for producing cider in the 19th century, only ceasing to do so during the 1960s. The old cider press is still in place in the restaurant, and there's an old stone mill outside, helping create a nice farmhouse atmosphere. A decent range of locally made ciders remains, but the real star is the truly amazing food.

THE SHOEMAKERS ARMS [1]

Pentre-bach, Brecon, Powys LD3 8UB

www.theshoemakersarms.webs.com

This once-troubled pub was saved from oblivion by a community buy-out, and is now a magnet that draws people from miles around. The beer may be perfectly kept, the views may be stunning, the pies may be awesome, but it's the attention to detail and unfailing warmth of the hosts that really set this pub apart.

THE SPORTSMAN [2]

17 Severn St, Newtown, Powys SY16 2AQ

www.sportsmannewtown.co.uk

The brewery tap for the excellent, multi-award-winning Monty's Brewery is utilitarian yet beautiful, with wonderful stained glass above the bar, and delicious beers and ciders on it. There's no kitchen, so you're allowed to order in food from local takeaways – a feature that's typical of the warm, friendly welcome here.

TAFARN SINC [3]

Rosebush, Pembrokeshire SA66 7QU

www.tafarnsinc.co.uk

High in the Preseli Hills, the red corrugated iron walls of this pub are an arresting sight. It was thrown up quickly in 1876 to serve the slate miners in the hills and the railway connection that took them down to the local towns. The mines and the railway are long gone, but the station has been re-created in the pub garden, with mannequins on the platform and steam train sound effects.

Also Try...

THE BELL

Skenfrith, Monmouthshire NP7 8UH

www.skenfrith.co.uk

GRAVITY STATION

6 Barrack Lane, Cardiff CF10 2FR

www.thegravitystation.com

THE HOPE AND ANCHOR

St Julian St, Tenby, Pembrokeshire SA70 7AX

THE OLD POINT HOUSE

Angle Village, Pembrokeshire SA71 5AS

THE PILOT

726 Mumbles Rd, The Mumbles, Swansea SA3 4EL

www.thepilotofmumbles.co.uk

THE SKIRRID INN

Llanvihangel Crucorney, Abergavenny, Monmouthshire NP7 8DH

www.skirridmountaininn.co.uk

BUNCH OF GRAPES 👥 🍺 🍴 🍎

Ynysyangharad Rd, Pontypridd CF37 4DA
www.bunchofgrapes.org.uk

When you're trying to reach it by car, The Bunch of Grapes is a mirage.

You follow the sat nav off the dual carriageway that takes you down the Rhondda Valley from Merthyr, and it's just around the corner as you enter Pontypridd. You curve to the left and you can see the building, almost making out the sign, not quite as it should be, reading:
BUN
CHOF
GRA
PE
S

And then you screech to a halt in front of a phalanx of concrete bollards that block the road, bisecting it. The pub stands a hundred metres away, not too far to walk, but the absurdity of the situation makes it seem much further. Locals know the solution is simple: you just have to go back the way you came, go up a very steep road in the opposite direction that then curves around, hugging the top of a small cliff, through a residential area before dropping back down at the other end of the road, and gliding into the pub's car park.

I'd love to say this quarantining of the Bunch contributes to its special atmosphere, but every time I go there I feel like I'm the only person who has ever had any difficulty navigating this secret route. The main bar is always full of regulars who nurse pints through the afternoon, while on the opposite side of the bar there's a restaurant that people from as far away as London come to try. All of them seem to be able to find the place with ease.

The Bunch was the first pub owned by Pontypridd's Otley Brewery, one of the first craft breweries to emerge in Wales, and one of the first in the UK to bring a smart, modern look to beer rather than traditional real ale tropes.

Nick Otley was a chef and professional photographer before he founded the brewery with his relatives, and everything they do comes with flavour and style.

A restaurant that's featured in *The Good Food Guide* and has won a stack of awards for its food doesn't necessarily sit comfortably with a down-to-earth backstreet community pub. And what a backstreet it is. But there's harmony here. Some of the harmony comes from the punters simply having trust in the family who run the place. But part of it derives from simple but brilliantly creative ideas that highlight how these two halves belong together in seamless fashion.

The restaurant bakes all its own bread and makes its own chutneys, and these are on sale behind the bar. There's something about the sight of a big wicker basket full of cooling loaves that just feels right and obvious in a pub, even though I've never seen it done anywhere else.

Everything else follows on from the same principle. The Bunch of Grapes walks a perfect line: it looks like an ordinary boozer, with little snugs and wooden partitions, local newspapers on the tables, and decoration that knows it's a backdrop and therefore tries not to get noticed. But photograph it under the right light, and it looks like a smart, design-led restaurant bar. Simple but versatile.

Backstreet pubs are those most under threat as the world moves on. We need fewer and fewer of them as people choose to spend more time at home. They're also the type of pub it's hardest to imagine gentrifying. Town-centre circuit pubs shed their skins every few years – it's in their nature. Not so the backstreet boozer. But this one has been reinvented without losing sight of itself, and made it look easy to boot.

OPPOSITE TOP: The mouth-watering menus at The Bunch of Grapes are on a par with any restaurant in Wales, and often beat them in culinary competitions.

OPPOSITE BOTTOM LEFT: A wall of beer taps incorporates an imaginative and thoughtful range of ales.

OPPOSITE BOTTOM RIGHT: Fresh bread on the bar. Why has no one else thought of this?

Homemade Soup
Wild mushroom & smoked garlic

Cardigan Bay Lobster bisque rouille

Starter
Fresh live Oyster on Crushed ice, With Charred Lemon & chilli Jam.
£1.75 each.

Starter
Tempura of Soft Shell crab, red pepper & Samphire, with Rice Wine Vinaigrette
£7.00

Starter
Warm Confit Leg of Wye Valley duck, with Watercress & Victoria plum Sauce
£6.20

Dessert
Baked Caramelised figs in lemon, rosemary & balsamic, With Vanilla Cream and Almond

Stuffing, grain mustard mash, Wilted Curly Kale, Onion & perry jus
£15.80

Main
Pan fried Welsh Wild seabass fillet, Cardigan Bay Lobster & Crab bisque, Royal Norfolk potatoes, & Carrot, parsnip & beetroot Crisps
£16.50

Main
Pan fried breaded Welsh Dover Sole, with tempura samphire & homegrown yellow Courgettes, potato Wedges & charred Lemon
£17.50

Main
Chargrilled 8oz fillet of Welsh beef, with Sauteed Pied Bleu & Pied de Mouton mushrooms, Watercress & Smoked Dauphinois
£21.50

risotto Balls - With fig ice Cream & rum syrup.
£5.50

PUB INDEX BY LOCATION

PUB INDEX BY NAME

ACKNOWLEDGEMENTS

Picture Acknowledgements

Illustrations by Jeremy Sancha: page 3 inset panel, 4-5, 8-9, 18-19, 36-37, 92-93

Page 1 Alamy/Nature Photographers Ltd; 2-3 Anchor Bar; 7 Alamy/West Yorkshire Images; 11 top left Jacqui Small LLP/Ashley Western, top right The Lion & Lobster/Richard Heald Photography, bottom left Adnams, bottom right Kings Arms; 12 Tracy Elliot-Reep; 13 The George Inn, Norton St Philip; 14 Harvey's Brewery; 15 top left Duke of York, top right The Eagle, bottom left The Salisbury, London; 16 top Mary Evans Picture Library, bottom left Anchor Bar, bottom right Draft House, London; 21 top The Anderson, Fortrose, bottom Beer Lens/Robert Gale; 22 Nicholson's Pubs; 23 left Alamy/Roberto Herrett, top right Alamy/Mick Sinclair, bottom right The Southampton Arms/Helen Cathcart; 24 top Fuller, Smith and Turner PLC, bottom The Fat Pig; 25 top left Alan McCredie, top right The Southampton Arms/Helen Cathcart; 26 top left Lamb & Flag, bottom left BrewDog Aberdeen/Sam Brill, right Photograph by Stuart Askew, 2015. Reproduced with permission of Wye Valley Brewery Limited ©Wye Valley Brewery Ltd; 27 Wayne Pilling; 28 Georgina Woodhead, Curiousbygeorge Photography; 29 top left S A Brain & Co Ltd, top right Hallamshire House, bottom right Beer Lens/Robert Gale; 30 John Hipkiss, 31 BrewDog; 32 top Beer Lens/Robert Gale, bottom The Bridge Tavern; 33 top left North Bar, bottom left Pint Shop, right The Southampton Arms/Helen Cathcart; 34 Everards Brewery; 35 Beer Lens/Robert Gale; 41 top The George Inn, Bottom left The Oxford Bar, bottom right The Lamb; 42 The Castle; 43 top The Fleece Inn, bottom left The Royal Standard of England, bottom right Georgina Woodhead, Curiousbygeorge Photography; 45 The George Inn; 47 top Alamy/Tracey Whitefoot, bottom Fuller, Smith and Turner PLC; 48 top The Oxford Bar, bottom left The Royal Standard of England; bottom middle The Peveril of the Peak, bottom right Nicholson's Pubs; 49 The Lamb Inn; 51 Nicholson's Pubs; 53 top left above The Black Boy, top left below The Grafton, top right Very English Ltd/ Amanda Tarrant, bottom The Driftwood Spars; 55 top The Talbot Inn, below left and right Chris Gittner; 57 top The Pebbles, bottom Jacqui Small LLP/Ashley Western; 59 Jacqui Small LLP/Ashley Western; 61 top left above The Clachaig Inn, top left below Tracy Elliot-Reep, top right Georgina Woodhead, Curiousbygeorge Photography, bottom The Wasdale Head Inn; 62 Tracy Elliot-Reep; 63 top The Hatchet Inn, below Jo Randall; 64 Chris Gittner; 67 top The Driftwood Spars, bottom Alamy/Bjanka Kadic; 69 The Ty Coch Inn; 71 top left above Beer Lens/Robert Gale,

top left below Paul Palmer-Edwards, top right, bottom Jacqui Small LLP/Ashley Western; 73 Thornbridge Brewery; 75 top The Butcher's Arms, bottom left Alan McCredie, bottom right The Drover's Inn; 76 left Beer Lens/Robert Gale, right Liz Vater 77 James Collinwood Photography; 79 Mark Bolton Photography; 81 top left Chloë King, top right Photograph by Stuart Askew, 2015. Reproduced with permission of Wye Valley Brewery Ltd ©Wye Valley Brewery Ltd, left centre Wayne Pilling, bottom left The Anderson, bottom right The Queens's Head, Eye; 82 The Anderson; 83 top Jason Olive, bottom left The Bridge Tavern, bottom right Courtesy of Jo Hone Photography; 85 The Bridge Beer Huis; 87 left top John Hipkiss, left centre Richard Heald Photography, top right Matt Austin, bottom The Tickell Arms 88 left The Southampton Arms/Helen Cathcart, right above Julie Beaume, right below The Fleece Inn; 89 Justin Slee Photography; 91 The Gurnard's Head/Paul Massey; 95 S A Brain & Co; 98 top and bottom right Beer Wolf Books, bottom left Liz Vater; 100 left Alamy/Anthony Morgan, right The Barley Mow, Bristol; 101 left Alamy/Jack Sullivan, right Matt Austin; 103 Tim Sears; 105 top left and right Christopher Cornwell; centre The Kings Arms, bottom left Hand Beer Bar, bottom right The Lundy Company; 107 The Halfway House;109 top left The Pebbles Tavern, top right Georgina Woodhead, Curiousbygeorge Photography, centre left The Royal Oak, centre right ALAMY/IDP Devon & Cornwall, bottom left and right Small Bar, Bristol; 111 Courtesy of Jo Hone Photography; 113 top left St Kew Inn, top Right Woods, centre left Warren House Inn, bottom The Trout Inn; 115 The Square & Compass; 119 Mike McWilliam; 120 top left and right The Butcher's Arms; bottom Fuller, Smith and Turner PLC; 121 left The Black Boy, right Wayne Pilling; 123 The Hatchet Inn; 125 top The Fox goes Free, centre and bottom Richard Heald Photography; 127 The Snowdrop; 128 top left Very English Ltd/ Joanna Copestick, top right The Reine Deer, centre Chloë King, bottom The Royal Standard of England; 131 Very English Ltd/Joanna Copestick; 135 Jacqui Small LLP/Ashley Western; 136 Alamy/Urban Images; 137 left The Bull, right The Grafton; 139 Paul Palmer-Edwards; 140 top Taylor Walker, bottom The Harp; 143 Jacqui Small LLP/ Ashley Western; 144 left Fuller, Smith and Turner PLC, right top The Pelton Arms, right bottom, Fuller, Smith and Turner PLC; 145 Taylor Walker; 147 The Seven Stars; 148 top The Southampton Arms/Helen Cathcart, centre left The Snooty Fox, centre right The Trafalgar Tavern; bottom left Jason Olive, bottom right The White Horse; 151 Jacqui Small LLP/Ashley

Western; 155 The Murderer's; 156 top left The Anchor Walberswick, bottom left ALAMY/Cath Harries, right Very English Ltd/Joanna Copestick; 157 The Butt & Oyster; 159 Very English Ltd/Joanna Copestick; 160 top The Dabbling Duck; centre Greene King PLC, bottom left The Elm Tree Tavern, bottom right Adnams; 163 The Queen's Head, Newton, Bottom right Liz Vater; 164 left and right Tessa Prior; 165 top left Pint Shop, top right Very English Ltd/Joanna Copestick, bottom Jo Randall; 167 James Collinwood Photography; 168 top left The Signal Box Inn, top right The Station Hotel, centre The Tickell Arms, bottom The White Horse, Neatishead; 171 Very English Ltd/Joanna Copestick; 175 The Coopers Tavern; 176 left Photograph by Stuart Askew, 2015. Reproduced with permission of Wye Valley Brewery Limited ©Wye Valley Brewery Ltd, right The Borehole; 177 left top The Burton Bridge Inn, left bottom The Brunswick, right The Castle Inn; 179 The Crown Inn; 180 top left The Cider House, top right The Craven Arms, bottom The Fleece Inn; 183 The Nag's Head; 184 left John Hipkiss, right The Royal Exchange; 185 left Tony Lord, right The Victoria, Beeston; 187 top ALAMY/Steve Sant, bottom left Batham's Brewery bottom right, ALAMY/Steve Sant; 191 Beer Lens/ Robert Gale; 193 top Tim Hampson, bottom Beer Lens/ Robert Gale; 194 left Baltic Fleet, right Andrew Clegg; 195 left Hawkshead Brewery, right Hole in T'Wall; 197 Julie Beaume; 199 top left The Kirkstile Inn, top right The Peveril of the Peak, bottom The Wasdale Head; 201 Greene King PLC; 205 top Beer Lens/Robert Gale, bottom The Fat Cat; 206 left Liz Vater, right The Feathers; 207 left The Bridge Tavern, right Justin Slee Photography; 209 Heather Griffin; 210 left The Kelham Island Tavern, right The Lion Inn; 211 Hallamshire House; 213 The Strines Inn; 214 top The Rat Inn, bottom left North Bar, bottom right above Will Forrest, bottom right below Chris Gittner; 217 Picturesbybish; 221 Marc Lawson; 222 left above and below Bradley Quinn, right above and below Lunny Images; 223 The Cross Keys Inn; 225 top ALAMY/Eye Ubiquitous, bottom left and right Alamy/Helen Cathcart 226 The Duke of York; 227 Brad McClenaghan; 229 The Harp Bar; 232 top left The Anderson, top right The Applecross Inn/Jack Morris Photography; bottom left The Ben Nevis Inn, bottom right ALAMY/Graham Uney; 233 The Clachaig Inn; 235 BrewDog; 236 top Gryffe Studios; centre left The George Hotel, centre right Old Forge; bottom left The Oxford Bar, bottom right The Stein Inn; 239 Alan McCredie 241 West; 245 The City Arms; 247 The Clytha Arms; 248 Tafarn Sinc; 249 left The Shoemaker's Arms, right Russ Honeyman; 251 Otley Brewery/Nick Otley

Author's Acknowledgements

Pete would like to thank: Charles Campion for sterling help in the Midlands, Chris Gittner for being wingman across the north, Jeff Pickthall for help even further north, Claire Keenan and the team at Tourism Northern Ireland, Adrian Tierney-Jones, Susan Stewart for Glasgow, Jo Copestick for perseverance in making this idea happen and contributing so much to it, Paul Palmer-Edwards at Grade Design for a great job, and all at Jacqui Small Publishing for bringing it to fruition. Finally, biggest thanks go to Liz Vater for support in more ways than anyone would believe, and Mildred for assessing dog-friendliness.